ENDORS[barcode: MW00598029]

Diane Gardner's book describes the pathway of a woman who, surrounded by obstacles on her journey, broke through unto a life of personal peace and fruitfulness in living. My awareness of her present life and influence confirms the fact that her public and private influence has profited many. I unhesitatingly suggest that *Overcoming the Enemy's Storms* will become a practical handbook of encouragement and breakthrough for those who read these pages.

DR. JACK HAYFORD, Chancellor King's University, Former Pastor and past president of International Church of the Four Square Gospel, Bestselling Author, Song writer, Spirit Formed weekly television program, Weekly Life Way Radio program, mentor to leaders worldwide.

Diane's book is more than her testimony. The story of her life can help people in their walk of faith, to handle the problems the Adversary brings their way. This book can help others make the right decisions when they come to life's crossroads, so they will know what is expected of them by God. Diane is a person of great personal and biblical integrity, true to what the Word of God says. She is definitely a leader that is highly qualified, highly gifted, and highly capable. I am impressed with her discernment of spirits and her insights. She is active and alert to the ways of the Enemy. She has an ability to respond to situations and do what the situations calls for.

DR. DICK MILLS (1922-2012) DD, DSTh, prophet, evangelist, Bible scholar, whose prophetic insight was sought by heads of nations, well-known ministers, television, radio and magazine personalities, and marketplace business persons.

Diane Gardner models the peace that she teaches. She has a passion for the Word of God and her tenacity in holding fast to her faith in turbulent times is inspiring and convicting. What a joy to have personally witnessed her steadfast faith in the midst of her trying circumstances. Read this book and learn how to stand when you've done all you can, *Overcoming the Enemy's*

Storms is certain to inspire you to keep your hope alive and to go to the next level in God.

DEBORAH SMITH PEGUES, MBA, CPA, speaker, businesswoman, author of more than 15 books including *30 Days to Taming Your Tongue* (over 650,000 copies sold) and *30 Days to Taming Your Anger*.

Diane Gardner is a remarkable woman, and she is highly qualified to write *Overcoming the Enemy's Storms*. As she shares some of the darkest times in her life it is always with a desire to show us how we can overcome, how we can fulfill our destiny, and how we can become beautiful women of God. I highly recommend this book.

REV. JOYCE GILL, MThS, prophetic exhorter, missionary, internet worldwide ministry, publisher, co-author of Bible School Manuals and books with over 20 million copies sold in 20 languages. Author *Victory Over Deception, A Guide to Christian Writers and Publishers, Miracles are Still Happening*.

Diane has created a valuable resource in her book, *Overcoming the Enemy's Storms*. As a financial expert and a military wife, I have witnessed storms of all kinds that threaten to rob us of our praise, our peace, and our purpose. Diane Gardner has created a roadmap to navigate the storms that the enemy brings our way, and she helps us enter into the calm and peace of God's protection and provision. I highly recommend this book for anyone who wants to live the victorious life, no matter what the circumstances!

ELLIE KAY, B. S., author, speaker, spokesperson, America's Family Financial Expert, frequent guest on secular and Christian television and radio programs and magazines. *60-Minute Money Workout, Heroes at Home: Help and Hope for America's Military Families, Lean Body, Fat Wallet*.

It is an honor to hook my name to Diane Gardner's work and written testimony. *Overcoming the Enemy's Storms* is refreshingly transparent, filled with anguish-producing failures followed by Christ-honoring recoveries. It is intensely human and profoundly spiritual at the same time. I know Diane

Gardner and have for many years. Her story is the real deal. It incarnates James 5:11 that says: *We count those blessed who endured . . .* followed by this discovery: *The Lord is full of compassion and is merciful* (NASB). After reading the long list of heart-breaking and life-crushing events herein, you too will be amazed at the powerful grace that has brought Diane where she is today—a woman of faith, vision, and great joy. She is forward looking and changes the lives of the people she touches. Read this book and pass it on—please!

DR. DALE VAN STEENIS, PhD, DTh, international mentor, speaker, missionary, humanitarian, director of Leadership Strategies International (LSI), author of *Miracles Around the Globe,* and *Heard: The Power and Promise of Christian Prayer.*

As the reader of this book one will feel sorry for Diane who wrote it, another will determine "not" to ever again have a "pity party" of your own and hopefully, the best response will be an awareness of God's grace, which is made available to all who will receive and administer it. The tragedies and unfair treatment that Diane openly shares did not produce a bitter, unreachable woman, as it has in so many others. By accepting and dispensing grace she has become a more understanding and faith-filled woman of God, mother, and minister. As you read *Overcoming the Enemy's Storms* you will learn how to overcome.

I recommend this book because I know its author and walked with her through some of the storms.

DR. IVERNA TOMPKINS DD, DLitt, speaker, author, mentor to ministry and marketplace leaders, Pastor Emeritus and senior associate executive pastor in Phoenix, Arizona.

The "dark side of love" is vividly portrayed through the honest, transparent discourse of a life whose tragedies and defeats are upended in victory through the empowerment of divine intervention.

DR. MADELINE MANNING MIMS, DD, MDiv, speaker, four-time Olympic gold and silver medalist, award winning gospel artist, president of

United States Council for Sports Chaplaincy and a chaplain to athletes at the Olympic Games since1988, author of *The Hope of Glory*.

Diane Gardner is a great example of a woman who has continued serving God under intense pressure. In her book, *Overcoming the Enemy's Storms*, she writes about her feelings when the enemy attacked her calling and her family in ways most people never experience. Her story is a testament to the grace of the Lord.

DR. LISA GILFILLAN, DMin, MA, missionary, speaker, co-founder Good Shepherd Ministries distributor of the world's largest video/DVD Bible School, over 140 nations, International School of Ministry (ISOM), Director of Women of the World (WOW).

In her memoir, *Overcoming the Enemy's Storms*, Diane Gardner makes her life transparent to us. It is her hope that we will benefit from the trials she has experienced. Yet, through it all, Diane has found that God's grace is sufficient for the difficult circumstances the Enemy has thrown at her. Her inspiring story will help others find hope, peace, and God's grace.

SUSAN TITUS OSBORN, MA, director of the Christian Communicator Manuscript Critique Service and author of over 30 books including *Wounded by Words, Too Soon to Say Goodbye* and *Breaking Invisible Chains: Overcoming Domestic Violence*. She has taught Christian writing at conferences in the US and abroad.

OVERCOMING
THE
ENEMY'S STORMS

Healing Through the Grace of God

DIANE GARDNER

To Karen Sue,
May His grace surround
you and flow through
you as you read and
share these miraculous
testimonies of
grace.
Revelation 13:11
Diane
Gardner
May
2015

WESTBOW
PRESS
A DIVISION OF THOMAS NELSON
& ZONDERVAN

All Scripture is taken from the New King James Version (NKJ) of the Bible unless otherwise noted.

WestBow Press books may be ordered through booksellers or by contacting:

WestBow Press
A Division of Thomas Nelson
1663 Liberty Drive
Bloomington, IN 47403
www.westbowpress.com
1 (866) 928-1240

ISBN: 978-1-4908-1501-5 (sc)
ISBN: 978-1-4908-1500-8 (e)

Library of Congress Control Number: 2013921011

Printed in the United States of America.

WestBow Press rev. date: 01/15/2014

Contents

Dedication

To all who's teaching and supportive words imparted to me as an insecure, fearful, young woman the knowledge that God had purpose for my life and wanted to use me to heal others for Him.

To the memory of two of my mentors that taught me perseverance and grace. They are now a part of that great cloud of witnesses in heaven cheering me and others to our finish line.

Dr. Evelyn Carter Spencer "Rev. Ev" (graduated to her reward 1998) was an evangelist, teacher, who taught me the ways of the Holy Spirit and challenged me to maturity like none other in my life. She understood God called me to minister emotional healing and deliverance. Therefore, she taught me to be sensitive to the various ways God wants to heal.

Her love and sensitivity to the Holy Spirit allowed her to be used cross culturally and across denominational lines. Her passion was to be available to God anywhere.

She taught me to be transparent with God and people. Through her example I learned to have the tenacity of an overcomer.

My other mentor, Dr. Dick Mills (graduated to his reward 2012), was a unique prophet, author, and world-renowned scholar, whose wisdom was sought by government heads, religious leaders, and others. He was a wordsmith and had over 7,000 Scripture promises memorized and gave them as prophetic promises to people as God directed him whether on a plane, in a restaurant, on the phone, or in the pulpit.

I will always cherish not only the times he ministered at my church but the times I took he and his wife Betty to lunch simply to be in their presence and hear their wisdom. Each time we met or he spoke at my church he invested in my spiritual training by giving me a book with a timely theme for what God was saying to the Body of Christ. Or he gave me the latest Bible translation.

God used him to prophesy the Scriptures into my life, giving me valuable guidance.

Brother Dick, as he was affectionately called, taught me longevity in faithfulness to God, to treat everyone with the same respect, and to give someone an encouraging word or what he called a "good word" everyday.

Both Rev. Dr. Evelyn Spencer and Rev. Dr. Dick Mills prayed for and encouraged me during some of the trials mentioned in my memoir. I was strengthened by their correction, prayers, faith, and love.

Foreword

Eric Wilson, *New York Times* best-selling author of *Fireproof*

You are in for a treat. While reading *Overcoming the Enemy's Storms,* your life might be changed forever, and I don't say that lightly.

In 2008, my seventh novel hit the bookshelves and became my first bestseller. That book, titled *Fireproof* (based on the screenplay of the hit film), opened new doors for me. It also revealed the shallow nature of this business. As a Christian, my goal is not, and should not be, to promote myself but to honor Jesus, and yet this industry demands that you do promote yourself. How is a minister, musician, writer, or bricklayer supposed to reconcile this tension? This question still plagues my daily decision and demands that I ask God for wisdom.

Along this path, I am asked to attend certain events, one of which involved Pastor Diane Gardner. I never imagined the stories that were stirring in her heart and mind. Real-life stories. Stories full of twists and turns and conflict, enough to fill the scripts of a dozen Hollywood films.

Overcoming the Enemy's Storms isn't just gripping storytelling; it is an account of one woman's mistakes, successes, and the numerous ways in which God has led her through life's floods and fires to come out of the furnace without even the hint of smoke on her.

Diane's story is fast-paced. It is honest. She isn't promoting herself but the One who has the true power to change lives from within. She doesn't candy coat her own faults, and despite the ups and downs of her journey, she doesn't point fingers at others. She points only a finger at only One. The Only One. She points to the saving grace, the redeeming power, and the life-changing forgiveness that only Jesus can bring.

Violence, sexual sin, rape and abuse . . . these are all realities of a fallen world, realities Diane has faced, but as she makes clear, none of us need wallow in the role of a victim. Each of us can find freedom in *Overcoming the Enemy's Storms.*

Don't stop now. Turn the page. And let your life be changed.

Eric Wilson
Nashville, TN
May 2013

Acknowledgements

Thank You, Lord Jesus, for making a path for me to follow even on the stormy seas. You were my Way, my Truth, and my Life. I love You with all my heart. Be glorified through these testimonies of Your grace in the pages of this book.

I'm still faithful to the Lord for over forty-one years with Him because of the example of you who have helped me stay the course by strengthening the fibers of my character with your influence in my life over the years: Iverna Tompkins, Beverly "Bam" Crawford, A. L. and Joyce Gill, Fred and Betty Price, Tal and Dee Klaus, Dale and Gloria Van Steenis, Carol Cartwright, Stan DeKoven, Mary Ann Flynn, Bob and Frieda White, Donna Edward, Joe and Barbara Jordan, Garnett Simpson-Grier, Miss Lillie Knauls, John Kilpatrick, and the Monday night Bible teaching and worship classes for eight years that strengthened my passion and purpose whenever I was weary. These are only a few whom God used.

Rev. Joyce Gill and Rev. Liberty Savard as authors and ministers, you were the ones God used during my sixteen "silent" years. At times I showed my writing to no one else but one of you and then I buried it back in the drawer. You encouraged me and kept striking a match to my smoldering embers of hope. Thank you both for allowing me to frustrate you and you still believed in me.

Deborah Smith Pegues, I approached you so I could purposely be a blessing to a bestselling author as a way of releasing a fresh anointing in my life for writing. I was seriously stuck for almost a year. It worked, I got unstuck! God honored my faith and also gave me a wonderful mentor, encourager and friend. This is the first of many books.

I will eternally be grateful to Peter and Beverly Caruso, missionaries, authors, speakers. Over twenty years ago I attended my first writing workshop and purchased a book on writing by Beverly Caruso. I became open to the possibility that others could write besides those with a "writing gift." Later I visited with Beverly and she told me to start writing on anything I wanted to write about and when I was ready to pull things together and make a book call her. Sixteen years later in 2010 I called. By then I had a credenza full of files of my writings that had gone nowhere. Because of her extensive travel schedule she recommended Susan Titus Osborn's The Christian Communicator's Critique Service. This was exactly what I needed, one-on-one mentoring.

Through Susan's mentoring eventually my fears, intimidation, and poor writing skills melted away. God required me to write about issues that were hard to communicate. Susan, when you knew something was from God you encouraged me and helped me to tell the *depth* of my stories. Some things I had never told anyone. Heaven recorded how lovingly you opened my heart to write about unrevealed secrets.

The prayers of others have undergirded me, rescued me from the harassment of the Enemy, and helped me to hear from God. Thank you to all of you who prayed for me and my book. Most of all I thank all those who understood the value of your consistent intercession. I want to give special mention to: Liberty Savard also her Tuesday night prayer group. ACOB led by Rev. Darlene Palmer (you've been in the labor and delivery room with me. This is your victory too!). Mary, Betty, Helene, Joyce S., Miss Lillie, Sherry, Carlton, Kisha, Ruth, and Johnny, I am forever grateful. You are all overcomers.

A big thank you to those who corrected my rough drafts, over and over again you all know who you are, you're the ones whose eyes are crossed and brain is mush.

Many of you have given me finances as God directed you. Thank you so much. Believe me it was hard when God dried up my income from my speaking engagements to block my calendar so I could be still and write. He sustained me through the obedience of His children.

I want to give special mention to whom God asked to be financial partners:

Joyce S., your financial generosity and sensitivity to the Holy Spirit's timing is always an encouragement to me. Big rewards from heaven are coming your way. Carlton, you prayed and obeyed, thank you.

In memory of Maria (graduated to her reward 2010) who transcribed messages from cassettes and CDs so my information and dates could be as accurate as possible. One of her final wishes was the first financial gift for my book to be edited. This was a big encouragement. Thank you, Rick for your faithfulness to follow through with Maria's wishes. Our heavenly Father has multiplied His blessings to you.

Introduction

I almost drowned when I was twelve. A wave snatched six-year-old Patti from the sandy beach as we played next to each other. I grabbed her arm to save her, and the next wave took me out. I vividly remember to this day what it felt like. I recall an overwhelming feeling of helplessness as I tumbled under water. Each wave dragged me farther and farther out into the Pacific Ocean.

Suddenly someone grabbed my arm and swam aggressively straight up to the surface. I coughed up the salty water that had filled my mouth when I yelled for help on my last trip to the surface. I gasped for air and took a deep breath. The dizziness began to leave my head. My rescuer asked as she slipped her arm around my waist, "I've got you. Are you OK?"

I answered, "Yes, thank you, thank you so much!"

She said, "You're safe now. I'll do the work to get you back to shore. Climb on my back and hold onto my neck."

I couldn't help in the effort—I hadn't learned to swim. The best I could do was trust the lifeguard to know what to do for me and follow her instructions.

The storms in life sometimes come like those waves—totally unexpected—and we are swept away with an overwhelming feeling of helplessness. We aren't prepared and don't know what to do. The best we can do is trust our Savior to know what to do and follow the instructions in His Word.

This scenario of unexpected turbulent waves has been replayed in my life time and again. That's why I'm telling my story. Through *Overcoming the Enemy's Storms* I want to be the hand that grabs your arm and guides you to the surface past your pain, past your grief, past your disappointment, past your shame, past your self-pity, past your guilt, and even past your pride—to safety.

Join me in the following pages as I share my journey about the times I got pulled under by my agreement with the Enemy, and the times I called on the grace of God and walked on the water with Jesus.

There were storms I never dreamed I would face. Throughout these storms I came to realize that God and the Adversary both have a purpose for our lives. How we choose to respond to the vicissitudes of life will determine the outcome of any storm, i.e., whether we become a victim or an overcomer. This book will also help you to let go of the pain or the shame of someone else's actions.

Overcoming the Enemy's Storms reveals the nature of God our loving Father whose heart was broken when I made decisions that followed the Enemy's calculated plans for my life. God's grace was there all the time, but I didn't always access it.

I approached my book like a television documentary or research paper. I dug for over a year through journals, videos, cassettes, court papers, calendars, and the back of my mind. There are lots of dates because there are many storms and many answers to prayers. If you can't identify with one storm keep reading.

I'm praying for you as you read my memoir. I want to awaken in you a resolve to know God's Word and serve Him with passion, and purpose. If you have a victim's mentality this book is your breakthrough. From youth to seniors I want to see an army of women make the decision to become an overcomer. Let nothing stop you from your purpose. When you get weary pick this book up again and say, "If Diane is still standing so can I!"

God's Word will give you the courage to impact today's culture for His glory. It's time to influence governments, churches, the arts, businesses, media, education, and families through your prayers, your faith, your love, and your commitment to God's Word.

But thanks be to God, who gives us the victory through our Lord Jesus Christ (1 Corinthians 15:57).

About the Cover

The floods have lifted up, O Lord, the floods have lifted up their voice; the floods lift up their waves. The Lord on high is mightier than the noise of many waters, than the mighty waves of the sea (Psalms 93: 3-4).

On Saturday July 17, 1999, Rev. Jan Painter spoke at our church for the first time. Before she concluded the service she looked at me and said, "Last night I had a dream about you, your ministry, and your home. God showed me houses used for ministry training centers designed to send people to minster around the world. The final property was your house, Diane. You met me at the door in a long hostess dress. The home had extremely high ceilings and was beautifully decorated with things from around the world. I noticed a large picture of Jesus hanging on the wall as I first entered. As I looked closely I noticed He was barefooted because He walked on the stormy sea. His hand was extended toward whoever looked at the picture as if to say, *'Come walk on the water with Me.'*

"In the dream the picture came alive and Jesus looked at me and said, 'I have invited Diane to walk on the water with Me through the Enemy's storms. As long as she keeps her eyes on Me, she will walk through the storms on the water in victory.'"

For years I carried an image in my mind of the picture of Jesus in the prophetic dream. I could imagine Jesus with His hand extended inviting me to walk through the storm on the water with Him.

In July, 2008 I saw a picture painted by prophetic artist Leslie Marks of Visual Praise Gallery of Fine Art. Her husband Bill shared with me that this picture was painted while she was under the anointing of the Holy

Spirit at a conference. I excitedly shared with him the part of my prophecy that included the picture of Jesus walking on the water in a storm with His hand extended to me as an invitation to join Him. He smiled as I shared.

Over the next year I thought of that painting and reflected back on Jan's prophetic dream. I purchased the painting and now it hangs on my living room wall.

When I considered the cover for *Overcoming the Enemy's Storms* I thought of my painting. I contacted the artist and paid for permission to use the painting as my book cover. I hope this book cover will be a reminder that through life's storms our eyes should be focused on Him, our minds should be healed by Him, and our guidance should come from Him. Then we can successfully overcome the Enemy's storms and walk on the water with Jesus.

The Bible tells us the Apostle Peter received the same invitation to walk on the water in a storm with Jesus. He did so miraculously, but when he took his eyes off Jesus he sank.

> *And Peter answered Him and said, "Lord, if it is You, command me to come to You on the water." So He said, "Come."*
>
> *And when Peter had come down out of the boat, he walked on the water to go to Jesus. But when he saw that the wind was boisterous, he was afraid; and beginning to sink he cried out, saying, "Lord, save me!"*
>
> *And immediately Jesus stretched out His hand and caught him, and said to him, "O you of little faith, why did you doubt?" And when they got into the boat, the wind ceased* (Matthew 14:24-32).

The passage doesn't say Jesus *carried* Peter back to the boat—not at all. He walked back to the boat in the storm on the turbulent waves with Jesus. He was upheld by only one Word from the Lord: "Come."

PART I

Curtis

Chapter 1

Stranded

So the serpent spewed out of his mouth like a flood after the woman, that he might cause her to be carried away by the flood. (Revelation 12:15)

Sunday, October 27, 1996

I sat on the bench outside the baggage claim at Ontario International Airport and shivered from the cool, damp October air. I glanced at my watch: 9:30 p.m. My son Curtis was due at 8:30 p.m. I called his beeper but did not receive a response. I tried Carlton's beeper three times to see if he knew where his brother was, but he didn't answer either.

A woman sat on the bench next to me and smiled. "Hi, I'm Sandy."

"Hi, I'm Diane. You were on the Seattle flight, right?"

"Yes, I was visiting my daughter. I'm waiting for my son."

"What a coincidence. I'm waiting for my son, also. Looks like I'm stranded, so I'm frustrated. If you'll excuse me, Sandy, I'll call Ken from my church and see if he can pick me up. My oldest son, Curtis, is always on time and responsible. If something happened, I can't understand why he didn't call. This is unlike him." After making the call, I hung up. "Ken and Linda are coming. Do you need a ride?"

"No. My son was working, but he'll be here. Thanks anyway. Were you in Washington for business or pleasure?"

"On business, I'm a Bible teacher. I spoke at a women's retreat."

We stopped our conversation and watched a man in a beige sports jacket walk in front of us for the third time to make a call from the nearby payphone. "I wonder if he might be stranded and need a ride? The other guy in the brown bomber jacket might be with him. I saw them talking."

"Yes, I noticed." Sandy stood up. "Oh, my son's here. It was nice to meet you." She shook my hand and left.

As soon as Sandy left the man in the sports jacket hung up the phone, walked over to my bench and looked down at me. "Are you Diane Gardner?"

I raised my eyebrows. "I don't think I know you. Have we met?"

"We're looking for Diane Gardner," he said. "You are the only passenger left at the airport. I'm Detective Smith." He pointed to the man in the brown jacket who now stood at the other end of the bench. "This is my partner, Detective Lott, and we're from the Corona Police Department."

He flashed his badge and nodded at Detective Lott who flashed his badge, but said nothing. Detective Smith pulled three pictures out of his sport coat pocket and sat down next to me. The first picture was a man's driver's license.

"Do you know this man?" he asked.

I felt uneasy. *No one gives up their driver's license to anyone. Was there a car accident involving this man and Curtis? Does the detective think I know something?* "No, I don't recognize him."

"Do you drive a red Cadillac with license number . . .?"

Why did he ask me about my car? Oh no, was Curtis in a terrible wreck? I took a deep breath. "Yes, I do."

"Do you have two sons, one Curtis and the younger Carlton?"

I hesitated. "Yes . . . they are my only children."

The detective showed me the other two pictures. "Is this your son, Curtis, and his ex-wife, Karen?"

"Yes, that is my son and daughter-in-law."

He stared into my eyes. "Well, Ms. Gardner, I'm sorry to tell you this, but Warren, the man whose license I have, was shot in the head at close range today. We think he's your ex-daughter-in-law's boyfriend. He's in the hospital having surgery and is in critical condition. This took place outside Karen's apartment in Corona around 1:00 p.m. Curtis allegedly shot him, kidnapped his ex-wife, and drove off in a red Cadillac. A neighbor gave us the license number. DMV shows the car is registered to you."

His partner shifted his weight. "Three children were abandoned at the scene and taken in by a neighbor," Detective Lott said. "The children told police it was their daddy who shot Warren and took their mommy with him. Mr. Warren's son is with his grandparents, and your grandchildren are with Karen's parents."

I felt as if time and my heart had both stopped. I jumped up and stumbled to the edge of the curb. I looked heavenward and released my emotions. "No! No! Jesus, No!" I released a deep groan. *How could this happen?*

Detective Smith came up beside me. "This entire airport is surrounded by Ontario Police. We were prepared to arrest Curtis if he picked you up. I have more bad news. Because this is a kidnapping, before you get home, this will be on the evening news on all channels."

I swallowed the lump in my throat. "How'd you know I was here and that Curtis was supposed to pick me up?"

"We did research to find Curtis's family. Through DMV records we found Curtis's brother in Riverside and brought him in for questioning. We confiscated his beeper to monitor any contact from Curtis. It went off repeatedly and when we showed him the number, he said it was you. Carlton wanted to leave because he said Curtis was scheduled to pick you up at the Ontario Airport. We told him he had to stay at the station, that we would take care of you."

I felt like my head would explode. I needed a place to cry and talk to God. "I need to go to the restroom; right now!"

"I can't let you go by yourself because Curtis may call you," Detective Smith said. "Detective Lott has to accompany you and stand in the doorway."

I nodded, rushed inside the building, and headed toward the restroom. Just then, Ken and Linda pulled up. Linda got out of the car and followed Detective Lott as he followed me. They stood at the door to the restroom. He informed her he was a detective and told her a little about Curtis.

Once I entered the restroom stall, I let out a wail of grief that I'm sure carried down the empty terminal corridor. "No, no, no!" I said, over and over. My mind wanted none of this to be real. I cried and screamed for what seemed like an hour, but it was only fifteen minutes.

I called on the Lord between my deep sobs. "Jesus! Have *mercy* on Curtis! Forgive him, Lord! Your Word says in 1 John 5:16: *If anyone sees his brother sinning a sin which does not lead to death, he will ask, and He will give him life for those who commit sin not leading to death.* "God, he has sinned against You. He has sinned against others. I ask You to preserve his life by the blood of Jesus. Cleanse him of these sins. Have mercy on the man who was shot, and have mercy on his child and family. Have mercy on Karen, my grandkids, and her parents. Have mercy on Carlton. Have mercy on me! I need your help, Lord." I wiped the tears away. "Oh God, if Curtis hasn't killed Karen already *please* help him to listen to You and *not* kill her. Deliver him from yielding to Satan's voice anymore!"

I sighed several times and cried again. I thought of what Detective Smith said about the television news programs. "God, please rescue me and cover me from the media. Rescue me so they don't come to my house and harass me, Carlton, or my neighbors. Please keep them from coming to Your church. Protect me, protect Carlton, and protect everyone in the church from reporters and media. Let them interrupt not *one* church service. Protect us by Your precious blood, Jesus, by Your angels, and for Your Name's sake. Protect my grandkids from any further trauma. Holy Spirit, you are my comforter and helper. Comfort me and help me; now!"

I remembered James 4:7, which is one of my favorite verses when the storms of life hit. *Therefore submit to God. Resist the devil and he will flee from you* (James 4:7).

I had submitted to God. Now I needed to resist the Devil. "I come against any further plans of the Enemy to destroy Curtis and Karen. In Jesus name, I rebuke any further assaults from Satan!"

A few minutes later, I calmed down and emerged from the stall. Detective Lott held the door open, and Linda stood just inside the door with tears in her eyes. I walked over and hugged her tightly.

My voice broke between words. "Thank you for being here. I thank God for my brothers and sisters in Christ, my church family."

We walked toward the sliding glass doors to exit, but Detective Lott stopped us. "I'm sorry, but they can't take you home. We need you to come to the police station. After we question you, Carlton can leave with you."

I pointed toward Ken and Linda's car. "May I ride with them?"

He hesitated. "Well, if they stay right behind us on the way to the station. I will need to take your cell phone with us."

On the twenty-five minute drive to the station, I told Ken and Linda about my encounter with the detectives. I was still in a state of shock.

We entered the old cement building and walked the bare corridor behind the detectives to an open area. As we stepped into the room, I saw my twenty-five-year-old son, Carlton. When he saw me, he jumped from his chair, rushed over, and hugged me tightly.

"Mom, you kept beeping me, and that guy had my beeper, so I couldn't answer you." He pointed at a police officer. "The police thought it might be Curtis, but when they showed me the number, I told them it was you. I said Curtis was supposed to pick you up at the airport, but if he couldn't, then I needed to do it. The detective wouldn't let me leave. So they said they would send someone to pick you up and that I couldn't call to tell you."

Tears ran down my cheeks and I hugged him again. "I know Carlton, they told me."

"They keep asking me the same questions, but I told them I was out of town most of the weekend. I haven't seen Curtis since before I left."

"Yes, I know you visited your friends from your summer job at Port Hueneme."

"That's what I told them when they pulled my truck over and asked me if I was Curtis's brother. Mom, I got to Riverside this afternoon and ate dinner while I watched the football game at a restaurant. On my way home they stopped me."

An officer approached us and pointed toward me. "I need you to talk to a detective, alone."

Fortunately, one of the Corona police detectives, Detective Jay, was a member of my congregation so they allowed him to question me. We stepped into a small musty smelling enclosed room.

"When was the last time you saw Curtis?" he asked.

"Wednesday afternoon I spent time with him and my grandkids before I left Thursday for Seattle."

"What activities did you do and where?"

"We played games and read to the kids at Curtis's house in Riverside."

"What did you talk about?"

"Mostly about things the kids had done that week. I asked him to pick me up when I returned tonight. He said he would call me on Friday to confirm."

Jay put his leg up on the chair next to me.

"And what was your Friday conversation like?"

"He seemed upset after a conversation with a friend at Father's Rights, Inc. of California where he does volunteer work. The organization helped him during the divorce, but I think the Enemy used this 'friend' to agitate Curtis. On Friday the guy told Curtis he was a victim. I believe that fed his distorted sense of injustice. I asked Curtis why he was so upset and he said he and the guy were discussing how women betray men. I asked Curtis not to listen to him, but he ignored me. I was troubled with his attitude.

"God impressed me to pray for both of my children and I did, but only for a few minutes and not on a deep level because I wanted to study for the retreat. Now I realize I tried to obey God *my* way. God wanted me to open that deeper door of prayer and resistance to the Enemy, and I didn't humble myself like God wanted. He always helps me, but I don't always understand how serious things are. Curtis still may have done what he did or maybe it would have been less tragic if I'd have prayed and listened. I reject condemnation, but the fact is I'll never know."

I let out a big sigh of regret and continued. "Let me finish allowing you to do your job. Curtis agreed to pick me up at the airport. I told him where my spare keys were if he chose to use my car instead of his grandparent's old clunker. Their car doesn't go over thirty-five miles an hour."

"Where's his Lexus?"

"As you know Curtis had an expensive Beverly Hills divorce lawyer. And since he was self-employed he wasn't paid when he took off work for court or to keep his kids, so the Lexus was repossessed. Since then he has been driving his grandparent's old spare car."

Jay rubbed his chin. "When I heard what happened, I wondered why he was in your car." Jay put both feet on the ground. "Please wait here. I need to talk to my boss."

I whispered a prayer. "God, thanks for Your grace. I appreciate that Jay knows Curtis and me personally and questioned me with genuine compassion. He didn't treat me like an accomplice or a criminal. Bless Jay, Lord."

A few minutes later an officer walked in and asked me to step into the room where everyone was seated.

Detective Jay stood in the middle of the room. "Ken and Linda, you are free to leave. I'll give Pastor Diane a ride home."

"Diane, when we get home, we'll call people to pray," Ken said.

"I want to be with you when you see the news reports on television," Jay said. "I'm really not sure how it's going to go down with Curtis. I hope the arrest is peaceful and there isn't a showdown." He took my right hand in both his hands. "I know you can understand these things because you have helped many people deal with law enforcement. I want to be there for you, so I will take you home. My boss wants me to stay an hour or so to see if Curtis calls the house or your cell. You understand why, right?"

"I understand, Detective Jay. Thank you."

"Carlton, you can follow us in your truck," Jay said.

I rode home in silence. *My life as I've known it and my relationship with Curtis, Karen, and my grandchildren has changed forever.* We arrived at my home around midnight. As we drove up, we saw three cars that belonged to people from our congregation. I stepped out of the unmarked police car and waived at everyone, but didn't speak.

"I thought I heard them say Curtis's name on the radio," Michael said.

"I saw something on TV. I came to see if it was really our Curtis," Ruth said.

Carlton unlocked the front door and we followed him into the house.

"Yes, it is *our* Curtis they are talking about," Jay said.

Ten of us sat around the television. The news reports were horrendous. Every few minutes there was a report with *my* son's picture and the description of *my* car. Every reporter sounded as if they were shouting at me. "Armed and dangerous, armed and dangerous. This suspect is armed and dangerous."

I knew he was armed. I could never minimize that horrible fact, but I hated hearing those words over and over like he was on a shooting rampage. I felt sick knowing my child, who knew the Lord, allowed his mind to become so darkened by the Enemy that he would deliberately seriously hurt other people. Curtis had given in completely to the temptation to do evil. He ignored all the warnings from His heavenly Father.

Let no one say when he is tempted, "I am tempted by God"; for God cannot be tempted by evil, nor does He himself tempt anyone. But each one is tempted when he is drawn away by his own desires and enticed (James 1:13-14).

That night, as I sat in my family room and looked at the television with everyone else, I knew I needed to get some relief from my pent-up feelings. I decided to whisper a prayer every time the reporters talked about Curtis. "Holy Spirit, Jesus said You are the Comforter so I give You my pain. I give You my grief. I give You my shame." Later, I put the Enemy on notice and declared. "Curtis and Karen will live and not die."

Those at my home began to reminisce about the last time they had seen Curtis.

"You all know the last time we saw Curtis was only a week ago," Richard said. "He was at our dedication for the church building we just moved into. He was on the platform with his mom and brother as they prayed over our building. He prayed a beautiful dedication prayer. He kissed his mom, said goodbye to us, and left to attend his church down the street."

"Before church that day, I asked him where his kids were," Mark said. "Curtis said they were with their mom because they had joint custody."

Kathy moved to the edge of her chair. "In June the county officials chose us out of six churches that presented proposals to rent the old March Air Force Base off-base chapel until time for demolition and redevelopment. The newspaper ran an article about the base conversion and winner of the proposal with our name as the one chosen. Curtis and his kids came to our old building to help us celebrate the favor of God on our ministry. He was laughing and talking with everyone."

"Five weeks ago Curtis helped us load a truck with a refrigerator, stove, and ceiling fans from the old vacant military houses across the street from the church," Palmer said. "Curtis worked hard right alongside us. He seemed alright to me."

Suddenly everyone stopped. "Look!" someone said. "The Los Angeles police chief is about to be interviewed by the reporters. We're over an hour away from Los Angeles, in Riverside County, so what does L.A. have to do with this?"

"One of our own was shot today while off duty," the L.A. police chief said into the camera. "He was shot at some apartments in Corona and is in the hospital in grave condition. Take a good look at the picture of this suspect. He is at large."

"Oh no!" I said.

The police chief continued. "Believe me, we will do everything within our power to apprehend this man. This is also a kidnapping. The suspect drove off with his ex-wife in the car, so we are working closely with all Riverside law enforcement departments. I'm turning you back to Riverside for the phone numbers and description of the getaway vehicle."

In shock we watched the news, prayed, cried, and watched the news again on another channel. It was worse than a bad nightmare and secretly I wished I could wake up soon.

At 2:00 a.m. Detective Jay received a call. He pulled me aside from everyone. "The police received a call from a security patrol in Riverside. He saw a vehicle that fit the description of your car parked at the abandoned military houses across the street from our church. A police helicopter is hovering over the car with the spotlight on it. I need to go." He paused, pursed his lips, and took my right hand with both his hands. "I'll call you as soon as I can." Then he left.

The church and abandoned houses were eleven miles from my home. Jay turned down Harmon Street, the dark isolated street off Van Buren Boulevard, which separated our church from the deserted military houses. As he headed toward the helicopter light that hovered over my abandoned car, he heard screams coming from the darkness. He stopped his car, rolled his window down, and drew his gun. In the moonlight he saw Karen run from behind the school next door to our church, screaming hysterically. Jay called her name and she recognized his voice.

"Jay, Detective Jay, thank you, thank you," she said through her sobs.

With his gun still drawn Jay got out and opened his back door to let her in. "Where's Curtis?"

"He's gone! He ran away! He told me to stay behind the school until he left if I wanted to live."

"We have law enforcement patrolling the area. You're safe now."

Jay opened the glove box and grabbed a stack of napkins to apply pressure to Karen's bleeding hand. "Keep these napkins on your wound with pressure, even if it hurts, it'll help slow down the bleeding. I'm calling for the ambulance, and I'll stay with you until the ambulance arrives."

She continued through her sobs. "Jay, he beat me. I've never seen him like that. Curtis went crazy, yelling and screaming at me for hours about our divorce. Then he yelled some of the same things we saw in a movie last year where the guy shot the girl in the hand. So he shot me in the hand I used to sign the divorce papers. He was evil."

"Is that what happened to your hand? I'm sorry he did that. Karen, I'm here because they spotted his mom's car."

"That's . . . what . . . Curtis said. The police or someone shined a light on the car. So he said, 'This is it! They've found us! There's a light on the car so we've got to go.' The car was parked a distance away from the house he held me in."

"What happened when the light shined on the car?"

"Curtis grabbed me. We ran across the street and ducked behind the school. He told me to stay there if I wanted to live, and don't come out until he's gone."

"What happened when you first left the apartments?"

"The child locks were on the back doors so I couldn't open them. Curtis drove to an empty field and then pulled me out of the car. I looked around to see where we were, and it was near Lake Matthews, between Riverside and Corona. Then he put me in the trunk so he could get some gas and no one could see me. After that he drove over to these empty houses across from his mom's church. It's like he knew where he wanted to take me."

Karen paused. "Jay, where are my kids? He left the kids and Warren's son standing on the sidewalk crying. I asked him not to leave them, but he said someone will call the police, and they'll take them in. Where are they?"

"A neighbor got your emergency contact phone number from your purse and called your parents. The kids are with them. My department contacted Warren's parents."

Karen sighed in relief. "Where is my boyfriend, Warren? I know he was hurt bad."

"Last I heard, he was in critical condition in surgery at the hospital."

She identified the red Cadillac as the car Curtis had her in, and then showed the police the house which Curtis held her hostage. They went in to gather evidence. The ambulance arrived and took Karen to the same hospital as Officer Warren. They examined her and treated her hand. Then Corona police detectives questioned her.

At my home everyone left by 3:00 a.m. Carlton was emotionally exhausted so he fell asleep immediately. I went to bed too, but thoughts and questions bombarded my mind. *When would I hear from my son? When would Curtis be arrested? How would the arrest happen? Will Curtis resist with a showdown? How do I get to sleep now or the next few nights? When will I see my grandchildren? How do I handle the constant calls I will receive from the police department asking if I've seen Curtis? How can I serve my congregation when I feel like this storm is going to wash me away?*

I finally fell asleep for two hours. When I awakened, I began to wonder what I could say to Warren's parents. I know they love their son as much as I love mine. What could the family of the violator say to the family of the victim? Telling them I'm sorry my family hurt their family sounded so shallow.

I sent a bouquet of flowers to the hospital with a note which read how sorry I was that this happened. I don't know if they received the flowers or refused to accept them. What do you do when you are the parent of the perpetrator? There's a depth of sorrow we feel for the victims, but where is our legitimate outlet?

Even to this day, I pray for Warren, who I heard is confined to a wheelchair and unable to function. I also pray for his family when the Holy Spirit impresses me to do so. Otherwise I have confidence that God has surrounded them with those who love and pray for them. I use Proverbs 4:23 as a guide on how to pray for Warren: *Keep your heart with all diligence, for out of it spring the issues of life.* To keep my heart means to release the pain as soon as I recognize it has surfaced. I also don't allow the Enemy or my own emotions to torment me about Warren.

Little did I know, my storms had just begun.

Chapter 2

The Showdown

Oh my God, I trust in You; Let me not be ashamed; Let not my enemies triumph over me. Indeed, let no one who waits on You be ashamed. (Psalm 25:2-3)

Monday, October 28, 1996

I tossed and turned after going to bed around 3:30 a.m., plagued with worry over Curtis. I only slept two hours. On that Monday morning, my sister, two brothers, sister-in-law and their children arrived at my home to be with me. I appreciated their support, especially my brother Kenneth, who was a Christian. My Muslim family members joined Kenneth and me in prayer.

All of us sat in front of the television to see if the police had found Curtis. From early morning until my family left around bedtime, every news channel interrupted its regular programs with the story of the "armed and dangerous" man on the loose.

As my family and I watched the television news, suddenly we saw the inside of my church building. It took my breath away.

"What happened? Why are they in *my* church?" I explained to my family. "The March Joint Powers Authority (MJPA), staff is the only ones with the keys to the building. They are the property managers for my landlords. They already met Curtis. I introduced them weeks earlier when appliances they gave us were moved from the abandoned military houses."

They must have let the police in, but they also have keys to the abandoned school next door. Why didn't the MJPA staff offer the police the keys to the vacant school? I don't get it. This is getting crazier.

The police department called out the Special Weapons and Tactics (SWAT) team. Throughout the day news footage showed the SWAT team inside *my* church, strategizing about how to capture *my* son. *This is an evil satanic irony.* The police believed he barricaded himself inside one of the three hundred abandoned military houses. We watched as they kicked in the doors and ducked between the houses. The same footage was on every channel, over and over.

"Some members of the SWAT team believe they heard a shot come from one of the houses," a reporter said. "The suspect may have committed suicide. They are looking now for a dead body."

Showdown with the Fear of Suicide

When I heard this news, I sat quietly in the corner of my family room on a kitchen stool. My family members sat on the couch and loveseat. Fortunately, no one said anything immediately about those negative words. That gave me time to focus before the atmosphere got negative. I knew at that moment I had to choose sympathy or victory. I could not have both. I could start crying over their speculations and have everyone "love" on me and comfort me, but there would be no healing, and I would feel worse. Or I could settle my mind and emotions and not allow them to start racing with fear or anxiety about the SWAT Team and reporters' speculations.

As I got quiet, I didn't believe Curtis had taken his own life. I didn't have a sense of the "tearing away" or "separation" death brings to our hearts. So I refused to receive the news, not because of denial in my head, but from a knowing in my spirit. *Holy Spirit, You are the Spirit of Truth, and You know all things. Is this true that Curtis killed himself or attempted to do so, because I don't sense it?* I waited in silence for a few moments.

I felt nothing and I heard nothing. Just as my family began to make comments about the news report, the phone rang. It was a close friend in Los Angeles, the founder of a large well-known ministry.

My sister answered the phone for me. "Diane, its Dr. Crawford. Do you want to take this call?"

"Yes, I'll take it."

"Hello, Diane, of course you know I'm praying for you. Have you heard the current news? They said Curtis may have committed suicide. What do you think? How do you feel about what they are saying? I called to pray with you."

"Thank you so much. Yes, I've heard. I was praying about that when the phone rang. My heart sank the first time I heard the word suicide, but I refused to allow my emotions to run away with anxiety and fear. Honestly, I considered what is in my heart more than the words from their mouths. I don't *sense* any separation from Curtis that would indicate he is dead. Besides, that's not the covenant I have with God.

"For many years I have said to the Lord, 'I confess that my children will *not die* prematurely. I will die a ripe old age, and my children and grandchildren will bury me.' I quote Psalm 118:17: *I shall not die, but live, And declare the works of the LORD.* I believe also that Curtis shall not die, but live and declare the works of the Lord."

"I will be in agreement with you on that promise," Dr. Crawford said.

"Thanks. Until I hear differently, I believe God will rescue him from Satan and from himself."

"I wanted to check on you. I'm glad you are handling this in faith and in courage. I'll keep prayful. Let's pray together now."

Her powerful prayer comforted me.

When I watched the television and saw the SWAT team in my church, I was thankful to God that almost two years earlier I obeyed Him and returned to my maiden name. I was impressed to do this for over six months, but I thought how troublesome to change a name I have had for twenty-seven years. The impression grew stronger and finally I realized it was God and obeyed. I took my divorce papers to the Family Law office and changed my name. When I did this I felt a release from the covering that my married name provided. I felt vulnerable and yet free.

That day, I was glad the sign on my office door said "Gardner" and did not match Curtis's last name. I imagined what it would be like if there was a church marquee with my married name and television cameras everywhere.

Then I thanked God for my answer to the prayer I prayed in the airport about protection from media harassment. *They'll know soon enough that we are related. Even if some already know, it isn't the topic of conversation with the media or the police at this point.* The SWAT team continued its search until after dark. By that time most of the doors to the abandoned houses had been kicked in.

Again, I went to bed worried about Curtis. *Would he turn himself in to the police? Would he keep running? How would the arrest happen? Would Curtis surrender peacefully or would there be a showdown? When would I hear from him? Was he OK?*

Curtis had become a fugitive and a vagabond like Cain who, after killing his brother, was banished to a lifetime of wandering in another land. Genesis 4:10-11 says: *And He* (God) *said, "What have you done? The voice of your brother's blood cries out to Me from the ground . . . A fugitive and a vagabond you shall be on the earth."*

The next day, Tuesday, an article on Curtis filled a large portion of the local section of the newspaper. It asked for any information on his whereabouts. My son had become the main fugitive in the Inland Empire—Riverside and San Bernardino counties. I decided not to read the details that morning. I figured the news certainly would not be any different than the television news from the night before.

Instead, I took the whole local section of the paper and held it up toward heaven. While tears ran down my face, I turned my face upward. I don't remember saying anything. I had prayed all I knew to pray and said all I knew to say. I made this gesture as a sign of surrender to Jesus, the only One who could have anything to say at this point. All I could do was groan and utter deep guttural sounds.

Romans 8:26 (MSG) says: *He* (the Holy Spirit) *does our praying in and for us, making prayer out of our wordless sighs, our aching groans.*

I continued with the groans, sighs, and tears until I felt the release of the Holy Spirit. With one big sigh of relief, I felt finished—sort of like when a conversation ends and we know we're done. The Holy Spirit was having a conversation with Father God about me, through me, and I let Him finish. Then a peace filled my mind. *And the peace of God, which surpasses all understanding, will guard your hearts and minds through Christ Jesus* (Philippians 4:7). I felt strengthened.

The fear of Curtis ever committing suicide never entered my thoughts again.

Showdown with the Adversary

After my time of surrender, I received a call from my administrator, Darlene. "Pastor Diane, a MJPA staff member called me. They said we were cleared by the police to return to the church building. So I'll leave and meet you there."

I drove to my church in a borrowed Corvette, owned by a couple in my congregation. I like to drive fast, fancy cars, but this situation took all the fun away from driving a Corvette. I arrived about an hour after the call. Darlene was already at work in her office. I wanted to give her an understanding of what I was about to do. I knew a *showdown with the Adversary* was in order that day.

I was determined to clear the horrible spiritual atmosphere resident in my church building and surrounding area. I wanted no darkness around—the feelings of shame, fear, defilement, or grief. I needed to take back the territory from the Enemy. I refused to walk into my church building and feel overwhelmed with pain about the SWAT team. So I needed to face the Adversary head on and set my boundaries before he could use this any further as an assault against my emotions.

I didn't want people giving fuel to what Satan meant as a mockery against God and me.

"Hello, Darlene, I didn't come today to do office work, but to do spiritual work. I have a battle to fight with Satan. The Enemy put it in Curtis's mind to violate others, and Curtis is at fault because he obeyed those evil thoughts. I asked God for mercy and protection for him.

"Some of Curtis's actions were motivated by Satan to specifically assault me and my calling. Years ago, before you came, I taught workshops for the California State Office of Criminal Justice Planning on the Religious Community and Victims of Violence for Governor Deukmejian. This was a networking model to bring together the religious community, law enforcement, and clinical professionals to heal the victim and the violator of a violent crime. I was a part of a Think Tank Workshop who produced a booklet called A Transfer of Knowledge used by professionals statewide. I don't have a clue how many victims and violators were helped, but the Enemy knows. That's why I say *some things* were directed to mock what God has done and will do with my life.

"For example, my son is now the violator, Warren and his family, Karen, her family, my grandchildren and I are victims of a violent crime. This is what I call a Satan-inspired *irony*.

"Curtis had his grandparents' car for months, but on that day he switched cars so he could use *my* car in his crime. I feel like I participated in Satan's plan when I told him where my keys were. I'll take time to forgive myself for that later.

"There are lots of desolate places between Corona and Riverside, but the Enemy made sure he brought Karen *here*, across from *my* church. Satan knows God favored me with this building because God told me He has given me spiritual authority over all the land MJPA staff oversees. The Enemy used Curtis to shed innocent blood on *this* land and caused it to become defiled before God. These ideas came directly from Satan to mock God."

"I understand," she said.

"I came to church today for only one reason, and when I am done, I'll leave. I need to have a showdown with the Adversary today. He has come to mock God's favor in granting *me* this building. We've only been meeting for worship here three weeks. God has called us to introduce people to the Prince of Peace in this building instead we had guns, assault rifles, and a SWAT team in the building. We've already been shown on television and in the paper for a negative reason. I will believe God one day we will be featured for good reasons. I forgive Curtis, but I am *angry* at him. And I *really hate* the Devil."

The children's church/banquet room was where the SWAT team set up their command center on Monday. I walked around the room to survey things and think through how I wanted to approach the Enemy. My words would be my weapon of choice. I wanted to make sure I caused damage to the kingdom of darkness.

The SWAT team left the tables in square horseshoe formation. The set up reminded me of a war room scene from the movies where strategic planning took place. The significance of the warfare strategy performed here, on my tables, in my church building, to capture my son, almost overwhelmed my emotions.

The room reeked with the smell of cigarettes and onions. The trash cans overflowed with cigarette butts, bags from fast food restaurants, coffee cups, and soda cans.

Then, the words came to me. I stopped and planted my feet. "Devil, I'm here to have a *showdown* with you. I'm sure I'll shed many tears for many years over different aspects of this incident with Curtis. But I refuse to shed one tear about the SWAT team using my church building as its command center to capture *my son*! I know this was your strategy sent to mock God and me! You thought this storm would take me under, but I'm not ignorant of your devices! I won't let it work! I'll not spend an ounce of emotional pain or energy on *this* issue!

"By the authority God has given me through the Name and by the blood of Jesus, I rebuke the demonic spirits who have an evil contract concerning this! I rebuke your plans! I cancel your demonic assignment over this building and this land!"

I took a deep breath, but I wasn't finished. Not by a long shot. "I come against every spirit assigned to mock God and mock me. I come against the thief who has tried to steal my God-given influence in this region, in Jesus' name! I will *not* leave Riverside. I will *not* leave this church building one day sooner or one day later than God intends! My landdords will *not* ask me to leave either. Satan, you defiled this land through the shedding of innocent blood. That blood cries out to God for vengeance. I come against that defilement and command the land to be cleansed by the innocent blood of Jesus Christ, which cries out for mercy!"

My resolve got stronger and I spoke louder. "I will never be heartbroken over this specific betrayal, nor hold Curtis accountable for listening to you about this property. He was a pawn in your hand and yielded to your destructive plans. You wanted this storm of betrayal by my son against me, my calling, and my car, to wash me away emotionally. Well, it didn't work!"

I walked around the room and at times stomped my feet. "Satan, this battle is strictly between you and me. Curtis is no longer a part of this betrayal and mockery. I defeat you with the Sword of the Spirit which is the Word of God, because Jesus said in Luke 10:18-20 (MSG): *See what I've given you? Safe passage as you walk on snakes and scorpions, and protection from every assault of the Enemy. No one can put a hand on you.*

"There *will not* be another battle over the issue of Curtis's betrayal of this property. There will not be another battle over his use of my vehicle, which I know was your idea. I declare my *victory* today by the authority of the Name and by the power of the blood of Jesus!"

With those words I was finished with the Enemy.

It was time to talk to my Father. "I release Curtis from accountability to me for the defilement and curse put on this land. I release Curtis for using my car in his crime. I ask You to forgive Curtis for his disobedience to your warnings, for doing evil, and for shedding the innocent blood of Warren and Karen. You are a righteous judge on behalf of the cry of innocent blood. Curtis is to be judged by You for shedding that blood. But the blood of Jesus speaks of mercy. I ask You,

Father, have mercy on him and forgive him. Your Word says: *God Who is Judge of all . . . to the sprinkled blood* (of Jesus) *which speaks [of mercy] . . . a better message than the blood of Abel [which cried out for vengeance]* (Hebrews 12:23-24).

"Lord, I ask you to mark Curtis's forehead as you marked Cain's according to Genesis 4:15: *And the Lord set a mark or sign upon Cain, lest anyone finding him should kill him.* I ask You that no one be able to kill Curtis because of Your mark on him. I submit everything to You, Father. I trust You. Amen."

I lifted my head and arms toward heaven. I put my arms down and looked around the room one last time, let out a big sigh, and walked out in confidence that I had accomplished a victory.

I went back to Darlene's office. "Please clean up the room where the SWAT team was. Dismantle the tables that are in horseshoe formation, dump the trash, and spray air fragrance. I will *never* complain to you or anyone else about the SWAT team having been here. I'll only mention it under the direction of the Holy Spirit when He wants me to give a testimony of victory. The Devil's assault to overwhelm me emotionally on this issue didn't work. If others in the congregation mention this to you, tell them to speak of Satan's *defeat* and Jesus' *victory,* and nothing else. The showdown is over, and Jesus and I have won."

I paused while I stared at Darlene. "Thank you for agreeing with me. This battle over any feelings of betrayal, defilement of the land, and the evil planned against the purposes of God for me to have this church is over!"

"In the Name of Jesus, I agree!" she said.

Showdown over the Land

A week after my showdown at the church I took my own prayer SWAT (Spiritual Weapons Assault Tactics) team from my congregation and collectively in unity had a similar *showdown* with the Enemy over the land. My team walked around the school property where Curtis had brought Karen to hide. We asked forgiveness and cleansed the land of defilement. We also walked between the houses and spoke the scripture passages that declared our victory over the Enemy. We repented for the bloodshed on the property because of Curtis. We sanctified, or set apart, the land and cleansed it for God's use for His desired purposes. We received communion as a sign of covenant, and then poured the rest of the grape juice on the land as a symbol of Jesus' blood cleansing it. Our desire was to make the land ready for God's blessings.

Jesus said the spoken word is what cleansed the disciples: *"You are already clean because of the word which I have spoken to you"* (John 15:3).

To this day I have never shed a tear about Satan's assault concerning the betrayal of the property or the betrayal of the use of my vehicle, which took me eight weeks to get back. It took the grace of God for the insurance company to pay for my car repairs. Because my car was used in a crime, and because Curtis had my permission to use the car, the insurance company teetered about whether they should pay. They mentioned if I said he stole the car, they would pay. But that would be a lie. He didn't steal it. The insurance adjuster and I discussed daily the same question and I gave the same answer. "Ms Gardner, did you give Curtis permission to use your car on that day?"

"The answer is yes and no," I said to the adjuster. "I gave him permission to use my car *only* to drive to the airport later that evening. I *didn't* give him permission to take it earlier in the day."

At the end of two weeks I said, "I pray for you to please be merciful toward me as you do your job." I've learned that humility goes a lot further than demanding what you believe are your rights. God gives me favor when I'm humble and yet firm.

Finally she said, "They are going to pay for the repairs on your vehicle."

The cost was several thousand dollars. Two days after the approval I met the AAA tow truck at the police station to have my car towed to the auto shop. There was black powder for finger print evidence everywhere inside the car and in the trunk.

Showdown with Shame

The Enemy wanted to disable me, to fill me with shame in my neighborhood, and my community. He wanted me to consider a move from the area. These were the thoughts the Enemy used to bombard my mind. Years earlier I learned one way I could take captive my thoughts was to say the opposite of what the Enemy says. I said, "I will not move from this area. God put me here and I'll not leave until He tells me! I will never leave because of shame!"

My trials made me stronger to embrace my authority as a believer. My storms made me wiser about the Enemy's tactics.

A few days following the incident I had papers about the building that were to be turned into the MJPA staff office. I could've had Darlene do it, but I would not have won my victory unless I had a showdown with shame and faced my landlords' staff. I asked the Holy Spirit for strength to face the ones who handed the keys to the SWAT team. In a whisper I rebuked the shame that came over me as I entered their office, "I say no to shame." I held my head high, looked each person in his or her eyes, and said hello. I handed the director the papers, smiled, and left.

Although they previously met Curtis, there was no mention of Curtis, the incident, or the SWAT team by either of us. I chose not to open any door of conversation the Enemy could use to stir up negative talk—I had to diligently protect my heart and the atmosphere between us.

The next showdown with shame came that Saturday night. All week on television, commercials aired announcing the return of a program called *America's Most Wanted* that had been off the air for a while. The news said people, law enforcement, and thirty-seven government officials put pressure on Fox TV Network to bring the show back.

Generally, the program focused on criminals missing for several years— people local law enforcement and FBI had been unable to find.

Since the program was returning to the air, the producers were looking for "hot new" material for the first show. I watched this program often and this was the first time I saw the writers chose to focus on someone missing for only six days. For their inaugural program, watched by millions on Saturday, November 2, 1996, they chose my twenty seven-year-old son, Curtis, to be the featured story. Suddenly, my personal problem, which became a community problem, was now a national problem! Now my shame was spread across America.

Curtis's last name was rarer than names like Smith or Johnson. Also Curtis's father, Chuck, or I had ministered nationally in several states over the past fourteen years, this made my married name recognizable in some circles. Therefore, I received calls from across the nation from those who asked me if I was related to the young man on *America's Most Wanted*.

"This man is armed and dangerous," said the host John Walsh. "He shot a Los Angeles police officer. He must be captured. Here is his picture. Take a good look and call us if you know or suspect his whereabouts."

I watched this show in the past and prayed for the criminals to be caught, the truth revealed, and the case closed. I prayed for the violators to receive Christ, be healed of their hurts, and have changed lives. I asked God to heal their families. I prayed for the victim's healing, if still alive. For their family's healing from grief, and to receive the grace to forgive so they could live in peace and this tragedy not destroy them. I prayed for everyone to be saved. Now the tables had turned. I was glad I hadn't been arrogant or judgmental toward the criminals. This is one time I truly wanted to reap what I had sowed. I wanted to reap compassion and prayers from people across the nation—from people who will never know Curtis or me, but would pray for us no matter what their opinions were of Curtis.

That Saturday night as I watched the show I felt overwhelmed with emotion and at the same time it seemed surreal. I faced shame each time I left my home of eighteen years and saw my neighbors ignore me. Most

Diane Gardner

likely they didn't know what to say. I wondered what they would have done if Curtis had died. They probably would have come over and given their condolences and brought me cards, flowers, and food. But my tragedy was not a familiar issue like death. People know the protocol when there is a death. What's the protocol when the tragedy is a crime against others and you are the parent of the violator? We know to console the family of the victim, but the family of the offender can feel the same pain. Adam and Eve felt the pain of the violator's and victim's parents—the victim and the violator were their sons. In order to break the back of shame I chose to speak to my neighbors first, and they said hello—sometimes.

As I ventured out in public, I saw people I had known for years, or classmates of Curtis. Most didn't know what to say so when they saw me they walked the other way. Some said they were sorry to hear what happened. People generally didn't ask me any questions but expressed their opinion of what went wrong. Most men said they had been angry enough to seriously hurt someone so they surmised that Curtis didn't have an anger problem, but must have "snapped" for a moment. I wanted to scream at them. *It's not that simple! You listened to the voice on the inside that told you not to do it—Curtis didn't!*

Showdown with My Own Mind

For a year God had dealt with me about holding what He called an Emotional Healing Clinic in the Sacramento area. His goal was to bring a healing atmosphere to that region and healing to those who had influence in and around the Capital. We worked on the seminar for a year and we scheduled it for shortly after our move into our church building. It was time to host our first Emotional Healing Clinic Seminar, Thursday through Saturday morning: November 14-16, 1996.

Everything was set. We planned extensively. I made two trips to make arrangements with Center of Praise as our venue. My speakers,

Rev. Liberty Savard and Rev. Dr. Evelyn "Ev" Carter Spencer, and I were scheduled. Plane tickets were purchased for those coming from my church. Two tickets were for staff members, Pina and Arleatha who came from Texas. We circulated brochures throughout churches where I had spoken in Northern California. We prayed for months for God to cover the event. Only two weeks were left before our departure. What was I going to do?

I didn't feel at all like I could go through with the healing clinic. Every part of me had something to say. My mind said it was impossible. My flesh told me to wait and do a seminar after I was healed. Because the only thing my flesh wanted was to stay home, go to bed, and nurse my broken heart by licking my wounds. But I learned earlier that there was no healing power in my own saliva. I reasoned how easily the team could get credit for their plane tickets and use them another time, but my spirit said let's hear what God wants.

The seminar theme was: Jesus came to heal the brokenhearted and set the captives free. *How can I go forward with this seminar? I'm hurting too badly and I'm only in the beginning stages of my own healing. I'm probably in worse pain than anyone who'll attend. Just make a few phone calls and the pressure will be off my shoulders. I can get rid of this knot in the pit of my stomach. Everyone will understand the need to cancel under such tragic circumstances.*

Yet, if I backed out, I knew Satan could count this as a victory. He would rejoice that the people who planned to come and be healed couldn't receive. Although I knew Satan would rejoice, more importantly, I believed my heavenly Father would be disappointed. He would be grieved because I chose my feelings over my faith. I knew God would get more glory if I trusted Him to show me how to walk on this stormy sea. A scripture came to my mind: *The just shall live by faith; But if anyone draws back, My soul has no pleasure in him* (Hebrews 10:38). I didn't want my heavenly Father to see me as one who draws back. So I had a showdown with my own emotions.

"Lord, I surrender my flesh, my mind, my will, and my emotions to You," I prayed aloud. "I'm hurting terribly, but I choose Your will over the needs of my flesh. You said Your grace is sufficient. When I am my weakest, Your strength shows up more. I want You to be able to trust me to do Your will no matter what storms enter my life. I covenant with You that I will never draw back."

Then I gave myself a little pep talk. "Diane, 2 Corinthians 12:9 says: *My grace is sufficient for you, for My strength is made perfect* (mature) *in weakness.* Therefore, I put my flesh under subjection to the Holy Spirit. My flesh and carnal mind is an enemy to the will of God. I will not draw back, but instead move forward by faith. I receive in my weakness sufficient grace to bring God's power to others. I choose to set my mind on the Spirit instead of the flesh according to Romans 8:5: *For those who live according to the flesh set their minds on the things of the flesh, but those who live according to the Spirit, the things of the Spirit.* Flesh, you no longer get to cast your vote on what I will do. The Word of God overcomes you."

I told my congregation we would continue with our previous plans. Two weeks later around twenty people from my church, my two staff members from Texas, and I flew to Sacramento and held our three-day Emotional Healing Clinic. My mentor Rev. Ev, and friend, Rev. Liberty, taught wonderfully. Rev. Ev expressed to me publically how "godly proud" she was of me for choosing to trust God and not give in to my flesh and my emotions to quit.

God healed people emotionally and physically and challenged us to grow that weekend. I was the first captive who God set free as a result of the clinic. My broken heart received healing as I was strengthened through God's Word and His presence.

Showdown with a Plague

The last showdown was harassment against my house from the Enemy. It started the same day I returned from the Healing Clinic in Sacramento. The Enemy was upset that I moved forward to minister to others when I was broken and feeling his pressure to quit. My Texas staff member Arleatha sang at the seminar in Sacramento and flew home with me to sing at my church on Sunday. She stayed Saturday night at my home.

As we prepared for bed I heard a strange noise either in my master bathroom or outside the bathroom door, which opened onto the patio. I searched for the source. I called Arleatha to come into my bathroom and help me find where the racket came from. We opened the cabinet door under my bathroom sink and saw nothing, but the noise grew louder. We both got on our knees and looked under the cabinet. To our surprise the wall plaster around the pipe had been eaten away by rodents. We could hear them as they scurried inside the wall. We cleared the things from under the cabinet, and I told her I would buy rodent poison the next day after church and the problem will be over.

I bought the poison and put it inside the hole. On Monday five mice succumbed to the poison. I asked Richard to carry them to the trash. The noise was still there, so the next day I put more poison and killed six more mice. I called Jeff, a young man from my congregation, to carry them to the trash. The problem seemed to be over for a few days.

When the noise started again, I called a rodent pest service and they put traps in the wall. They said they would come back and remove the traps in a week. Every night all week I heard rodents who were caught in traps banging against the bottom of my bathtub. I didn't get much sleep.

The pest service came back and I explained the traps were too noisy, so they put poison in the walls. Each week they carried out dead rodents. When they could no longer reach them, they cut a hole in my wall so they could get deeper into the wall.

All my linens and towels smelled like dead rodents when I put them on the beds or dried off after a shower. Eventually, I put my bath towels, face cloths, and linen in plastic bags and moved them to another closet. I sprayed disinfectant regularly to mask the smell.

Over the next two years, I spent over two thousand dollars with the pestilence service. In addition, I spent time and money trying every home remedy people suggested. I came to the end of my rope. What do we do when we've done everything we know? We pray again, only more fervently.

I started by having a few people over to pray with me. We rebuked, renounced, and told the Enemy to leave my house alone. We quoted Psalm 91:3, 5-6: *Surely He shall deliver you from the snare of the fowler And from the perilous pestilence . . . You shall not be afraid of the terror by night, Nor of the arrow that flies by day, Nor of the pestilence that walks in darkness, Nor of the destruction that lays waste at noonday.* This time I didn't see any results.

I was so frustrated some nights when I couldn't sleep that I banged on the wall and yelled at my occupants hoping they would run away because of fear. That didn't work either.

I sought the Lord more diligently for a while and listened for my answer. One day, the Holy Spirit spoke to me. *This is harassment from the Enemy. He could not stop you from moving forward with your life and calling after Curtis. The Enemy was angry you had the Healing Clinic, so he sent this harassment.*

"What's the main purpose for this harassment?" I asked. "And what's my main weapon to use against the Enemy?"

To rob you of money, prayer time, and sleep. Your weapon is patience.

I thought of Romans 5:3-5 (MSG): *There's more to come: We continue to shout our praise even when we're hemmed in with troubles, because we know how troubles can develop passionate patience in us.*

"Thank You," I said. "From now on I'll not spend another dime or spend prayer time on this harassment. I'll play the Bible on CD or praise music every night and use ear plugs. I'll drown out the noise as much as possible."

During this time I sensed God wanted me to sell my home. *How can anyone sell a house that smells like dead rodents? And what about the big cutout in the family room wall that's hidden behind my couch?*

In faith I took down some of the wallpaper and painted. I prepared my house to go on the market. Some wallpaper had been removed and one room was painted. Then I sorted through twenty two years of boxes.

Meanwhile, in June 2000, I was invited by Dr. Kluane Spake to accompany her on a biblical study tour of Egypt hosted by Dr. Catherine Clark Kroeger, a Bible scholar, professor at Gordon-Conwell

Theological Seminary, and expert on biblical equality between men and women. *How could I leave this mess? I don't have any money for the trip. But what an opportunity to study under someone so well respected and has written her own Bible commentary of the New Testament. Lord, please show me what to do.*

Every detail came together in such a way that it was definitely God. A friend of our ministry purchased my plane ticket. People in the church and others gave money for the trip. Jeff, whose family I had known for years, volunteered to house sit while I was gone. He offered to remove all wallpaper from my master bedroom and both bathrooms, and then paint while I was in Egypt. He volunteered without me asking. This was the kind of work he did while working his way through school. I was thrilled.

I came home to all three rooms beautifully painted. Jeff said while I was gone he carried out several rodents and could hear them every night. We prayed together for wisdom on what I should do next if my home was to sell.

Rev. Jan Painter, a guest speaker at my church, came in July, 2000. During one of the services she pointed to me. "Pastor Diane, God says to tell you that you'll sell that house now. It'll sell *this* year."

In 1995 I had the house on the market for ten months and not one offer. Nevertheless, I moved forward in faith and had a garage sale, as I simultaneously carried rodents out the back door. I felt as though they were building a shrine to themselves inside the walls.

I took the next big step of faith and called a realtor and signed a contract. This happened the first weekend of October. The realtor asked, "Do you want me to put the sign up today?"

He never knew how much faith it took for me to have the showdown with this harassment and to tell him yes.

"Yes, let's do it!"

I didn't have a clue what I was going to do about the rodent problem, but I was convinced God would give me some kind of wisdom before the first client was brought through the front door and could smell the dead rodents.

The sign went in the ground one Sunday evening. Two days later I noticed I didn't hear any rodents. Three days later I invited Jeff over so we could listen together and he could look in the hole inside the wall. There were no more rodents!

"I see lots of droppings but I don't hear one rodent or see any," Jeff said.

"Jeff, I know this sounds bizarre, but I believe they left the moment the "for sale sign" went into the ground. They have been here since the day I returned from the Healing Clinic we held in Northern California in November 1996. That's one month shy of four years! If I ever doubted this long ordeal was *not* a spiritual warfare assault, I sure don't doubt it now. You're my witness and proof they are suddenly all gone. Wow!"

I joyfully called the pestilence company to come and patch up the wall where they had cut open. They were amazed that they didn't hear or see any rodents.

Several people who had been to my home numerous times during those four years were the ones who came to help me pack. They noticed there was no smell of dead rodents. They also were witnesses to my miraculous deliverance from that harassment from the Enemy.

The young widow with three children who purchased the house came by at 3:00 p.m. on December 31. As God said through Rev. Jan, my house sold that same year, on New Year's Eve.

I saw the new owner and her children in the store several months after she purchased the house. I asked how things were going. She said everything was beautiful, and she was so happy. I was also happy to learn that the harassment plague never returned. The assault was only directed at me.

I thank God for the power to overcome the Enemy's storms no matter how long they last. The Devil is impatient, and we have the fruit of patience. With faith and patience we can outlast any storm.

My brethren, count it all joy when you fall into various trials, knowing that the testing of your faith produces patience. But let patience have its perfect work, that you may be perfect and complete, lacking nothing (James 1:2-4).

Chapter 3

The Arrest

Then the Lord said to Cain, "Where is Abel your brother?"
He said, "I do not know. Am I my brother's keeper?" And
He said, "What have you done? The voice of your brother's
blood cries out to Me from the ground . . . A fugitive and
a vagabond you shall be on the earth (Genesis 4:9-12).

The entire time Curtis was a fugitive, I could pick up the newspaper on any given day and see Curtis's picture along with a headline that read: "Have You Seen This Man?" One morning stands out in my mind. I was sitting at the breakfast counter on a barstool as I talked to Carlton. He loaded the dishwasher with our breakfast dishes while I walked out to get the newspaper. As I entered the house I opened the paper and immediately saw pictures of Karen and Curtis. I let out several blood curdling screams from the emotional pain I felt. It was like my heart was bursting open.

I clutched the paper and stroked it in a nurturing embrace, as if to comfort their hurts the way a mother wants to. My arms ached to hold them. My lips wanted to kiss them and bring our pain together in prayer to Jesus. I yearned for Him to heal us.

"Mom, are you OK? Why are you crying so loud?" Carlton asked.

I stopped for a moment to catch my breath. "I'm letting out my grief. I know I'm loud, and the neighbors can probably hear me, but none of them can heal me, so I choose not to be embarrassed. My heart is hurting worse than I know how to explain. This is the only way I know how to give my grief to Jesus. Only God can go deep into the heart of my mind and heal me. I've got to give Him this pain so He can give me my healing. If I don't let this grief out, then I will become physically ill from all this internal pressure.

"I don't know when I'll see Curtis or the grandkids again. Even if I called Karen's mom to try to arrange it, she would be too afraid Curtis might find them to let me see my grandchildren. I need Jesus to heal my broken heart right now!"

The reality of Isaiah 53:3-4 ministered to me: *He is despised and rejected by men, A Man of sorrows and acquainted with grief . . . Surely He has borne our grief And carried our sorrows.*

I continued to cry as Carlton stayed close and nervously wiped the same countertops. This lasted somewhere just under an hour. Then the feeling suddenly lifted. I sighed in relief and knew I was finished, at least with this pain. My emotions were wrung out, my throat sore, my eyes red and puffy, and my nose red. But the deep pain in my heart was released, and I was thankful. "Thank You, Jesus, Lord, I thank You so much for healing my broken heart and releasing the pain of my grief," I whispered.

"Are you done now?" Carlton asked.

I nodded my head.

"Good. I thank Jesus for helping you. I hope one day I will learn to let the pain out of my heart and give it to God."

My frequent meditation became, *He will not be afraid of evil tidings; His heart is steadfast, trusting in the LORD* (Psalm 112:7).

I needed to make some quality decisions and resolve some issues if I was going to be steadfast, trusting in the Lord. I resolved to agree with the Bible that says God is good, even in a bad situation—He is still good. The Devil was the one I needed to fight, not others. I resolved to do whatever was necessary to be an overcomer. I determined I would not hold onto grief, sorrow, or shame, but let it go as soon as I recognized it. I had to say audibly what I trusted God to do.

My heavenly Father knew where Curtis and where my grandchildren were, so I called on the power of the Word of God to help me sleep at night. *When you lie down, you shall not be afraid; Yes, you will lie down and your sleep shall be sweet* (Proverbs 3:24).

I resolved to continue with the purpose of God in my life to let the Lord know I love Him and will serve Him no matter what. As a senior pastor, I determined to be in my pulpit every Sunday no matter how I felt. I wanted to send a message also to the Adversary that he could not jerk me around. I made a quality decision to continually receive healing from stress so it will never send me to the hospital or doctor because my body was breaking down from the emotional pain. I wanted to come out of this with no stress-related illnesses.

While Curtis was missing, often I thought about the times I saw how God dealt with him and warned him about the Adversary's influence in his life. I thought about the promise God gave us in 1 Corinthians 10:13 and how Curtis resisted accepting this promise. There is the kingdom of light (also called the kingdom of His Dear Son) and the kingdom of darkness. Two plans: the Adversary had a will and plan for Curtis, and God had a will and plan for him. Curtis's cognitive will was the deciding factor.

No temptation has overtaken you except such as is common to man; but God is faithful, who will not allow you to be tempted beyond what you are able, but with the temptation will also make the way of escape, that you may be able to bear it (1 Corinthians 10:13).

God provided the promise to make a way of escape from the evil temptations in Curtis's flesh. The Adversary influences the flesh. God spoke a warning like He always does for every one of us, because He is faithful. We must humble ourselves to obey the warning, or we harden our hearts. *Today, if you will hear His voice, Do not harden your hearts* (Hebrews 4:7).

Curtis followed Cain's pattern of hardening his heart to God's warning mentioned in Genesis 4. God spoke to Cain and to Curtis *before* they committed their crimes. God warned them to change their minds and to stop listening to the Devil's words of jealousy, rage, and murder. But Cain and Curtis chose evil over good, pride over humility, destruction over God's love and life.

Genesis 4:5-7 (MSG) says: *Cain lost his temper and went into a sulk. GOD spoke to Cain: "Why this tantrum? Why the sulking? If you do well, won't you be accepted? And if you don't do well, sin is lying in wait for you, ready to pounce; it's out to get you, you've got to master it."*

As I read Genesis 4, I noticed Cain was born in sin because his parents disobeyed God. Unlike us, they didn't have generations of sin, such as: abuse, addictions, incest, rejection, etc. Adam and Eve had the only flawless parent—God. They were the least dysfunctional of any parents in history. Cain lived in a sinful environment, but with much less sinful influence than anyone else in history. He had no peers to pressure him to sin—no outside stimulus to contaminate him. There was no television, radio, drugs, alcohol, or Internet to influence him toward evil. He was keenly sensitive to the spirit world with direct face-to-face access to his heavenly Father.

Yet, the Adversary was able to deceive Cain completely simply by evil thoughts and vain imaginations. When Cain yielded his will to the Enemy's plans he accepted a hard heart (a heart of stone) and darkness. This caused him to reject God's warning. As always God provided a way out *before* he sinned. Cain rejected the warning, followed through on the Enemy's thoughts and killed his brother, Abel.

God was faithful and gave him a way to escape like He does for all of us. He also warned Curtis several times that Satan had big plans for him, and Curtis had the power to resist the Enemy. God never intended Curtis, Karen, their children, or any of us to be this brokenhearted. But Curtis was like Cain.

God never wanted Adam and Eve to bear the loss of both of their sons on the same day. They lost Abel through death, and they lost Cain through imprisonment. Cain chose to open the door of sin. He chose to submit to sin rather than rule over the Enemy.

One year before the tragedy with Curtis, a member of my church told me she saw a serpent coming through the sliding glass doors in Curtis's and Karen's home. It was a warning to say they had opened the door to the Enemy. I asked her to please tell Curtis. She decided it would be too uncomfortable for her because of Curtis's pride. So she asked me to speak to him. I shared with them her vision and prayed over them, but I could tell they didn't take it serious.

Curtis and Karen respected Pastor Wayne, who had performed their wedding ceremony. They attended his church for three years. After their separation, Curtis was in church every other Sunday with his children, Chris (three) and Cyndi (two). But Curtis was not handling his emotions well. He desperately needed someone to give him wise counsel. About ninety days prior to Curtis becoming a fugitive, I made an appointment to see his pastor who I had known for several years.

"Pastor Wayne, I'm concerned about Curtis's thinking and where it might lead," I said. "He's not allowing God to heal his pain. Instead, he is pulling away from God. His car has been repossessed, and he may lose his home. It seems the main person he is confiding in is a man at the Father's Rights Group, where he volunteers. This man is *not* good for Curtis and helps fuel his anger. He desperately needs someone to listen to him, give him sound advice, and pray with him. As you know Chuck, Curtis's dad has moved to Georgia. When I shared with him he doesn't want to understand what Curtis has become.

"I know you have more than a thousand people in your congregation. Do you have a men's program or a quality man or two you can connect with Curtis? This is urgent!"

"I talked with Curtis a few months back before they started their divorce." Pastor Wayne said. "I understand you're a concerned mom with a son going through a divorce, and you're worried. But I don't have any men's ministry, and I don't know any men who want to mentor or disciple any young men. Curtis is kind of prideful so I'm not sure he would want to listen to anyone anyway. Just tell him to make an appointment to come see me and stay close to me."

"OK, Pastor Wayne, I'll tell him."

I invited Curtis over to my home for us to have our talk. "Curtis, I'm extremely concerned about the level of anger and pain I see in you.

I talked to your pastor about it. He said for you to come see him and stick close to him. You must let Jesus heal your broken heart."

"OK. I'll call soon and go see Pastor Wayne."

The appointment with Pastor Wayne never materialized. But the grace of God through the Holy Spirit's work is relentless. He warned Curtis again two months after my conversation with Pastor Wayne. And three weeks before the shooting incident, I asked Curtis to come to my home.

"Curtis, I'm not talking to you only as your mom, but also as a minister." I looked deep into his eyes. "God revealed to me that the Holy Spirit is grieved. The reason is the Devil is talking to you, and you are *not* resisting his words. You are embracing the Adversary's evil thoughts. I believe you need a strategy to resist the Devil. You should ask someone to pray with you in your home. Take dominion over the evil spirits. I have some things you can do."

"Sure, Mom, I'm listening."

"You can begin with James 4:6-8 which says: *But He gives more grace. Therefore He says: "God resists the proud, But gives grace to the humble." Therefore submit to God. Resist the devil and he will flee from you . . . Cleanse your hands, you sinners; and purify your hearts, you double-minded.*

"Take this passage and any others that God reveals to you. You'll need someone who knows how to pray and resist the Enemy to come over to your house and pray with you. You've got to rebuke the darkness that is trying to take over. God says the Adversary wants to destroy you, and he wants you to do some evil things, but God's giving you this warning because He loves you. He wants you to rule over those evil thoughts—to take authority over the Enemy. I believe you have opened the door through bitterness, rage, and pain. Please shut the door now, honey. God is giving you a serious warning."

Curtis thought for few minutes. "Mom, I'll give that some thought. Thanks for praying for me all the time. See you later."

I thought about these conversations hundreds of times while Curtis was a fugitive.

February, 1997

Four months after Curtis disappeared; I was ministering in New Zealand for the first time. This was a speaking tour of ten churches on the North Island. My trip was a ministry forerunner to acquire churches that wanted to host my Beautiful Women of God Seminars. I had been invited to bring my seminar and team of eight ladies in August to hold four two-day seminars in various regions. This was an exciting and fruitful time.

My host couple, Pastors Guthrie and Jennifer, gave me a memorable birthday at the aquarium and then a wonderful restaurant. That evening in the car on our way to their home I received a call from Darlene. She spoke slowly. "Happy Birthday, Pastor Diane, I hope you're having a nice time."

"Yes, I've had an enjoyable day and the seafood we ate tonight was great. What's going on? You don't sound like we're celebrating my birthday."

"I hate to disturb you during your ministry trip and on your birthday, but I thought you might want to hear this from me instead of someone else. Today your daughter-in-law Karen was on the *Montel Williams Show* with John Walsh from *America's Most Wanted*. He brought three victims with unsolved cases to the show. They showed Curtis's picture many times. I recorded it for you. I'm sorry to have to tell you this."

I paused a moment, "Thank you for recording the program for me. I'll pray about all this tonight. Bless you, goodbye."

I prayed that night. "Father, Curtis has become an embarrassment to the local police department. Even the FBI and a bounty hunter have been looking for him at the homes of his relatives in other states. The police have searched my home twice and warned Carlton and me that we'd be arrested if we harbored Curtis.

"God, please protect Curtis from any officer shooting or beating him because the department's pride is bruised. I hear *America's Most Wanted* is still involved. Please turn that around to Curtis's good. If at all possible, have John Walsh and his crew there whenever Curtis is arrested so there will be television evidence that there's no harm to him. Jesus, if there is any way, I'd like to hear from Curtis or know where he is by Mother's Day, please. Amen."

A woman near San Diego, California, watched the program and thought she had taken a picture of Curtis at a party in Mexico. She called the phone number given on the show. Corona Police Department officers drove the two hours to San Diego and picked up the picture. They brought the picture to Karen to confirm it was Curtis. Over the next two months they contacted the Mexican authorities and began working on their strategy to capture him.

Mother's Day Weekend, 1997

On the Saturday before Mother's Day, I spoke at Dr. Crawford's women's meeting. I shared about my confidence in God and faith in His promises. I revealed to the ladies that my son had been missing for seven months. "I asked my heavenly Father some time ago to please allow me to hear something about my son Curtis, as my Mother's Day gift from God," I told them. "Mother's Day weekend is here and I expect to hear something about my fugitive son."

Three months after the airing of the *Montel Williams Show*, Curtis was arrested. When he was brought across the border, John Walsh and the *America's Most Wanted* crew were there, filming the handover of Curtis to the American authorities. This happened the same day I spoke to the ladies in Los Angeles on the Saturday before Mother's Day.

The police department in Ensenada, Mexico worked in conjunction with the Corona Police Department and found where Curtis worked. They devised a plan to bring him to their station for questioning. On the designated day, they arrested him and drove him to the border, turning him over to the American authorities.

On a visit to Curtis six months after his arrest, he related this story to me. "During my transportation by Mexican authorities an officer in the car threatened me before we got to the border. He said he would take me to a dark place on the road and shoot me, then tell everyone I attempted to escape."

The officer didn't follow through on his threat possibly because *America's Most Wanted* was waiting to televise Curtis's arrest by the American authorities.

I thank God for answered prayer. God can take anything meant to bring shame to us, and through our faith and trust in Him, turn it around to work for our good or our children's good.

Once Curtis was arrested and Karen knew where he was, she allowed me to see my grandchildren. We met at different locations, but mostly the Corona Police Station. Then I took them to have fun at designated places. After a few months, I was able to have them come to my home on occasion and spend the day with me.

May 29, 1997

Curtis was brought to the Riverside County Jail, where I began my prison ministry in 1975. Now in 1997, my own son was a prisoner there.

I was cleared to visit the jail two weeks after the arrest. I could feel shame covering me like a blanket. It seemed I could hear constant mocking from the Enemy.

You came to this jail for years for other peoples' children, and yet, you could not keep your son from coming here. The day you gave your life to Christ, you told the pastor's wife you wanted God to help you raise your children so they would not become juvenile delinquents and end up in jail like your brother. Even though Curtis never joined any gangs or became strung out on drugs, he still ended up in jail. You thought you had some kind of guarantee, but you didn't. I won and you lost. What good did it do to serve God all those years? Now what are you going to tell people about God's grace? Because his arrest was televised, the entire nation knows Curtis is headed to prison. You should quit trying to help people. No one wants to hear from you anymore. You have too much shame to stay in this community. Why don't you move where no one knows you're his mom?

The questions were unrelenting and oppressive, but I didn't answer the Accuser. He didn't deserve an answer. I kept telling shame that it had no place in my life because Jesus bore my shame. "Shame, you cannot stay in my life! I choose to put my trust in God and not be put to shame! Shame, you are a thing that I don't want. Go from me now!" By faith I knew I was effective, but my feelings felt captive to shame. I realized how captive I was when I walked into the jail for the first time to visit Curtis and felt as if a blanket covered me. Nevertheless, I was determined to be an overcomer.

I entered these same doors for many years with joy in my heart and a sense of purpose in my mind to bring the love of Jesus to the inmates. I didn't know how I was supposed to feel this time. Should I feel numb, determined, frustrated, or shameful?

When I sat down, feelings of shame rose over me to the point of tears. Then I felt anger at my son for the trauma he'd put everyone through. How could he be so selfish? How could he give himself over so completely to the Enemy when he had been taught better?

I had already laid all these thoughts at the cross, but now they stirred up again. I said to myself, *Get a grip, Diane. I know better than to allow my mind to wander and feed my emotion's negative thoughts. Stop it! This will be the first opportunity I have to speak to Curtis in seven months. It is what it is, and nothing can change the circumstances no matter how much I wish they weren't real. I will not ask him why he did this, because it would only be trying to give some kind of answer to my emotions. I cannot make a bad situation feel better. I'll let Curtis know I am glad to see him and I love him. I'll let him talk about whatever he wants to talk about. Our relationship is what is important.*

I used the restroom before going in so I would not have to interrupt our time together. Once I was inside the restroom, I heard a woman come in from the outside. Talking loudly, she begged the officer to use the restroom. I glanced back and saw it was a lady whose clothing was torn and her hair was matted. I wondered if she was homeless.

She came in and took the stall next to me. As soon as she sat down, she let out a loud scream. "Ahhhh! Somebody help me! Somebody come in here! Officer, there's a man in the ladies restroom! Hey you in the stall next to me, I know you're a man. I can tell you have on men's black patent leather penny loafers. What are you doing sneaking into the women's restroom? Are you trying to do something to us ladies? I'm telling the officer as soon as I get out of here. Help! Help!"

I started to laugh so hard I almost fell off the toilet. I have a deep low voice so she still wasn't convinced I was not a man. I wasn't able to tell her because I couldn't stop laughing.

She bolted out the door without washing her hands. She was convinced I was there to do her or some other woman harm.

"Officer, you've got to go check the women's restroom because there's a man in there. I saw his shoes in the stall next to mine. Go check, hurry!"

"There's no man in there, so you can just calm down," he said. "I'll take care of it in a moment. You have a nice day."

"Be sure and get him out of there before he bothers some woman." She left the building.

It took me a while to stop laughing. *Thank You Lord, I now have a merry heart. It broke the shame and silenced the accusations from the Adversary. I feel better now. Thank You for Proverbs 17:22a that says: A merry heart does good, like medicine . . .*

I exited the restroom and the officer chuckled. "You don't look like a man to me."

"But obviously my shoes look manly." I held my foot up so the officer could see my black alligator penny loafers. We both laughed.

By the time an officer called my name to go inside to see Curtis, the shame was gone. I sat on the cold steel stool in front of the glass and watched Curtis come through the door in an orange jumpsuit with leg and wrist cuffs. They took off his wrist cuffs. He shuffled to the steel stool, sat down behind the thick glass window, and picked up the phone.

I picked up the black phone on the wall next to my right ear. "Hi, honey, I have missed you. I love you."

"Missed you too, Mom. Love you, too."

The next couple of moments were silent and awkward as we sat there staring at one another. *Where do I start in such a serious and uncomfortable time?* I decided to tell him about the homeless lady who thought I was a man. We enjoyed a good laugh together.

Then he started to talk about things he saw when he was a fugitive, places he went, and interesting people he met. The jail staff listened to the conversation, and every three minutes the phone went silent for a few seconds to remind us we had company on the line.

Of course we had to guard our words and not mention anything about the incidents without a lawyer. But it would have been nice for Curtis to say, "Sorry, Mom."

I had to let it be OK in my heart without longing for an answer or an apology. The only answer could have been the same kind Cain might have given to Eve. His conversation could have started: "Mom, you did your best, but of my own free will I gave myself over to the anger and rage that allowed the Enemy to convince me that killing my brother, Abel, would make my jealousy feel better. I rejected God when He warned me. He didn't violate my will. It was my choice to obey. I didn't take God's way to escape.

"Instead, I allowed my heart to become filled with darkness, and I chose the darkness instead of the light. Mom, don't blame yourself and don't blame God. Don't carry guilt. Don't receive false guilt and condemnation for *my* actions. I made a conscious choice as an adult to harden my heart to the voice of God. I'm banished to a city that's my prison for life. Our relationship is forever changed. Any relationship with your future grandchildren will be forever different. I've caused you the lost of both sons in one day—me to a prison of a lifetime of wandering in another land and Abel to death. It's not your fault."

Thankfully, I only lost one son.

The Trial, June, 1998

Curtis's first public defender quit because of a conflict of interest. He knew one of the people involved. Curtis fired the second public defender because the lawyer had little contact with him and things were not going the way Curtis wanted, so he became his own lawyer. After this he was able to receive all the correspondence concerning his own trial and no longer had to guess what information his lawyer possessed. He sent papers to a high school friend, Marvin, to assist him to get the right papers filed on time for the court.

Curtis spent as much time as they would allow in the law library, filing papers that were to be presented and bringing the right papers to the hearings. I was at each hearing. My life was on hold while I centered my schedule on postponed and rescheduled court hearings.

I was outside the courtroom one day waiting to hear about Curtis who, after going over all his paperwork now asked to be assigned a lawyer. Suddenly the prosecuting attorney from the D A's office bolted through the door and stopped in front of me. "Walk with me, and we'll take the elevator while I tell you what happened.

"The judge ordered Curtis to go to trial *today*. He's now facing a triple life sentence with *no lawyer*."

"Oh no. Curtis told me he was going to ask for a lawyer today."

"He did, but the judge said no. This will complicate things for Curtis *and* for me. We are in courtroom 207 in three hours. Go out and get him some civilian clothes to wear and take them to the jail in two hours. Curtis has to show up in court ready to defend himself. This was the judge who assigns courtrooms. Curtis was arrested a year ago, so the judge said he was not going to allow Curtis's trial to be delayed any longer. I'll see you in three hours."

I went home, ran in the door in a panic, fell to my knees and sobbed in fear for Curtis. I cried out to the Lord for help for twenty minutes. Terror gripped the pit of my stomach. Then I called at least six law firms until I got someone who said he was available that afternoon. I quickly shared about Curtis and was told I needed to guarantee I could come up with $100,000 over the next month and several thousand dollars as retainer fee in thirty minutes. He would go to court and tell the judge Curtis had a lawyer and ask for things to be postponed. He said to call back in ten minutes and let him know about the money. There was no equity in my home and I had no cash. Besides Curtis had no public defender because he wanted to run things himself for a while and now it backfired. I called the lawyer back five minutes later and told him I could not find that kind of money that fast and thanked him.

I surrendered the situation to God. I prayed again for the right judge and for God to supernaturally intervene so Curtis would not be given a triple life sentence. I rushed through a department store and quickly bought some clothes I hoped would fit Curtis and dropped them at the county jail. I proceeded to courtroom 207 and waited. I was the only one on the benches. Curtis was as frightened as I was, and because he was anxious he became obnoxious.

The judge addressed Curtis as the lawyer and read his charges.

"I want a lawyer," Curtis said. "I need a lawyer. I won't go forward without a lawyer."

"It's too late. The other judge has ruled that you be brought here for your trial to start, and I have no control over that decision. You must move forward."

"I will refuse to show up for court."

"As an inmate you have that right. As your lawyer you do not. You will be made to come to court with the proper paperwork each time we are in session. Looking at your papers filed, I can see you are an intelligent young man so I know you understand the law on this issue. Correct?"

"I need a lawyer. I need a lawyer."

This pattern continued all afternoon. The judge became frustrated with Curtis.

When we left the courtroom the prosecuting attorney turned my direction. "Walk with me on my way out. I don't want to bring Curtis's little kids to court as witnesses and have them point their fingers at him and tell the jury what their daddy did. The way things stand Curtis will surely get triple life and no possible parole. He has no lawyer for me to talk to so I'll make my offer to him through you."

He paused for a few seconds. "The previous plea bargain that Curtis refused is already completely *off the table*—twenty-eight years straight.

He would have served eighty-five percent of that and had a definite release date. Curtis told his court appointed investigator, Mr. Steve that he wanted his day in court instead.

"Now the offer is twenty-years, *plus life*. This includes an automatic ten-year sentence for any crime with the use of a gun, which is the law. Ten years for the kidnapping. That is usually an automatic twenty years. But I will offer ten, then life for premeditated attempted murder. This means Curtis can still go up for parole in about thirty years. If we go to trial, he is guaranteed to never get out."

He stopped in front of the courthouse. "Give Curtis the offer tonight and show up at my office in the morning at 8:00 a.m. with his answer. Whatever he decides is what I will take to the judge in the morning."

As I walked through the doors of the jail that night I prayed. "Holy Spirit, I ask for Your help to share this with Curtis. I ask for you to touch Curtis's heart to do what's best for him. Lord, have mercy on him."

I picked up the black phone attached to the wall. "Hello, honey, I talked to the assistant DA after court today."

"What's he doing talking to you? He's the opposition."

"You're right, but you don't have a lawyer, and he wanted to offer another plea bargain. He wants to know your answer so he can take it to the judge first thing in the morning, whether it's yes or no."

"OK, what's he offering this time?"

"He said it's an automatic ten years for the use of a weapon in a crime. It's twenty years for kidnapping, but he will cut it down to ten years. So that's twenty years. You must serve eighty-five percent of the twenty. Then the life sentence starts. They are not congruent but consecutive. The minimum on a life sentence before you go up for parole is eight years. So what he is offering instead of a triple life sentence with no parole is twenty years plus life. That's what he will take to the judge in the morning.

"He said, 'If you take the plea bargain, then your kids don't have to come to court and testify against you.'"

He rolled his eyes. "I don't know if I want to do that or not."

"Honey, you don't have a lawyer and can't get one now, so the playing field has changed. The Amplified Bible gives a definition of one of the names of the Holy Spirit as Advocate, which means lawyer or one who fights for you. Let's kneel down in respect of who He is and ask for His help in this decision as your Advocate. He is also your Helper. We need His help right now. Don't you think?"

He shrugged his shoulders, "I guess so."

I knelt down next to the stainless steel stool I had been sitting on with the phone still in my hand. "Curtis, you don't have time for pride. We only have a few minutes. Can't you respect God in these few minutes?"

He shrugged his shoulders again, and then knelt down next to his stool. We couldn't see each other, but we had the phone receivers to our ears.

"Curtis, this is your life. I'm afraid for you. You ask for the Holy Spirit to be your lawyer and helper. Ask Him also to protect your kids from any more harm. I'll agree with whatever you pray."

He began. "Lord, I don't have a lawyer, and I want my day in court to tell my side, but not without a lawyer. I need You to be my Advocate and Helper. Help me to do what's best for my future and protect my kids from any harm. Amen."

It was my turn. "Lord, I agree with Curtis's prayer. Help me know how to talk to the assistant DA on Curtis's behalf. Amen."

We stood up. I waited on him. The guard appeared in the window of the door and knocked to signal the end of our visit.

"Tell him yes, I'll take the plea." He put his hands behind his back to receive the handcuffs.

"OK I'll tell him. Bye, honey."

June 16, 1998

I was at the DA's office at 7:50 a.m. At 8:00 a.m. the assistant DA came in and looked at me with raised eyebrows. "What's his reply?"

"He accepts the plea bargain."

"Good, I'll tell the judge this morning in court. I'll tell his investigator Mr. Steve, because he'll be in the courtroom with Curtis."

Mr. Steve's job was to gather evidence in Curtis's defense to help with his case. He worked with each lawyer and worked with Curtis when he was his own lawyer.

The previous day Curtis's father, Chuck arrived from Atlanta, Georgia and came to court that morning. Warren's parents sat on a bench just a short distance away from courtroom 207. Karen's parents, Betty, our former secretary, Kathy, our former prayer coordinator, Betty, a former member of our church and my hairdresser were all present. They had known and prayed for Curtis since he was a child. We huddled around the courtroom door to pray for Curtis and wait on the outcome.

Suddenly the courtroom door opened and Mr. Steve came out and stood directly in front of me with a puzzled look, "Ms. Gardner, we only ask a relative to come in if the person before the judge is a minor. They cannot say anything to the judge or lawyers, but the minor can discuss things with the relative or guardian. Since Curtis has no lawyer for him to discuss things with, the judge has asked for you to come in to be there for Curtis. You cannot say anything to anyone except Curtis. This is highly unusual. In fact, this is the first time I've ever seen this happen, and I have been at this job for over thirty years."

I knew it was the grace and favor of God that had intervened. I had asked God not to let Curtis be alone at this crucial time and He answered my prayer.

Curtis accepted the plea bargain when it was read by the judge. Those standing outside were allowed in for the sentencing which took place immediately.

Curtis has been in several prisons throughout the state of California. He has served over half of the thirty years he must serve before becoming eligible for parole. But all is not well. He has spent a lot of time in solitary confinement known as Security Housing Unit (SHU). Sometimes he caused the problem, and sometimes he was unjustly detained. One four-month sentence in Solitary Confinement was extended to twelve more months with the excuse of "lost paperwork." In isolation he became more paranoid and withdrawn.

Shortly after his transfer from Southern California to Central California in November 2007, Curtis's cellmate was found dead in their cell. They determined there was enough evidence to bring Curtis to trial. I wept for two days when I originally heard this news. I wept for Curtis, I wept for the man who died, who may not have known the Lord. I wept for the man's family. I wept for myself because of another major storm concerning Curtis. I turned my focus to the Lord so I could release the pain and depth of my disappointment. I needed to do this if I was to walk through this storm as an overcomer.

I attended his two week trial in March 2012 in Central California. The charge was first degree murder, but the jury could see that wasn't true. The jury found him guilty of voluntary manslaughter, which carried a maximum sentence of eleven years. Curtis never said he regretted killing the man, he only said that he felt it was "him or me." This may be why the jury did not come back with a self-defense verdict. The judge gave him the eleven years, and then to everyone's surprise, said he believed Curtis is not to be back on the street and tripled the eleven years to thirty-three years.

It knocked the wind out of me. I'm sure it did the same to Curtis. His lawyer immediately filed an appeal.

As one of my favorite ministers Joyce Meyers, often says, "It is what it is. Face it and move on."

Jesus said: *These things I have spoken to you, that in Me you may have peace. In the world you will have tribulation; but be of good cheer, I have overcome the world* (John 16:33).

Chapter 4

Children of Trauma

But the mercy of the LORD is from everlasting to everlasting On those who fear Him, And His righteousness to children's children. To such as keep His covenant, And to those who remember His commandments to do them (Psalm 103:17-18).

Six months before Curtis disappeared; he looked like any young man in his mid-twenties who had recently received joint custody of his two children. He rented office space in Riverside as a self-employed businessman. It seemed he became more self-sacrificing. He made the financial sacrifice to work more from home in order to be more available for his kids. He changed Cyndi's diapers, learned to comb her hair, read books to Chris, and cooked meals. I babysat when he worked at the office.

But everything changed ten days after his divorce was final. On that fateful October 27, 1996, in the afternoon after church Curtis was selfish beyond my wildest imagination. My grandchildren watched their dad kidnap their mom and abandon them as they looked at the wounded body of their mom's boyfriend.

Three-year-old Chris, two-year-old Cyndi, and four-year-old off-duty Officer Warren's son, were left traumatized. Three innocent children became deeply scarred, and *my son* was the vessel the Enemy used.

One of Satan's pleasures is to destroy innocence in all forms. Satan hates children and seeks ways to violate their innocence. He searches to find a willing vessel where he can use their unresolved issues as entry access points to cause physical abuse, sexual abuse, verbal abuse, neglect, or trauma. He is our true Enemy—not the human vessels. Although we don't excuse their acts, God wants us to forgive those who Satan uses and fight the real *source* of the evil.

For we do not wrestle against flesh and blood, but against principalities, against powers, against the rulers of the darkness of this age, against spiritual hosts of wickedness in the heavenly places (Ephesians 6:12).

My heart was overwhelmed with questions that all started with one word, *How? How* could my son go that far into the dark side of the Enemy's territory? *How* could he yield himself to Satan so completely? *How* could he disregard every warning God gave him? *How* could he totally ignore the impact his actions would have on his children? Chuck and I worked hard to help him know the Bible and love God. *How* could that not give us some kind of guarantee that he would be a benefit to society and a blessing to God's kingdom?

I saw signs of wrong judgments, emotionally unhealthy actions, and anger issues in Curtis as early as elementary school. When he was sixteen, Chuck and I sought advice from a counselor friend. At the end of our talk I asked our friend to counsel Curtis. He recommended a counselor he knew was good with youth.

Chuck and I thought it was proper he take him to the counselor since Curtis was a boy. They went to two sessions and quit because Chuck said Curtis was playing mind games with the counselor and wasn't learning anything. He said for the amount of money we were spending he thought it was a waste of time and finances. He was right because Curtis is extremely intelligent and loves playing mind games. He was also wrong because as counselors ourselves, we knew it could take two sessions before a person believes a counselor is authentic and is comfortable enough to open up.

Discontinuing counseling was a regrettable mistake. I should have taken him at least once myself to bring his emotional problems to the table. It took me years to convince Chuck that Curtis needed help so he would agree to take him to that counselor. Afterwards, I sought other counselors, but I allowed Chuck and Curtis to put up roadblocks, such as football practice, and other activities that became priorities. The issue was not limited to the mind games and the cost. It was also Chuck's pride and unwillingness to allow someone to probe the painful emotional side of our family. It was too uncomfortable for him. I had pride also by not wanting to talk about our family, but I was desperate for help and willing to move beyond my pride. We were good people and good parents, but we had too many defenses. Our unresolved issues and unhealed hurts left us too emotionally unhealthy to help ourselves become an emotionally healthier family.

My biggest regret is I didn't continue my search for a counselor or stick with the one we had and allow God the opportunity to heal all of us. We needed someone who could go to the core of the deception and pain in his heart and ours. I regret that I didn't pursue spiritual help for Curtis, also. I needed help for him to truly understand the ways of the Enemy and build in him a desire to resist him and simultaneously build a passion to understand intimately the love of God. Someone to help Curtis communicate about his relationship with God because as parents we quizzed him after each learning activity but we didn't thoroughly take time to watch how he applied what he learned.

Curtis was born-again at age five, he experienced an intimate encounter of being filled with the Spirit at age seven. That morning Carlton and I watched in awe after our morning devotion before school. Curtis lifted his hands and worshipped God for several minutes as he praised God in a beautiful prayer language. He put his arms down and sat motionless for several more minutes with a wide smile on his face. He was "lost" in the Spirit. I led him to the car and to his class because he was somewhat oblivious to his surroundings. At ten he was water baptism. We didn't build on these experiences and teach him the significance of the God encounters. A home run in softball or a good tackle in football was praised and celebrated much more than his spiritual accomplishments. It's normal but a "big mistake."

He prayed heartfelt God-inspired prayers as a youngster. He memorized many scriptures, attended private Christian schools, and was active at church. He knew he was loved by his parents, brother, grandparents, extended family, and church family. In spite of this Curtis at times was filled with anger.

We didn't lead a dual life. As parents we tried to live out our faith in an authentic way. We attempted to live by the Word and serve God from flawed but sincere hearts. A lot was right in our family's life, but our strongholds needed to be healed.

When that fateful event happened, my mind was bombarded with seemingly insurmountable guilt. Suddenly, I remembered every time I made an immature decision in my parenting. I recalled the times I overcorrected Curtis. Before I received some of my own emotional healing, my discipline was based on my emotions and good intentions and not the Word of God and wise counsel. I felt he would have become a better adult if he had parents who were healed from their own childhood issues. Yet I knew that was not the whole answer.

Curtis didn't fit the stereotypical pattern of a violent criminal. Chuck and I were saved when Curtis was three years old. He was from a two parent household. He had not been abused or molested. He didn't do drugs or alcohol; he was never a gang member. I refused to put locks on my children's doors so they could never isolate themselves or disrespect us as parents by making us beg access to their rooms. Of course we respected their privacy and knocked on their door before entering.

My emotions were like a rollercoaster. One day I believed we were good parents and blamed Curtis for the way he turned out. The next day I knew we had failed miserably as parents. But did our failure lead to his hardened heart? I just didn't know.

One thing I did know—I underestimated how relentlessly the Enemy fought for control of his life. The Adversary pursued Curtis from conception. I never realized the full extent of Curtis's identification with the Enemy's picture of who he was. His image of himself was not based on becoming a man of God.

I turned to the Bible for resolution. *Don't let anyone under pressure to give in to evil say, "God is trying to trip me up." God is impervious to evil, and puts evil in no one's way. The temptation to give in to evil comes from us and only us. We have no one to blame but the leering, seducing flare-up of our own lust. Lust gets pregnant, and has a baby: sin! Sin grows up to adulthood, and becomes a real killer* (James 1:13-15 MSG).

I took steps to free myself from unhealthy guilt and condemnation: I forgave myself for the areas I felt guilty. I surrendered to God every unanswered question. I resigned myself to the revelation that the Adversary will always be after my children. He hates all humanity, but he hates women and children more.

Satan tempts us, God warns us against the temptation, and our will (soul) is the deciding factor—not how we were parented. The Adversary's greatest desire was for me to carry guilt and shame for my son's choices. I chose not to do that. It was a fight, but I overcame. But that doesn't mean the children involved didn't suffer. They did.

Previously I shared how Curtis became his own lawyer, therefore, he was given all the paperwork pertaining to his case. He copied papers and wrote letters of instructions which he sent to a fellow business owner and high school friend, Marvin.

Marvin's office was put under surveillance by the police to see what connection he had to Curtis. Eventually, they raided Marvin's place of business and took him in for questioning. They confiscated his computer and the papers in his office. He was released, but not before they read everything sent from Curtis.

I was unaware this had happened. A few days after the raid I called Karen's beeper and left a message about the time we agreed that I would pick up my grandchildren at the Corona Police Station, our usual meeting place. I didn't hear back for half an hour so I called her beeper again. About twenty minutes later my home phone rang and it was a male voice.

"I'm Mr. Greg, the investigator for the district attorney's office. I received a call from Karen. She asked that I return her call to you. There have been some changes, and she has asked that you not call her number anymore. She will be getting a new number right away. She also said you will not be seeing your grandchildren anymore."

I felt the wind knocked out of me. "Ah . . . I don't understand. She's the one who set this date for me to babysit the kids tomorrow because she had an appointment. Why are you the one who's calling to tell me this?" Under my breath, I whispered a prayer. "Lord, help him not to hang up until I know what's going on."

"I really shouldn't be giving you any information that the DA's office has access too, but I'll tell you this part. There was a raid on an office Curtis is in constant communication with. A letter was found with Karen and the kids' Social Security numbers, all of her known addresses, plus the address, and phone number of her parents. The letter requested the party find Karen and forcibly make her not testify against Curtis since she is the only eye witness. Because of this threat, we have provided a safe place. That's all I can tell you. Goodbye, Ms. Gardner."

I hung up the phone in shock. "Oh God, help us! Have mercy on us! Jesus! Jesus! Jesus!"

I paced the floor and prayed. Then I called Curtis's investigator, Mr. Steve, to see if he knew anything about the letter. He confirmed what Mr. Greg had shared. "Curtis has really messed up big time. This will hurt his case. He sent a letter suggesting his friend find Karen to persuade her not to testify against him. He put personal information in the letter like Social Security numbers, addresses, etc. Karen told the DA that Curtis and Marvin knew some questionable and dangerous people and any one of them may have seen the letter. She believed her family's safety had become jeopardized. So it looks like they may go into hiding until the trial."

I heard nothing about Karen or my grandchildren for two months. No return calls from her family. Then all their numbers were disconnected. One morning I picked up the newspaper and read where Karen had gone to the county recorder's office and made a scene. She was upset because they had published her and my grandkids' new names while they were being processed into a phase of the Witness Protection Program. The police said since the names were published she had to chose new names and go through the process again.

What? A phase of the Witness Protection Program? *My* grandkids? Will this drama ever end? I got up from my chair and walked in circles for a while.

I called the investigator Mr. Steve. "Steve, I had a serious shock this morning when I saw an article in the paper that said Karen and my grandkids were given new names and now will change their names again. Please tell me you know something about what's going on?"

"Ms. Gardner, I recently found out this happened over the last two months," he said. "Karen and your grandchildren were relocated with the help of the police. They entered a type of witness protection program. They received new identities, new Social Security numbers, and an undisclosed residence. Her parents have moved and changed their phone numbers also."

A year passed and I had not seen my grandchildren—my heart ached. I called local and federal agencies to get some understanding of the legal rights of grandparents. I found some advocates for grandparents' rights. But they needed at least one Social Security number or some current information to trace them and help me. When I couldn't provide the information to get started I thought maybe I could borrow money and hire a private detective and he or she could do some digging around and find them. But that would be difficult with no current names, addresses, or Social Security numbers. Finally I gave up. I realized this was the worldly way of finding answers. I could borrow money to make things happen and still end up empty-handed.

At last I settled in my heart that God was the *only* One who knew where my grandchildren were. He alone is the God of my restoration. So I completely surrendered my relationship with my grandchildren to the Lord. I made my mind up to patiently endure, like Abraham and Sarah. I went boldly in faith to the throne of grace with my face wet with tears. I determined they would always be tears of faith and no more tears of self-pity, grief, or unbelief. I asked the Holy Spirit to show me whenever my tears were rooted in self-pity. I said to the Lord, "I will be restored to my grandchildren while they are young. I will influence them for Christ. My hope is in You alone."

Each time I cried I asked Him about the source of my tears. When He revealed it, I surrendered my improper motivations to the Lord, whether it was self-pity, fear of the future, disappointment, etc. I asked to be healed from the source and I chose to let go of the lie. I talked to the Holy Spirit about my faith and trust in Him. I prayed until He healed me, and I could let go of the pain.

I became unwavering in faith for God to work a miracle and get the glory for the testimony of restoration with my grandchildren— no matter how many years it took. I held onto Hebrews 4:16: *Let us therefore come boldly to the throne of grace, that we may obtain mercy and find grace to help in time of need.*

I reflected back to when Curtis and Carlton were still in elementary school. It was then that I began a pray regiment for their mates and declared "Each son will marry the right woman and I will have a good relationship with my daughters-in-law. I'll have favor in their sight. My sons will *not* have children by anyone other woman than their God-given mate. I believe I will be able to influence my grandchildren for the Lord and they will be born-again at a young age."

I was prompted to declare this after experiencing many counseling appointments from women who were distraught because they had no contact with their grandchildren. I noticed several daughters-in-law because of jealousy or immaturity had convinced their sons to become estranged from his family. Therefore I determined to have preventative faith. Put my faith in the Father before a problem could arise.

I was glad I had taken that initiative for years. So I comforted my heart by reminding myself that the foundation of faith for this situation was laid years earlier.

I encouraged myself until I had a heart full of faith. I knew without a doubt one day I would be reunited with my grandchildren, the question was when it will happen. I quoted God's promises and covenants, concerning my children's children. Psalm 103:17-18 was one of my favorites: *But the mercy of the LORD is from everlasting to everlasting on those who fear Him, And His righteousness to children's children, To such as keep His covenant, and to those who remember His commandments to do them.*

This scripture made my heart leap with faith. It is *not* about my children, but my children's children. There is nothing in this verse that says my kids had to live right for the promise in this verse to be fulfilled. As long as I, a grandparent, kept His covenant and as long as I walked in the reverential fear of the Lord, He would show mercy to my children's children (grandchildren). So I prayed this scripture passage over their lives.

God lives in eternity where there is neither time nor distance. And prayer is an eternal thing. No time or distance can restrict the influence of our faith-filled prayers; God's grace is released through faith-filled words. Words that show God we trust Him and are willing to take the dominion Jesus purchased by His blood. We speak words of an overcomer in any storm. Even if I didn't know where they were, the covenant was still true and was activated on their behalf!

God sends his warring angels to where our grandchildren are to minister to them. We can believe for them to know God and be born-again. Whether we ever see them this side of heaven or not, but we can believe for restoration. This truth excited me.

The Lord is a generational Father. He makes covenant with us for the good of the generations, not only for us. His covenant dealings were with Abraham, Isaac, *and* Jacob, the grandchild.

I thought about Cornelius in Acts 10. His prayer and his giving of resources and finances were a memorial that blessed his entire household. I gave offerings to ministries and to the poor and put "grandchildren" in the memo of the check. I know my prayers and giving showed God the seriousness of my faith in Him to restore my "household." Like

Cornelius, I was not trying to buy anything from God but to allow my life to reflect my faith in Him.

James 4:7 says, *Therefore, submit to God. Resist the devil and he will flee from you.* I submitted to God, and then I resisted the Devil. Because Satan is a thief, I told him he could *not* rob me of my covenant rights to influence my grandchildren for God. I declared, "You will *not* silence my voice!"

I longed for my children and grandchildren to come under the umbrella of my covenant obedience to God. I wanted favor and blessings to come to them because of me. I wanted them to understand their blessings and favor didn't come from their good looks, personality, ingenuity, or luck, but from God.

One day I received a surprise phone call—near my birthday in February 1999. It was Karen. "Diane, I want to wish you a happy birthday. I know the only thing you have left of Curtis is his children. I'm sure you miss them a lot. I thought about when you went through your divorce, you never spoke badly about Mr. Chuck to me or Curtis. That always impressed me. I want to believe I can trust you not to tell Curtis where the kids and I are. My children and I have a counselor, and I've talked to her about you seeing the kids. Would you see the counselor with me to find out if something can be worked out for you to see the kids?"

"I am more than happy to do that. I know it took a lot of courage for you to make this call. Thank you. This is the best birthday gift I could have received!"

"Well, I am not making any promises, but this call is to say I want to try."

I hung up the phone and excitedly lifted my hands and praised God. "Thank You, Lord, for Karen! Thank You for answering my prayer of faith over this last year! She has a kind heart and You have moved her heart to go beyond her fears to reach out to me. I bless You for Your grace that brought me that phone call. You are great and You are miraculous."

I saw the counselor, who was a nice Christian lady, a total of three times. I answered every question, jumped through every hoop, listened to every concern, and apologized where I had offended Karen. I apologized on behalf of Carlton and any other of my family members who offended her. I apologized for what we did do and what we neglected to do.

After the third session, I had to ask the question. "Have you made a decision? Will I be able to start seeing my grandchildren soon?"

"I still feel afraid that Curtis will know where I am," Karen said. "You may feel sorry for him one day when he is missing his children, and you might tell him where we are. I know he can't do anything but he had some bad people in his life, and I don't know if he is still in contact with any of them."

"Karen, I understand your fears. This is a terrible situation brought on by Curtis's selfishness and him listening to the Adversary. There is nothing I can do to help you feel better. It is impossible to make a bad situation feel good. I know there are so many unanswered questions."

I leaned a little closer to her as we sat on the couch together. "As a senior pastor, it is my job to keep people's secrets. As a biblical family counselor, I keep secrets. Keeping confidences is a way of life for me. As a child of God, if I give you my word, I will keep it because ultimately I will answer to God Himself for what I do. Either I have proven myself trustworthy or I have not. Ask your counselor what she thinks. Fears and emotions aside, it will be good if this can be settled today—if we can have the faith to try."

We both had tear-stained faces.

She turned to her counselor sitting in a leather overstuffed chair across the room. "What do you think?"

"Karen, you have valid concerns, but Diane is right. There is nothing new that can be said. The topic has been fully explored. It is time for a conclusion. She has agreed not to tell anyone when she meets with the kids. She has agreed not to ask the kids any questions about where they live and what they do. She has agreed not to tell Curtis that she has seen his children. She is willing to meet you at any place you designate to pick up the children. It would be good to give her a yes or no today. Take your time."

After sighing a few times, Karen turned toward me. "Yes, you can see the children. But I want you to use my mom, for the meetings. Every time I see you, it reminds me of Curtis, and sometimes it causes nightmares."

Yes! I thanked Jesus for His favor and answered prayers as my heart raced with excitement. But calmly I said, "Thank you, Karen. I know this was a big step of faith for you to make this call and set up these meetings with your counselor. I appreciate you."

We hugged and cried.

Four weeks later, I met Karen's mother Lois, on the playground of a park in Corona. Chris was five and Cyndi was four. He remembered me, but she did not. They responded to me as if I were a stranger. I pushed them on the swings, waited at the bottom of the slide, and tossed a foam Frisbee I brought.

It had been two years since I'd seen them. My heart was racing as I looked at the most beautiful children in the world. I only wanted to hold them, rock them, pray over them, and never let them go. But they responded like children of trauma. They had no smiles and very little expression. It took them both some time to warm up to me. We played for about an hour. I took lots of pictures of them. When we parted I realized how preoccupied I was because I left my cell phone in the park. I returned to looked for it, but it was gone—just like their innocence.

Lois commented that some of the playfulness and curiosity of children their age was not there. She also said they still had nightmares about abandonment, but the counseling was helping them. I was extremely thankful that Lois was committed to helping me reconnect with my grandchildren.

Over the years they've received much counseling. They felt depressed, rejected, and abandoned. And I was sure they faced kids who bullied them about their father being in prison.

I can't imagine how much pain it must cause children when they are asked why their father or mother is not around and they respond by saying they are in prison. What a burden so many of our children, grandchildren, nieces, and nephews must carry. We should open the conversations for dialogue and prayer concerning this subject more often. God wants to heal their hearts.

A few years later as we played a game of ping pong at my condo, Chris and I had a disagreement when he was eleven. He got upset with me then blurted out from nowhere, "People say they love me, but they don't! You don't love me! Don't you realize I think about my dad every day?" Then he burst into tears. We had not mentioned his dad prior to his outburst. It broke my heart. I prayed with him, but he refused to let me hug him.

Chris threatened suicide as a preteen and as a teenager. Things have been rough for Karen and her kids. They have had the love and support of family and friends but they missed the healing which comes from a loving supportive church family. They've also not fully understood the depth of healing that can come only from a loving heavenly Father and through His Word. This goes far beyond counseling. My hope is one day the Father's love will become a daily reality.

They are good kids, beautiful, and above average in intelligence. Do I sound biased? They are maturing and will do well. The sparkle in their eyes eventually came back. They have had numerous struggles in their journey, but God's hand is on their lives. Over the years I was able to help them know who Jesus is. Each became born-again as preteens.

I chose to continually speak over their lives the opposite of what the Enemy has done. I speak a blessing. I decree the name of Jesus whose name is above the name of trauma. Sometimes I say, "Trauma I command you to leave Curtis's children now! Trauma will not define their future or their purpose. I destroy every destiny thief and destiny pirate. I destroy the symptoms of PTSD. I command their lives to be covered by the blood of Jesus Christ! I choose to trust the power of God to make a difference in their lives!"

To know that I could declare the truth beyond what I saw and felt was my key to sanity. *You will make your prayer to Him, He will hear you, And you will pay your vows. You will also declare a thing, And it will be established for you; So light will shine on your ways* (Job 22:27-28).

Today, they have both graduated from high school and are attending college. I believe God will lead them to fulfill the call of God on their lives. I believe the trauma of the past will not define their life but be a stepping stone to stand tall and help others from the storms they've experienced.

God opened the door in 2004 for me to take them from California to Atlanta for their cousin Jeana's first birthday. I have taken them on subsequent trips to visit Uncle Carlton, Aunt Kisha and their cousins.

Up to now they have not visited their dad. I have attempted to take them several times, but either the permission papers had not been notarized by Karen, the prison went on lockdown, their schedule of activities changed, or there was another snag. A few times they changed their minds. Chris said the more he thought about it he felt it would make him too sad if he saw his dad in prison. Curtis and Carlton blamed me for Chris and Cyndi never seeing Curtis. That's sad, but God knows the truth.

God will open the door someday for them to see their Dad, and prepare Curtis's mind to be positive and apologetic when they see him. They are adults now and can apply for an application to visit on their own.

For Thanksgiving 2010 I took them to Ohio where Uncle Carlton, Aunt Kisha and their three cousins now live. Carlton previously informed Curtis about the we would be at his home. Curtis was able to call while they were there. This was the first time they'd heard his voice in fourteen years. It was a pleasant conversation, but my grandkids said they were waiting for their Dad to apologize to them. He never did. Carlton didn't tell me in advance Curtis was going to call; nevertheless, I am thankful it happened.

What a rich blessing to have all five of my grandchildren together. I flew a professional photographer from my ministry who is also a friend of our family to Ohio for that Thanksgiving weekend. We had beautiful family portraits done and a rich time of food and fellowship. This was a time I will always cherish.

The pictures are a testimony that Jesus is a God of restoration.

I believe the healing process from their trauma will continue into adulthood. The more they surrender to Christ, the deeper healing will take place. Their experience with church has been limited. But in faith, I declare they *will* become the people God intended them to be from birth. They each have a powerful call of God on their lives as leaders in service to His kingdom. I believe they both will help others affected by trauma. I'm looking forward to watch their destiny unfold as they learn to seek God for His purpose.

Chapter 5

Prison Mom

"Fear not, for I have redeemed you; I have called you by your name; You are Mine. When you pass through the waters, I will be with you; And through the rivers, they shall not overflow you. (Isaiah 43:1b-2a)

I'm the mom of a prisoner, but I never want to become an imprisoned mom. I don't want to be imprisoned by my pain, imprisoned by my disappointments, imprisoned by my grief, imprisoned by my shame, or imprisoned by my unforgiveness. Neither do I want to be imprisoned by my children's decisions.

However, this is largely an impossible reality without the grace of God. By His grace I choose to live with the evidence of God's Word authentically played out in my life in a balanced way. I believe only God can reveal to me when I am out of His balance. I'm out of balance when my heart is heavy and needs to be emptied of the cares of this life. God cannot fill a spot that is currently occupied.

January, 1998

I remember a conversation I had with Curtis during his first several months in jail before his trial. I knew it was the right thing to do and the right thing to tell him, but being right didn't make my emotions feel any better. I prayed for God to prepare Curtis's heart to receive my words, and for me to be able to logically communicate my heartfelt decision without a lot of emotions.

As I sat on the metal stool and listened to Curtis talk about how terrible prison life was, I breathed a quiet prayer, "Lord, keep him close and cover Curtis with Your blood. Heal him of the traumas he is going through. Thank You for the angels that surround him. He will live and not die. I ask You for grace for both of us. Thank you, Jesus."

I looked through the glass window as I held the large black telephone receiver to my right ear. "I need to talk to you about something close to my heart."

"Yeah, Mom, go ahead."

"You've been in jail since Mother's Day weekend last year, and I've been here once or twice weekly. Also, I've been in court every time the judge set a date. Many of those dates were postponed by the lawyers after we were in the courtroom and I had taken the day off work. Your first lawyer had a conflict of interest and had to resign. Your new lawyer needed to start the process over again. All this has taken me away from my responsibilities."

I paused to let that sink in. "So far things are going well at my church. I have a good team, and I have trained them well. My assistant, Darlene, is doing a good job holding things together. But I have had no time to organize where we as a ministry are headed this year. New people have visited the church, and some have joined us, but I have not had time to connect with any of them. Curtis, what I need to express is I won't visit you as often, God has shown me I need to spend more time working and vision casting, or the ministry will suffer. I also need to prepare for my upcoming speaking engagements."

Curtis wrinkled his eyebrows and looked a bit puzzled.

"Yet, let me say I love you with my whole heart. I missed you terribly when you were gone for seven months. I will always be here for you. You are my son, and you will always come before any other people in my ministry. You and Carlton come before anyone else. I have always demonstrated that to you, haven't I?"

"Yeah, Mom, you were always there for us. You included us even when we didn't want to be included, and you always cooked for us first when you cooked for the church." He said with the corner of his lip turned up in a slight grin.

"As much as I love you, honey, I love God more. You cannot come before my love for God. Jesus gave His life for me, and I have turned my life over to Him. I don't belong to myself anymore, and my time is not my own either. I have to be where He wants me to be. I'm not only your mother, I'm God's servant. To put God first, I need to put my calling first. I'm not talking about people's needs. Instead, I'm talking about what God asks me to do *for* people. My ministry is my occupation *and* my service for God.

"Since you've been in court for months, I have put *your* needs before my love and service for Jesus. I've put you before His call on my life. I can't do that anymore. What makes it hard is that I'm the only one in court to support you. From now on I'll not be in court every time. I have to study, pray, and prepare. My congregation and I have got to get fresh insight so we can find out what God wants us to do next."

"Sure, Mom, you need to do what you think is best. I know you love me. Don't feel bad when you can't come to court."

"Thanks honey. I asked the Lord to show me how to prioritize my life, and I believe this is what He wants me to do. The Holy Spirit reminded me about Luke 14:26 (AMP): *If anyone comes to Me and does not hate his [own] father and mother [in the sense of indifference to or relative disregard for them in comparison with his attitude toward God] and [likewise] his wife and children and brothers and sisters—[yes] and even his own life also—he cannot be My disciple.*

"I repented of the ways I made you an idol and put you first." A recorded message interrupted me. "You have three minutes before this phone is cut off."

"So now you tell me God says you have to hate me to follow Him." Curtis smirked the way he usually did when he was making a sarcastic remark.

I smiled. "You know that's Old English for 'have less regard' for you or me than I do for God and His concerns. There are people whose lives He wants me to touch for Him. His timing cannot be put on hold—people's lives are at stake. My obedience to Him is crucial.

"When I obey, God brings blessings on my life, and benefits my children and grandchildren also. Never forget that Jesus loves you so much, Curtis."

"Sure, Mom."

"Thanks for understanding."

The phone suddenly cut off, and a correctional officer appeared in the window of the door behind Curtis. Simultaneously we stood up. I blew him a kiss and mouthed the words, "I love you."

He mouthed the words, "I love you too, Mom."

Curtis put his hands behind his back, took three shuffles backward, and put his hands through the small opening in the door. The officer cuffed his wrists. Curtis took three shuffles forward and turned around. The officer opened the door and ushered him down the hallway.

I felt my heart sink to a depth of disappointment that caused me momentarily to become totally numb. What a horrible sight. What a horrible life Curtis brought on himself. When Curtis and Carlton were young I sometimes visited my brother Johnny in prison. On each visit I said to myself, *I never want my children to end up in here. I'll do everything possible for that never to happen. That would be a mother's worst nightmare.*

I tried everything I knew for my children to never become a prisoner. But there are no guarantees in life. The Enemy often mocked me with tormenting thoughts about Curtis ending up in prison when it was my life's goal that he wouldn't.

From time to time when I sat in the courtroom with Curtis, my gaze was drawn to the young lawyers. They were a lot like him: intelligent, articulate, poised, confident, and arrogant. Oh, and handsome too. I imagined Curtis sitting in the lawyer's chair instead of the defendant's chair. *If only a few of his decisions had been different. If only he were less selfishness, had more emotional stability, and had a passion to help others.*

If only his thoughts were healthy instead of unhealthy—if that had been the case, he could easily be the lawyer and not the defendant. I knew if I continued with these thoughts, I would become depressed, so I didn't allow myself to ask *what if* any longer, no matter how tempting.

Curtis has had to do a lot of legal research and brought his findings to his lawyer. One of his lawyers told me Curtis was the most intelligent client he had in thirty years of practice as far as grasping the law was concerned.

As parents, Chuck and I laid down our lives for our children. We made many sacrifices and put their needs before ours. We taught by example how to be people of integrity and hard workers, as we walked out our faith and grew in Christ.

We wanted our children to have a passion to fulfill God's call on their lives. We wanted them to be good citizens, good leaders, good husbands, and good parents. We listened to sermons and studied books on parenting that made us feel like we had a *guarantee* that our family would be immune to some problems. A guarantee was implied that our children would not go to jail, join gangs, or do drugs if we taught them the Bible and kept them in church. These teachers and authors quoted statistics that implied if our children came from a two parent home with hands-on parenting then success was guaranteed.

That kind of thinking left Satan out altogether as our relentless adversary. It left out our children's free will to choose God's way or Satan's way. It left out our family's propensity for emotional or mental illnesses. Because of the Enemy, and human nature, the only guarantees we are left with are God's love, His Word, and the Holy Spirit's guidance in a storm. Yet, it is our responsibility to ask for, accept, and act upon His help in the storm. To complain about the size of the waves releases no faith for God to work and accomplishes nothing.

We need the grace of God to be an involved mother, grandmother, wife, sister, aunt or guardian, of a prisoner because only His grace can release the grief, shame, condemnation, and disappointments from the depths of our emotions—a sentiment expressed in 1 Peter 5:6-8: *Casting all your care upon Him, for He cares for you. Be sober, be vigilant;*

because your adversary the devil walks about like a roaring lion, seeking whom he may devour.

I've made my mind up, with God's help, to never be hospitalized because of stress related illnesses such as, a stroke, ulcer, migraine, heart problem, depression, or nervous condition because of my worry over *someone else's actions.* I've found the keys to victory for me—forgive and empty my emotions of the cares—fill that empty spot with God's love and grace. It takes God's grace to forgive, to truly live Matthew 18:21-22, to forgive again and again, seventy times seven in a day, if necessary. Forgiveness justifies no one's behavior; it frees them from accountability to us and makes them accountable to God. Forgiveness frees us from the emotional yoke that keeps us tied to that person.

I forgave Curtis because he knew the Word of God and chose the Enemy's way. I forgave him because he makes it a practice to ignore my counsel and warnings. I forgave him for his pride and rebellion. I forgave him for not writing to me for long periods of time although I write to him. And I forgave him for his ungratefulness toward God and creating his own "idol god" spawned by the Enemy's deception and his own imagination.

A major paradigm shift in my thinking came when the Holy Spirit urged me to choose to forgive Curtis for whom he has chosen to become, and forgive him for how he has chosen to live his life. That's a better approach than trying to forgive each individual incident. Each bad decision is a reflection of his wrong thinking because of who he has become. So I had to embrace that he is not who I want him to be.

For as he thinks in his heart, so is he (Proverbs 23:7).

Ultimately I was able to pray, "Lord, I forgive Curtis for choosing the path that leads to destruction. I forgive him for hardening his heart toward You, and me. Until he surrenders and allows You to replace his heart of stone with a heart for You, he will continue to believe the lies produced by deception and rejection that Satan has planted in him."

Enter by the narrow gate. For the gate is wide and the way is easy that leads to destruction, and those who enter by it are many (Matthew 7:13 ESV).

For over fifteen years, I've driven to various prisons throughout California to visit Curtis. Recently I drove seven hours to a hotel thirty minutes from the prison. I checked the recorded message for the third time that night before bed to make sure the prison was open. It said all visits were open. When I got to the prison at 8:00 a.m., I was told they had been on lockdown since 4:00 a.m. when a few inmates got into a fight. I drove seven hours back home.

In fifteen years in prison no one in California close to me has ever asked for Curtis to send them a visitation paper so they could visit him. I visit him alone. I have had a couple of people drive with me and stay in the area while I visited him. I'm grateful for that. A few have written him and I'm grateful for that also.

The times I get in to see Curtis, guards tell us where to sit. Guards listen to our phone conversations. And when he is not in solitary confinement and we have a "contact visit" they watch our every move. I also have to guard my words so Curtis doesn't fly off the handle. Such is the life of a prisoner and a prison mom.

As the mother of a prisoner, I celebrate holidays without Curtis's laughter. There are no family vacations with both sons and their families. None of my family portraits can include Curtis's smiling face, although when we can we take a picture in prison every couple of years. I don't see the simple pleasure of Curtis's interaction with his children, his brother, or me.

One day I picked up my ministry mail from the post office and laid it on the passenger seat. I was in my gym clothes as I headed for my workout at the gym. I felt happy and content with my day's schedule and my prayer time that morning was a blessing.

While at a red light, I glanced down at a copy of *Focus on the Family* magazine. It was the June issue, and they highlighted fathers and fatherhood. There was a picture of a father and his small son who smiled at one another. Without warning tears filled my eyes and I felt a stabbing pain in my chest. I drove a few blocks and saw a father walking down the street holding the hand of his young daughter—another knife wound to my heart. I've learned I cannot prevent what will trigger the pain of grief. I just have to determine to release it as soon as possible. Jesus bore my grief so I would not have to carry it. I have a choice when grief shows up.

At that moment I could dry my tears, shut off my emotions, go to the gym, get on the treadmill, and aggressively work to release my stress while I suppressed my pain. This is a temporary burial because one day the grief will resurface. Or I could go home and take the time I designated for the gym and get before the Lord and let Him dig out my pain. I went home. When I got there I held the magazine up to the Lord and began to wail, letting out my grief and disappointments to God. I asked the Holy Spirit, "What is the main issue of my pain I am releasing from my heart?"

I heard Him say, *You're grieving the loss of relationship between Curtis and his children. They will miss simple pleasures of life: playing catch, a walk holding hands, being taught to ride a bike, driving in a car with their dad, good night prayers, reading the Bible together, and the pleasure of a meaningful conversation with him.*

Afterwards I felt emotionally drained, but I was wonderfully healed. I took the time to grieve and empty myself in His presence so He could fill me with His grace. His grace cannot fill a place that is already full. It hurt, and it was hard, but it was worth the time. Now I can look at fathers who interact with their children and enjoy what I see. My pain is gone, replaced only by an occasional momentary sadness—without pain—when I think of the loss.

February 27, 2012

After serving over fifteen years in prison Curtis was in court again. I sat in the courtroom with Darlene for two weeks during his trial. Four years earlier Curtis and his cellmate had fought and Curtis's cellmate was found dead in their cell.

I emptied my heart of any anxiety and angst by calling on God to give me grace to look at the pictures of the man my son had murdered. Curtis was the only defense witness, so I wanted to be there to intercede for him while he testified. I reflected back to another person who suffered a type of "death" at the hands of my son, Officer Warren. He didn't die, but his brain was tragically damaged. The last I heard, he was confined to a wheelchair, unable to walk, talk, or care for himself. As I write this, it has been over sixteen years since that fateful day, and my eyes are filled with tears because of the darkness in Curtis's mind, and for the family of the man that was murdered.

For years I've prayed for Warren and his family as the Lord directed me. I have asked God to have others pray for him too. I empty my heart of the care each time I end my prayers so I don't carry the burden of what happened to him as heaviness in my heart. I have to diligently protect my heart.

This trial was another horrendous storm, but in the midst I saw the hand of God. Garry, the investigator on Curtis's case, was a strong Christian. I know he was one of the laborers God sent into my son's harvest field. He was gracious and loving, and yet firm with my son when he was obnoxious and ready to fire his eighty-year-old public defender. He intervened when the public defender wanted to quit because of his frustration with Curtis.

Curtis walked into the courtroom in the civilian clothes Carlton and I had purchased for him. It was the first time in over fifteen years that I saw him without the prison clothes. He looked handsome. Although I couldn't take a picture with a camera, I took one with my memory and I carry it in my heart.

I wasn't allowed to hug, kiss, or speak to him because it was a trial. And I wasn't able to visit him that weekend because the prison was on lockdown. I spent my entire tax refund on that trip to pay for myself and Darlene, hotel, food, and gas. I thank God I had the money and didn't need to go into debt. I've found God supplies financially if I pray in advance and ask Him for the money to see Curtis. I pray about the best time to visit. To help me lead a balanced life I've learned to plan at least a half day or more to visit a friend, take in a museum, stop at a fancy restaurant, anything fun on my trip. He'll do the same for you. It's wonderful to trust God and watch Him provide.

When I attended Curtis's trial, Darlene was able to take off from her job as a case worker and be with me in court. I was strengthened by her presence and thank God for her generosity. Afterwards she wrote me a note to tell her impression of that stressful time. I want to share it with you.

March 11, 2012

Darlene wrote:

I watched you during the trial and I was so impressed with your strength of character. Yes, it had been four years since the murder of Curtis's cellmate occurred, but the time lapse did not take away from the severity of it all.

I want to commend you for your fortitude. Your strength of mind allows you to endure pain or adversity with courage. It serves as an example to me and others.

Psalm 1 has been the focus of my reading the last two days. It says when we delight in the Law of the Lord and meditate on it day and night, we are like a tree planted by the rivers of water. We bring forth our fruit in our season. Our leaves never wither.

During the trial I saw your fruit of love, longsuffering, and kindness extended to Curtis. When we first arrived, he made it clear to his brother on the phone that he didn't want you there. When we first entered the courtroom Curtis smiled at me but not at you. But not once was there evidence of your fruit of love withering.

You remind me of Jesus.

I respect you,
Darlene

Although I'm the mother of a prisoner whom I love very much, I work to remember that Jesus has a rich, balanced, abundant life for me to live in addition to motherhood. Over the years I've traveled to foreign countries, continued my education, taken tennis and golf lessons. I started my writing career; I speak at meetings, and host my own retreats to coach women business leaders, and host seminars, etc. I'll serve Him and His kingdom, even though my schedule is interrupted by my prison visits. Carol Kent is another mother of a prisoner who was raised to know the Lord and now is serving a life sentence. She is the author of *When I Lay My Isaac Down* and *A New Kind of Normal.* She says her altered lifestyle, that now includes frequent prison visits, is "a new kind of normal."

Many of the storms I have included in this book have concluded victoriously. But, so far I see no end is in sight for the storms concerning Curtis. Yet I look to God's grace to give me the power to live with this sustained storm.

I declare, "God has His angels in the prison cell with Curtis. The Holy Spirit is there to touch his life with healing and deliverance. He will never be raped or killed. By faith, I envision Curtis ministering the Word and love of God to others, in the name of Jesus."

Years ago I heard a minister say something that increased my boldness. The Enemy will attack you and your family. Satan attacked Jesus' cousin, John-the-Baptist, and beheaded him. When Jesus was told John was beheaded, He left the crowd to grieve, but the multitudes found Him. Instead of asking them to leave Jesus had compassion and healed them all. I learned from this example that the best way to overcome the Enemy is to hit him where he hits you. When people get saved and healed, Satan's kingdom is destroyed. Jesus destroyed the works of the devil that day, big-time.

In 1975 my brother Johnny, after ten years of recycling trough prison gates, was arrested again for drug related issues. This time was different—not for him but for me—I was born-again by three years and understood by then I could sow seeds of faith and reap a harvest for Johnny on what I sowed. I asked God to send laborers across my brother's path. I sowed my time to become the laborer to minister to other people's brothers, and sisters in jail.

Today I'm a part of a faith-based prison recidivism program designed to keep inmates from returning to prison. My team and I teach a weekly series on the power of life and death is in the tongue. Also we teach the difference between our spirit, soul, and body, and how to yield each part to Christ.

We continue contact after they are released. We've received many miraculous testimonies of how God restored them to their estranged children and families. These inmates, some were in as long as thirty years, have gotten jobs, gone to school, started businesses. It's great to know these former inmates have started a new legacy for their family.

Jesus said we will be rewarded if we reach out to those in prison:

> "And He will set the sheep on His right hand, but the goats on the left. Then the King will say to those on His right hand, 'Come, you blessed of My Father, inherit the kingdom prepared for you from the foundation of the world: I was naked and you clothed Me; I was sick and you visited Me; I was in prison and you came to Me'" (Matthew 25:33-34, 36).

PART II

Carlton

Chapter 6

The Accident

And the dragon was enraged with the woman, and he went to make war with the rest of her offspring (Revelation 12:17).

Sunday, September 19, 1992

This Saturday night seemed like any other Saturday night. I was alone in my church office, praying for our church service the next morning. We were thrilled to be a part of a national movement with Charles and Frances Hunter to leave our sanctuary during our regular church time and witness on the streets house-to-house. I was excited to take everyone in teams of three door-to-door to pray for people in the community. We knew God was going to do wonderful things for those open for prayer.

As the senior pastor, a custom I patterned after Pastor Jack Hayford, was to fast my time and meet with the Lord on Saturday nights at church to pray and listen to any last instructions for Sunday service. For some reason, I couldn't stop praying that night.

When I looked at the clock again, I noticed it was 1:00 a.m. Sunday morning. Still, I continued to pray. *I need to find out why I feel the need to continue to pray. I hope I hear something soon so I can go home and go to bed.*

At 2:00 a.m., the office phone rang. *That must be a wrong number. But, then again, it may be someone who has an emergency and they didn't reach me at home.*

I picked up the phone expecting to hear a person asking for someone at a bar or hear a familiar voice in crisis.

"Does someone at your number know a young man named Carlton?" an unfamiliar male voice asked.

"Yes, I have a son named Carlton." A knot formed in the pit of my stomach. As a parent, a middle of the night phone call that includes your child's name is a parent's worst nightmare.

"I'm Dr. McCormick, and there has been an accident. A few college kids brought a man into the ER tonight and said he hit his head on the concrete sidewalk outside the home where there was a party. They told us he was new to Eastern Oregon State University, so no one knew his last name. They left before we could ask any more questions. My nurse looked for identification, but he had no wallet. The only item in his pocket was a card from a church. I took a chance and called. I hoped the call would be forwarded to someone, or there would be an emergency number on the voice mail. But I'm glad you answered. I needed to talk to someone immediately.

"Carlton has a serious concussion and is losing spinal fluid through a hole that has been punctured in his eardrum. He's partially conscious, but unable to talk because of swelling on the brain. I've got to have some questions answered before I can treat h—"

"Oh no! Jesus, help Carlton!" I took a deep breath. "Yes, doctor, what do you need?"

He recited his list of questions, "Spell his entire name. How old is he? Is he allergic to any medication? Is he currently taking any meds?" Etcetera.

I answered every question in a calm voice while my insides shook and my hands trembled.

"Once again, I'm so glad you were at this number," he said.

Carlton was 21 years old and entering his fourth year of college, his first at Eastern Oregon State. He had received a partial scholarship to play football. Friday he told me how excited he was about Saturday's first scrimmage game.

"We need to start work on him right away," Dr. McCormick said. "We'll run tests today, and I'll call you Monday with results. Here's the hospital information in Le Grande, Oregon."

I thank God I didn't ignore the Holy Spirit's nudge to stay at church and pray. Obviously I got no sleep that night. I stayed at the church and continued to pray. At times I found myself walking around in circles.

When I got home about 5:00 a.m., I knelt down by my couch. "Father God, my heart hurts for Carlton, because as his mom, I can't be with him now. Carlton is all alone, and no one is there to comfort him, pray with him, or hold him. But, Lord Jesus, You are there with him, and You have angels assigned. Thank You for being there with him. Help Carlton not feel abandoned. God, please pave the way for me to get there and provide the funds to pay off the credit card."

Jesus, Your Word says in Psalm 107:20: *He sent His word and healed them, And delivered them from their destructions.* Heal Carlton, deliver him from this destruction, and restore his brain cells. I surrender his life to You."

Talk about stress upon stress, Carlton's accident happened four months after Chuck and I separated. I called and gave him the information the doctor had given me. Then I called the airlines. I was able to put a twenty-four hour hold on two flights for Monday, one for noon and one for late afternoon. I wasn't sure how quickly I could get things organized to leave.

Our Sunday outreach to the community was a great success. Many people accepted prayer and some came to Christ. Monday morning I took care of church business and assigned responsibilities. As the morning wore on, I realized I could not make my noon flight. Disappointed, I called Alaska Airlines and told them I would have to take the 4:00 p.m. flight to Portland, Oregon.

Two hours after I changed my flight, Dr. McCormick called. "Ms. Gardner, the results of our tests are inconclusive. We are sending your son to Providence St. Mary Hospital in Walla Walla, Washington for further attention. They have better equipment for head injury patients. Here is their information." I thanked him and hung up.

"Wow! Thank You, Jesus! If I had taken the noon flight, I'd already be on the plane on my way to Oregon instead of Washington. And I'd have missed the doctor's phone call. Thank You for the divine delay."

When I called to reschedule my flight destination, I learned the airline didn't fly into Walla Walla. The nearest city I could fly into was Seattle, Washington, which is over 250 miles away. So I booked my flight to Seattle and ordered a rental car. I planned to stay in the hospital in Walla Walla and accompany Carlton on his flight home, whenever that would be.

My next plan of action was to cancel two upcoming engagements— one for 80 female ministers from around the world that Dr. Anne Gimenez was hosting in Virginia Beach and the other for a women's conference in Dayton, Ohio where I was scheduled to teach a workshop. Everybody involved would understand. My son needed me desperately. All I could think about was seeing Carlton and comforting him like only a mother can.

As I dialed the first number to cancel the engagement, I clearly heard these words: *Do you love Me?*

I hesitated because I was surprised. "Yes, Lord Jesus, I love You."

Do you love Me more than you love, Carlton?

"Yes, Lord, I love you more than I love Carlton, and I love my children a lot. But I love You more." I wondered where God was headed with these questions.

Then put the phone down and keep those appointments because they are divine connections for your future and others. Satan wants to get you away from My purpose and plan. Keep the appointments and be on that flight on Wednesday to Virginia. I'll take care of Carlton's needs.

I stared at the phone as tears filled my eyes. "I do love You, Jesus— not my will, but Yours. You said in Luke 14:26, *If anyone comes to Me and does not hate his father or mother, wife and children, brothers and sisters, yes, and his own life also, he cannot be My disciple.* Lord, I want to be a true disciple for You."

I called the airline and changed my return reservation for the last plane leaving Seattle on Tuesday night. *I'll spend less than twenty-four hours with my son the only time he has ever been hospitalized in his life. God's ways are certainly not my ways, just as He said in Isaiah 55:8, For My thoughts are not your thoughts, Nor are your ways My ways, says the LORD.*

I arrived at the Seattle airport and headed toward the rental car counter when I heard an announcement over the loud speaker. "Horizon flight 555 Boarding for Walla Walla, Washington, last call."

I looked to my left and saw a sign from a small airline. The sign read, "Flights to Walla Walla." I ran over to the desk. "Do you have any more flights to Walla Walla tonight?"

"Yes, one more," the attendant said.

"I want to buy a ticket for that flight, instead of renting a car. My son is in the hospital in Walla Walla. I'll take a taxi from the airport to the hospital. Would you happen to have the number to a taxi service in Walla Walla?"

"Here's your ticket to Walla Walla. I'll call the rental car desk for you. If you'll wait just a minute, I'll call my co-worker over here for you because she's from Walla Walla."

Her co-worker arrived. "Could she have driven to Walla Walla in a rental car this time of night?"

"Absolutely not! The roads are too dark with few street lights, and some streets have no signs and you wouldn't be able to see the landmarks. You would've been lost until someone found you in the morning."

"I'm so thankful that I heard the announcement about Walla Walla. I'm thankful to you for sharing that information. I can see how much God is watching over me."

"Can she take a taxi when she arrives? She has to get to the hospital to see her son."

"The taxi service stops around 9:00 p.m. and it's after that time now."

"What do you suggest I do? How far is the hospital from the airport? I'll believe for God to work something out for me."

Before she could answer a lady seated nearby stood up and started talking as she walked over toward us. "I'm flying to Walla Walla on the same flight, and my parents are picking me up. We'll give you a ride to the hospital."

"Are you sure your parents won't mind?"

"If I told them I heard this conversation and I didn't offer you a ride, they'd be upset with me. They'll be happy to take you there."

"Thank you so much. I thank God for all of you." *Lord, I'm thankful to You for taking such good care of me.*

Her parents were a beautiful sweet Middle-Eastern couple who spoke a little English. She interpreted while they asked me questions about my son. At the hospital I entered Carlton's room and my heart sank at what I saw. I held back tears so I wouldn't upset him. He had tubes everywhere, but thank God, he was conscious and aware of his surroundings. I was grateful he recognized me and was able to say "Hi, Mom." But beyond that, his words made no sense. He became agitated when I couldn't understand him.

Carlton's dad Chuck, Curtis, and Carlton's girlfriend Kelley surrounded his bed. Chuck and Curtis left Riverside Sunday evening and as they drove through Northern California they picked up Kelley. They arrived about three hours before I did.

The doctor came into the room and spoke to us. "Carlton's brain has sustained a horrible blow, it has predominately affected his speech enter. It will take months for the swelling to go down. The rest of his brain is functioning well, so he'll think he's saying the right words, and his speech will be articulate, clear, and actual words, but they won't be the right choice of words."

"Doctor, he said to us a moment ago." Curtis quoted Carlton, "'I played football and they passed me the Q-tip and then I ran.' He was trying to tell us about the scrimmage football game he played the day of the accident.'"

"Exactly, and sometimes even fewer words will be correct."

"What what other things might be a problem?" Chuck asked.

"Sometimes, because he won't remember what you've said, he make react improperly. We explained the MRI process to him and in the middle of the test he got out of the machine. He started yelling about how he didn't like what we were doing to him. He obviously didn't remember my instructions.

"Also he has a limited short-term memory, so when he goes home, someone will need to be with him around the clock. He might walk out the house and forget where he is and wander off. Similar to dementia, he'll ask the same questions repeatedly or make the same statements repeatedly, not remembering the previous conversation. I understand he finished three years of college. He'll not be able to return to school because of his inability to retain information. Some of that will improve over the next eighteen months, but not enough for him to study and take tests. I'm sorry."

"What about football?" Curtis asked. "He loves the game and was recruited to play at Eastern Oregon State."

"Never let him play football again. If his head ever sustains a traumatic blow again, it could kill him instantly, or his brain could be irrevocably damaged. The other bad news is he'll have no sense of judgments of heights, danger, or common sense conclusions regarding cause and effect. This is another reason he has to be watched at all times, specifically for the next few months. He could climb on something and not perceive how far it is to the ground."

The doctor left the room. We stared at each other then all stared in silence at Carlton while he slept. We stayed the night in chairs around Carlton's bed. I held his hand and prayed through the night, dozing whenever possible. Carlton slept a lot and tried to communicate when he was awake, but it was frustrating.

Tuesday evening I did one of the hardest assignments the Lord has ever required me to do. I left the hospital room with my son attached to several monitors and didn't know when we would see each other again. I took a taxi to the airport to catch the last plane leaving Walla Walla and flew home.

Wednesday morning, September 23, 1992, I flew to Virginia Beach, and was picked up in a Rock Church International van and taken to the beautiful Founder's Inn adjacent to Regent University. I met women I long admired, including Joy Dawson, Devi Titus, and others. Some I had seen on television and others I had read their books. I was thrilled to be under the influence of a quality seasoned minister such as Dr. Anne Gimenez. When the retreat was over, I received a surprise request.

The driver's wife said as they drove us back to the Founder's Inn from the restaurant where we had dinner, "I'm excited to hear you speak to the ladies at church tomorrow, Pastor Diane."

"No, you must have me mixed up with someone else."

"No, Dr. Anne told me herself she was changing our four Sunday school classes and combining them into two classes. The women will be put in the gymnasium. We'll have about 600, so the gym will be perfect. The men will meet in the sanctuary and be taught by her friend that's the missionary to South Africa. She said you'll speak to the women in the gym. Pastor Anne also said, 'We'll have a powerful time in both places.'"

"Well," I said hesitatingly, "That's a scary surprise—but pleasant one."

So I heard at 10:00 p.m. Saturday night that I was to speak on Sunday morning at 9:00 a.m. That's difficult. I spent a good portion of the night praying about what message to give.

Sunday morning I arrived at The Rock Church International, and Dr. Anne saw me. "Diane, I told everyone you were speaking this morning, but I was told I forgot to mention it to you. Please excuse me.

"Here's the set up. We usually have four classes on various subjects, so I'm combining them into two. You'll speak in the gym to all the women. The men will be in the sanctuary with Missionary Rachael. I decided I couldn't have you be this close to my women and not have you speak into their lives. I'm so thrilled you're here and chose to join us on Sunday morning. I enjoyed your ministry last year when we were speakers together in North Carolina. You have a quality ministry. I hope that didn't catch you too much off guard."

"Yes, it did surprise me. But it would be my privilege to minster to your ladies. Thank you for the opportunity."

"So then, it's a done deal! Now instead of visiting my church, you have to work." She chuckled then said, "Follow me to the gymnasium."

What a divine set up by the Lord. He made clear the message He wanted: *Overcoming Satan's Assault on Women*. I had forty minutes, which isn't enough time to properly *teach* the message, so I *preached* it with passion and fire, hitting only the high points. I decided not to draw attention away from God's purpose to share what the Enemy had done. So I didn't mention anything about Carlton being in the hospital. Instead, I boldly encouraged the women to never let the Adversary stop the purpose of God in their lives. It was a powerful meeting.

The next day I flew to Ohio. I asked a few ministers I knew to pray for Carlton. One of them was a friend of ours and called Chuck to see how Carlton was doing. Chuck criticized me for not staying with Carlton; she echoed his point of view to me. She expressed her opinion to me and a couple of others. They agreed with her. No one *asked me why* I had made the choice to be in Ohio and not by Carlton's bedside. I was disappointed they formed an opinion without asking, but I could not feel guilty because God made it clear that He wanted me to keep my appointments.

There are times the Lord will require something of us that others don't comprehend or want to understand. At these times it is futile to try and defend ourselves. The Sunday school class at The Rock Church, my workshop at the conference, and when I spoke on Sunday morning at the host church Revival Center Ministries in Dayton, Ohio changed people's lives. Many were healed and others were encouraged to be an overcomer.

While in Ohio, I received a message on my home phone from the doctor in Walla Walla updating me about Carlton's condition. I returned the call and was told. "We've done all we can for Carlton, so we're sending him home to recover. He'll sleep a lot because his body is healing. His spinal fluid has stopped leaking from the hole in his eardrum, so we're happy about that. The pinhole in his eardrum is small, and it should close up over time. As far as his brain is concerned, whatever inabilities he has at the end of eighteen months will be his limitations for the rest of his life.

"Unfortunately, he is unable to fly anywhere. Flying will cause pressure to his eardrum and pressure to his brain and that would be damaging. Someone has to drive him home. Call me back and tell me what arrangements you've made and when someone will be here to pick him up."

I was in Ohio and wasn't due home for five days. What was I to do? All I knew to do was pray. Chuck, Curtis and Karen stayed a couple more days after me and then drove home for them to go back to work. They had been home five days when the doctor called on September 30, 1992.

I still lived in the home Carlton grew up in so he had a bedroom there. This was the best place for him to recover and as his mother I wanted to care for him. Because Chuck and I were separated difficult decisions like this one became exponentially more difficult to discuss. Besides, I didn't want to hear Chuck tell me if I were home I could get Carlton. Or that I shouldn't be in Dayton. I waited for the Lord to give me an answer before I called the doctor back.

Finally, an idea popped into my head the next morning. I called my brother who lived near Riverside. "Kenneth, the doctor said Carlton will be released from the hospital in Washington as soon as someone can get there. He says he can't fly because of the pressure to his ear and brain. I know you're off work for a while. Would you be willing to take three days and drive up there to pick him up? You can take my car because it has a large back seat for Carlton to rest on. Darlene can let you in the house to get my spare key."

"I think I can do that," Kenneth said.

"That's wonderful, thank you so much, I really appreciate you. When can you leave?"

"Tomorrow."

"Great! I'll be home Monday late afternoon. Hopefully I will see you then." I was glad Beverly, Kenneth's wife, took a couple of days off work and accompanied him on the trip.

After the plans were made and the doctor contacted then I spoke to Chuck and gave him the details and informed him when he could see Carlton.

I returned home on Monday, October 5. I arrived home about an hour before they arrived. God blessed me to be able to be there to welcome Carlton home. I threw my arms around him and kissed him many times. I hugged Kenneth and Beverly in gratitude. Carlton looked fine on the outside, only thinner and weak from being bedridden, but his sentences were usually jumbled. He went straight to bed.

I unpacked and took a hard look at the challenging storm in front of me. *Carlton will be like a dementia patient. He'll repeat himself over and over because he won't remember the answer. Many times he will use the wrong words and get frustrated because he can't get his point across. I can't let him walk out the door because he could wander away. I'll have to take care of him alone. The congregation is still suffering from losing Chuck as a pastor only a few months earlier. Finances are down and I'm not getting paid consistently. The church owes $5,500 in back rent. I don't have a clue how to recover from all this.*

I slumped down onto my couch and put my head in my hands. "Lord, You so beautifully touched others lives through me these last few days in Virginia and Ohio. Yet, I need Your touch as much or more than many of them. Touch me Lord. I come boldly to Your throne of grace to receive grace and find mercy to help me. All I know to do is tell You I trust You. So I decree that I believe I will never be late on my bills. The past debt will be paid off or forgiven. Carlton will be healed.

"Give me grace to be patient with him while he responds like a dementia patient." I looked up and sighed. "Lord, You said in Psalm 3 that You are the glory and the lifter up of my head. I look up to You. I will not borrow from tomorrow's worries because there's more than enough for each day. I'll take things one day at a time. I love You."

A month later I asked Carlton a question that was difficult for me. "Honey, I feel bad you may have felt abandoned by me. I was only able to stay at the hospital for less than twenty-four hours. I might need to explain why I left you."

"Mom, I don't remember anything about being in the hospital. I don't remember the accident. The last thing I can remember was the football game, and having a few beers while playing cards before the party. The next thing I remember is Uncle Kenneth, Aunt Beverly, and I went through the drive-through at a fast food place and he asked me what I wanted to eat. That's all I remembered until I got home and saw you."

My heart filled with joy as I spoke my praise to the Lord. "Thank You, Jesus, You said You'd take care of all his needs. You knew it wouldn't matter whether I was there or not because Carlton wouldn't remember anything because of the type of injury. Wow!"

I took Carlton everywhere I went. He fell asleep as soon as he sat in any chair and snored loudly. Sometimes I pretended I didn't know the six-foot man in the hotel lobby chair until it was time to go and I woke him up. When I traveled out of state for a day or two Curtis stayed with Carlton. Chuck was in a one bedroom apartment so had no room for Carlton.

My conversations with Carlton felt like a guessing game, trying to piece together his sentences so they made sense. He was continually agitated. Sometimes he had dizzy spells. The doctor said he couldn't drive until the dizzy spells left and more of his short term memory returned.

The medical bills were over $20,000. When each hospital, doctor, and lab bill came in the mail, I took them to the Lord and asked what I was to do with them? How could they be paid? I had anxiety over the mounting costs, but then I heard the Holy Spirit's voice. *These are not your bills. Why are you worrying? These are Carlton's bills. He's twenty-one. I'll help him pay them when he starts to work full-time.*

That took a load off my shoulders. I expressed to Carlton what the Holy Spirit said. We prayed together for God's help. Years later, he took care of the debts.

A professional photographer in my church named Joan took Carlton under her wing and "hired" him to work in her studio three days a week. She wanted to help stimulate his brain activity and benefit his sense of value by him working. They became close. She was patient with him as she repeated instructions over and over, even after he had written them down. Carlton was good with people, so he was a benefit to her business.

March, 1993

The State of California Department of Vocational Rehabilitation appointed Carlton a wonderful caseworker whose assignment was to assess which job training program he was capable of performing given his limitations. I thanked God we live in America where as a country we provide help for those in need. I think we're never as thankful as when we are on the receiving end.

Carlton and I listened as the caseworker read the two state doctors' recent evaluations of his limitations. She said the state has offered him a job training program that is available for people with disabilities. I wondered what would work for him. I was grateful for the opportunity, but Carlton was agitated.

"I don't want any of those jobs! I want to go back to school! I know the doctors' reports say I can't, but I have to finish!"

"Disability Rehab and I understand it's hard to embrace a loss like this," the caseworker said. "The stress caused by classes at school will be too hard on you. You have other talents, and I have the authority to let you try more than one training program to find your best fit."

Carlton became more agitated. "God already talked to me about my future. When I was fourteen the Lord showed me that I had to get my master's degree to fulfill His purpose. In a vision I was a wealthy businessman speaking to businessmen and women about success and how to serve God in business. Mom remembers me telling her that back then." He glanced in my direction.

I nodded, but I must confess God's purpose for his life was not on my mind when we entered the doors to rehab. I felt lost and a bit disheartened as we sat at the rehab office. This time Carlton had the faith God needed to do the impossible.

The case worker moved to the end of her chair and leaned closer to him. "I have more than one doctor's reports. They all say your short-term memory *will not* allow you to concentrate and hold information long enough to take tests or get decent grades. They recommend I find a suitable job you can handle."

He didn't back down. "But *God* said I *have* to get my master's degree! I haven't finished my bachelor's degree yet! Right now, I need your help to do that!"

"OK, if you insist. There are requirements because we'll *not* pay for someone who can't take tests and pass classes. You must understand that! You have to maintain a C average in all your classes. Are you willing to follow the rules?"

Carlton pounded the desk with his fist. "Yes! I've got to finish school!"

By now my hope was stirred. My faith had increased. I was never more thankful for what we taught Carlton when he was young about God's plan for his life than I was at that moment. Without a tangible God-given goal like the vision Carlton had as a teen, we may not have known how to walk through this storm. He had taken that truth and chose to be an overcomer.

He was told to seek God until you understand some things He wants you to know. Our main scripture was Jeremiah 29:12-13:

Then you will call upon Me and go and pray to Me, and I will listen to you. And you will seek Me and find Me, when you search for Me with all your heart.

Shocked at Carlton's dogged determination the counselor fell back in her chair and said, "OK, then, I can allow you to try two semesters, before I need to turn in my evaluation. If you cannot maintain a C average, I mean not one grade below a C in any class then the financing for school stops after the second semester. Then we'll see what other training you will need to get a job you can handle. You also must carry a full load of classes. Rehab will not pay for a failing student."

She opened her drawer and shuffled through the files to find the paperwork. "We'll have you start in July with summer school because it requires only two classes to carry a full load. That'll give you a chance to start slowly. Bring me your summer school transcript for evaluation. Then if you want to continue, we'll pay for the fall semester. Your grades at *that* time will make or break your future concerning school. No exceptions. You want to try this program?"

"Yes! That's great!" Carlton said with a big grin.

"I'll put in for rehabilitation to finance your two semesters."

Carlton jumped up and threw his arms around her. He felt confident because he had always received As and Bs without much effort.

Carlton's pride didn't allow him to listen to any of my advice. He plunged himself into California State University at San Bernardino, trying to handle things the way he always did. He thought all he needed was to study a little more. At the end of the summer semester, he took his caseworker the report card.

"Oh Carlton, you have a D and an F. This will not do. I told you the doctors' reports have expressed your limitations. Do you want to get evaluated for job training, or do you want to try one more school semester?"

"I want to try school again. I know I only have one more chance."

When we returned home, Carlton humbled himself. "Alright Mom, I'll listen this time. I'll write down the plan you said God gave you for me. I won't do my own thing."

We sat down at the dining table and got to work. "Last semester I sought God diligently for you because there's absolutely no way you could succeed on your own," I said. "I believe this will work for you, but you must do it without deviating from the strategy. God has a strategy for every difficult place. Your reward comes from your obedience."

"Yeah, I know. I'm ready to write."

"You must memorize some scriptures that will help your memory. The Word of God is full of life. Your brain cells need more life in them to regenerate and recover. Start with memorizing what God did for Daniel and the three Hebrew young men in Daniel 1:17-20: *God gave them knowledge and skill in all learning and wisdom.* (KJV), and John

14:26: *But the Helper, the Holy Spirit, will bring to your remembrance all things that I said to you.*

"You need to develop the skill to learn, and you need help, and the Holy Spirit is your Helper if you ask for His help. Rely on Him this time and not your intellect.

"Pray and ask for His help before each class, before each test, and before you study. You are yielding yourself to the Holy Spirit when you do this.

"Next, take a tape recorder to every class and inform your teachers that you had a head injury and want permission to record their class. Tell them you are not going to use this as an excuse because you will work hard to get good grades. You can show them the doctors' reports if they require them.

"Listen to the tape while you study, over and over again."

Carlton stopped writing and looked up, "Why should I say that about the doctors' reports?"

"So they know you're not trying to be dishonest in order to get an easy good grade.

"Next, when you cannot remember something while studying or during a test, stop, quiet your mind, then say, Holy Spirit, You are my Helper and I need Your help now. I did my part to study, and I trust You to bring this to my remembrance. Wait on a thought to come to your mind and write it down.

"Finally, read your Bible regularly. Speak healing scriptures over your brain cells. That's it, son. That's your study plan from God."

Carlton listened, followed the strategy, and worked extremely hard. His tenacity was admirable.

At the end of the fall semester we returned to Rehab to see his caseworker. "Here's my transcript for the fall semester. I took a full load of four classes."

She stared at the transcript for a moment, raised her eyebrows, looked up at Carlton then back to the transcript. "Oh wow, Carlton, the classes are all As and Bs. How . . ." She looked into Carlton's face with a puzzled expression. "How *in the world* did you ever make such a big improvement that quickly?"

"God gave me a plan, and I followed it. And I worked really hard. But primarily, I believe Jesus is healing my brain cells and resurrecting the ones the doctors said were dead." He said as he grinned from ear to ear.

"Well, I don't understand all that, but I know it's working for you. As long as you get these kinds of grades we'll continue to pay for your education until you graduate. Keep up the good work."

I'm grateful to God that the vocational rehabilitation program paid for the balance of his two bachelor degrees. He finished with a BA in international business, while he learned Japanese. He earned a second BA a year later in mathematics. He was able to start driving again by the time he finished the second semester. In that eighteen months after the accident he was in school full-time, working a full-time job, and still getting good grades.

At his first graduation party at our home there was not a dry eye in the room. All said how much they prayed for him and how godly-proud they were of Carlton's hard work and progress. Many said how glad they were to see the power of the Holy Spirit at work in such a tangible way. A year later we had another graduation party with the same responses.

After both graduations, Carlton applied for a job when he was in Atlanta visiting Chuck for Father's Day. In summer 1997 Carlton moved to Atlanta to begin a job for Kroger food chain as a store management trainee. He has received several promotions. He accomplished the instruction the Lord gave him at age fourteen when he received his master's degree in finance from Georgia State University in 2002. What an exciting milestone in obedience to God's directive!

He now lives in Cincinnati, Ohio and works at Kroger corporate headquarters. He belongs to a Bible study with co-workers where they take turns teaching.

Carlton met and married a wonderful beautiful lady named Kisha. She received her BA in sociology from Virginia State, and her master's degree in psychology from ORU in Oklahoma. Today they have three beautiful and talented children.

God's mercy, grace, and healing have been evident in Carlton's life. He restored Carlton's health to use him as a powerful tool in business and prophetic leadership.

Recently, Carlton uncharacteristically wrote a beautiful poem that I want to share with you.

Carlton's Poem

You knew I would come; you knew I would be here.
What type of person? What type of child? All a valid fear.
But you stood there, pressed on, and didn't give up,
Even became a Christian so as a mother you wouldn't suck.
You knew you needed help with me, and my brother, Curt.
Your love was so overflowing, your heart continually hurt.
You were always there with a hand extended to help,
With words of wisdom, hands of care, along with a switch or belt.
Through infancy, early childhood, preteen, and adolescent,
You were the key to the family remaining effervescent.
Through good times or bad, you loved us and prayed.
God, God, what can I do when my sons still misbehave?
I wonder what to do and still be strong.
I even asked the boys' father what I am doing wrong.
Two boys and a man (Dad) growing fast and apart.
Many times others lived in our house and also played a part.
I see such potential in my kids—such skills, grace, and gifts.
My kids are awesome, fun, and smart, but rebellion they must sift.

Thank you for the vacations, the trips, and the fun.
We did quite a bit in the water, snow, and sun.
You were hurt when the men around you waivered and said goodbye.
Not only to you, to others, and even to God because of pride.
Don't blame yourself or your actions for what your kids did.
Remember from the start their ancestors' heads are big.
Then you called out to God. This all happened why?
God said through this misfortune, I am preparing you to fly.
So through all you've been through, I know Mom you did swell,
Pastoring a church, raising children, and training us well.
I always see and admire you with high regard,
Since you are an awesome mother and a beautiful woman
of God.

Mom, thank you for loving me and still giving me advice.
Whether I agree or disagree, you still tell me twice—no thrice.
If I can be half the parent you are, I will do very well. Hey, I
could even write a book that will probably sell.

Chapter 7

Death Threat

And the dragon stood before the woman who was ready
to give birth, to devour her Child as soon as it was born.
(Revelation12:4b)

December 9, 2002

My early Christmas gift for Carlton and Kisha was to help them prepare their nursery for their first child. Carlton was a store manager for Kroger while he also worked on his master's degree in finance. Kisha evaluated families to say whether children should stay with their parents or go into foster care. They were active church members so had little free time.

I had only three days to complete the job—to prep the room, paint it, and apply Precious Moments border paper. It was great fun as I painted, sang to the Lord, and prayed for their family. Suddenly something in the atmosphere changed drastically. The more I prayed, the worse I felt. I became engulfed with a sense of gloom that filled the room. "What does this mean?" I asked the Holy Spirit. "Why am I feeling like something is wrong?"

Unexpectedly, I heard the word *death*. I felt grief followed by a sense of loss, which fell like a blanket over me. I knew the Adversary was planning something horrible. What could it be? *Will this be physical death in which Kisha's life will be in danger during the delivery? Will she go*

into postpartum after the baby comes and be subject to an emotional death?
Will the baby's life be threatened?

I asked the Lord these questions and waited to hear a response. To my disappointment, I didn't hear or sense anything further. I decided to be satisfied with what I'd heard. One word gave me enough awareness to know warfare was immediately necessary. I needed to respond to what I had heard, no matter how the Enemy brought it. There was no time to waste on my fear of the unknown. Often I want God to give me a paragraph when He speaks, although He knows one word is sufficient to get the job done.

Carlton, Kisha, and I needed to close every door of access to death. The Holy Spirit is our Helper, therefore, we would trust Him to lead us. 1 John 3:8b says: *For this purpose the Son of God was manifested, that He might destroy the works of the devil.* Jesus didn't destroy the Devil, but He destroyed the Devil's works—past, present, and future. And He gave us His authority to enforce His plan to destroy the Devil's works.

I searched my mind and spirit for any spiritual weapon I could use against the Enemy's works. I remembered a covenant agreement I made with God, concerning Carlton and his children when he was only six years old. This was the day he was expelled from kindergarten. I felt hopeless as a parent that day because I couldn't keep my Christian kid in a Christian school. He had already been suspended three times before he was expelled. Where had I gone wrong?

When Carlton and I came home that day from the principal's office, I sent him to his room and told him not to come out until I called his name, and I went to my bedroom. I cried for two hours, and then prayed. "Lord, I'm not coming out of this room until You give me a scripture concerning Carlton. I need something to hang on to." A portion of the promise He gave me that day was Jeremiah 32:39: *Then I will give them one heart and one way, that they may fear Me forever, for the good of them and their children after them.*

After I remembered this promise concerning Carlton and his children, I went back to the Lord in prayer. "Lord, You're a covenant-making, covenant-keeping God. You gave me a promise out of Jeremiah

32 when Carlton was six that You would give him a heart that is one with Yours and the fear of God would be in him for his good and the good of his children after him. Lord, stir the reverential fear in Carlton's heart that will bring humility and put down pride for his family's sake.

"I heard the word *death*. Show me how to cancel the Enemy's tactics. I'll not fear, but trust Your Word that is full of life. Life is greater than death. Help me know how to instruct Carlton and Kisha."

Carlton came home from work and brought the extension ladder upstairs from the garage. His job was to paint the walls near the vaulted ceiling.

As we painted, I shared with him what I heard from the Holy Spirit. "Carlton, as I prayed for you, Kisha, and your baby, I heard the word *death*. I had a deep sense of grief and loss. I believe this was the Holy Spirit revealing the Enemy's plan for your family. The door to the *curse of death* must be closed immediately! I thought about a few doors of entry the Enemy could use.

"Most of your life you spoke *word curses* about not having any daughters. You said, 'I only want boys, five of them, and I don't want any girls.' Your doctor says you're having a girl. We've got to address that negative judgment in your heart and cancel the influence of your words about not wanting a girl. This can be a door of entrance for the Enemy. Those words may have sounded funny when you were a young boy, but you said this also as an adult. If you made a vow not to have girls then you were putting a curse on your own seed because the sex of the baby comes from the male sperm. The Enemy heard those words and can use them as a weapon. You've got to cancel the influence of the root of that judgment and the corresponding negative words. The Bible says in Proverbs 18:21: *Death and life are in the power of the tongue.*

"Satan has power over anything hidden in darkness. So each thing must be brought into the light of Jesus to take the control away from the Enemy. I'm going to bring up some things that only God knows where you stand on these issues. You don't owe me any explanation. There is no condemnation from the Lord, although you should ask for mercy. Come clean with gut-level honesty before God who knows everything anyway. But to take anything out of darkness you must speak it out loud to the Lord. Then ask for mercy and come in true repentance and humility. Psalm 19:12 says: *Who can understand his errors? Cleanse me from secret faults.*

"A door can also open to death if you have ever helped a girlfriend get an abortion. If you did that and you caused the death of a child, you must cancel that curse. You may have agreed with or assisted someone who wanted to get an abortion. For example, you gave her money or took her to the clinic. Maybe you've counseled a girl or guy and said that an abortion was his or her best option. You've got to close the door to death through repentance. This will cancel any death assignment from the Adversary. The door to his plans can come through any of these avenues. I have closed this door already on my side of our family.

"In 2 Samuel chapters 11 and 12, King David had sex with Bathsheba then tried to cover it up by having her husband Uriah killed in battle. David then married her as his final cover-up. He opened the door to death and their baby died. Does this make sense to you?"

"Yes, I understand," Carlton said.

"Make sure you include these 'Six Rs': repent, renounce, rebuke, resist, restore, and rejoice. You might want to write those down so you can use these to defeat the Enemy."

"OK, please hand me that notepad and pencil. I need to repent for my sins, renounce my disobedience, and rebuke the Enemy. Then I need to discover what it is I'm resisting, what should be restored, and how to rejoice. Right?"

"You have those first ones absolutely right. Let me go over all of them to answer your question more fully.

"*Repent* and ask God to forgive you. Be specific about what you ask forgiveness for. Ask forgiveness for your part in (name the person or situation). Ask forgiveness for partnering with sin and not asking Him for guidance when faced with that situation. Ask God to forgive any young ladies involved. Ask forgiveness for putting a curse on your own seed each time you said, 'I don't want to have any girls.' Ask to be cleansed by the blood of Jesus.

"*Renounce* things like pride, deception, stubbornness, rebellion, criticism of the opposite sex, word curses spoken in secret, etc. You can say 'I renounce every time I came into wrong agreement with someone to cause death by abortion whether directly or indirectly. I renounce any time I came into wrong agreement with anyone when we talked about hurting anyone through a fight, or any means of harm that could lead to death. I renounce all association with the spirit of death in my generations.'

"*Rebuke* the spirit of death. Say boldly: 'Satan, I close all doors of access to death I have given you! I rebuke the spirit assigned to bring death to my family. I command every spirit to go, now! We will live and *not* die!'

"*Resist* by using the Bible. A useful weapon is James 4:7 that says: *Therefore submit to God. Resist the devil and he will flee from you.* This is how Jesus resisted him. Do you remember a good example?"

"Yeah, when He was in the wilderness in Luke chapter 4 and the Devil showed up," Carlton said. "Jesus quoted the Bible passages from Deuteronomy to defeat the Devil. He said four times, 'For it is written.' He defeated the Enemy with the Word of God."

I nodded in agreement. "That's how we rebuke and resist by Jesus' example, with one addition. He was sinless and we're not, so we also renounce our carnal nature, which is an enemy to God. Things like pride, stubbornness, disobedience, rebellion, fear, and doubt. The Holy Spirit will reveal to you what needs to be renounced.

"You can use your own words, but make sure you include the six Rs and scriptures like Jesus did when He resisted the Devil. For example you can say, 'The Word says: *Therefore submit to God. Resist the devil and he will flee from you* (James 4:7). I choose to submit to God through repentance. Now I resist you Devil, and you must flee from me!'

"*Restore* your soul which is your mind, will, and emotions. When you renounced those things you emptied the area the Enemy influenced in your soul's carnal strongholds. Then fill your soul with the Word of God. If you don't fill up with godly thoughts, then the Enemy will return to occupy that space again. Psalm 23:5 says: *You prepare a table before me in the presence of my enemies; You anoint my head with oil; my cup runs over.* You get restored by worshiping God then reminding yourself the victory you have over the Enemy, and declaring who you are in Christ.

"*Rejoice* is to praise and worship. You show God your faith in Him by praising and worshiping you have the victory before you see the evidence. That's what faith is. Praise God for what He has done. Thank Him for the warning. Thank Him that His Word and blood conquers death. Then lift your hands and worship Him for who He is. He's the giver of life. He has the final word because He is almighty."

Growing up Carlton was given age-appropriate information concerning some of the trials we faced as a family. We discussed how we overcame and received our God-given victories. He experienced our family's miraculous answers to prayer. Now it was his time to fight for his family. He needed a private time to be gut-level honest with God.

I went downstairs and shared the same information with Kisha. Her parents had taught her about spiritual warfare growing up also. "I hope you understand the seriousness of these next few moments you'll spend surrendering to God and warring with the Enemy over the spirit of death. You can overcome through the Word of God." I left her alone to fight.

The next day we finished the room with the Precious Moments border paper, and it turned out beautifully. I flew home early the day after. On the flight I thanked God for the warning. "Lord, You warn us so many times and we miss it. Thank You that you helped me not miss the warning about death. I love You, Lord."

December 12, 2002

The day after I came home, I flew to Sacramento, California to attend an annual board meeting for author Rev. Liberty Savard. I sat in her office library in her green recliner while I read her latest book and waited for the meeting. I was startled when my cell phone rang. It was Dr. Barnes.

"I had my annual checkup two weeks ago, but your personal call cannot be good news."

"Well, we don't know that yet, but I do need you to come in right away for us to run a battery of tests. When I examined you I mentioned that one ovary is swollen, and I don't know why. I don't believe it is ovarian cancer, but we won't know until you complete the tests. How soon can you get in here?"

"I'm in Sacramento for the next four days. I'll be home Monday night."

"I see on the schedule we can take you first thing Wednesday morning, 8:00 a.m."

For the previous several months I had felt exhausted. I figured my body fought to be healed, and this caused the exhaustion, but I had no other symptoms. I asked the Lord to expose the hidden problem and for it to be removed. These two scriptures were my weapons. Matthew 10:26b: *For there is nothing covered that will not be revealed, and hidden that will not be known.* Matthew 15:13: *But He [Jesus] answered and said, "Every plant which My heavenly Father has not planted will be uprooted."*

Dr. Barnes ran tests over the next month, but he could not come up with a diagnosis. He decided to schedule me for a hysterectomy surgery, but he didn't think it was cancerous. In August 1986, I had my first partial hysterectomy surgery in which a doctor removed a fibroid tumor and my uterus. He left my ovaries so they could keep producing estrogen, but now at least one ovary was sick.

February 7, 2003

Dr. Barnes removed my ovaries, lymph nodes, and appendix. One ovary had precancerous cells and was developing ovarian cancer. But thank God, the cells were contained inside the ovary. What was hidden was revealed and uprooted like the scriptures said. No chemotherapy was needed! The death threat over my life was cancelled! I was sent home on Wednesday, February 12. I had round-the-clock care from congregation members for a couple of days.

On Valentine's Day, a friend fixed me a holiday meal. After she left I began to throw up violently. This happened off and on for hours. Darlene took me back to the hospital about 1:00 a.m. After many tests, they discovered I had a bowel obstruction; this was probably caused by the morphine after surgery causing extreme constipation.

A nurse came in to give me more details. "Ms. Gardner, we have flattened your stomach to see if the obstruction will move so you can pass it. If it doesn't move, then we'll take you in for surgery and cut out that portion of your intestine. Your stomach is flat now so we'll put the stethoscope to your abdomen and listen for some activity. As soon as you can get up, we want you to walk. It will help a lot."

"I can't have another surgery now for two reasons," I said. "First, I don't want another surgery. Second, my third grandchild is due February 28, and I must be there. I've asked God to help me be at the birth or shortly after the birth of all my grandchildren. I believe He'll help me do that."

"That's quite a goal you have." She raised her eyebrows. "We can only wait and see what happens."

"Obstruction, move in the name of Jesus," I said. "I'll be at my granddaughter's birth, God willing." I went home on February 19, without the second surgery. I was limited because I couldn't drive for six weeks or pick up anything over three pounds.

A church member packed my suitcase a few days after I came home. God knew I trusted Him for my trip to Atlanta for the birth of my grandchild. I used my frequent flyer points to acquire a plane ticket for February 28. I needed a changeable ticket in case the baby came later.

Someone took me to a partners' meeting in Orange County of a ministry we both supported. When we got back to our hotel room I called home to get my voice messages. On February 27, 2003, I heard Carlton's excited voice. "Mom, Kisha's water just broke, and we're going to the hospital now. Love ya, bye."

I called the airline and found an available reward seat non-stop flight at Orange County Airport. I called Ruth. "Are you busy this evening?"

"Not especially, why?"

"Well, you are now. I need to be at the Orange County Airport in a little less than two hours, and it's a fifty-minute drive from my house. Kisha's water broke, the baby is coming. My suitcases are by the front door at home because I was leaving tomorrow. Use your key to my house. I'm at the Hilton Anaheim on Convention Way. See you soon?"

"I'm on my way."

I called Dr. Kluane who lives about an hour from the Atlanta airport. "Kluane, I need to know the best transportation to get from the airport to DeKalb Hospital at 10 p.m. Carlton and Kisha are having their baby. I want to be there right after the baby is born."

"Tell me when your flight comes in and I'll pick you up and take you to the hospital."

February 28, 2003

When we arrived at the hospital, Kisha was still in the last stages of labor. It was a dry birth so the baby crowned but came no further. With the medication, Kisha's body had difficulty producing pressure to push the baby out. Around 11:00 p.m., the doctor decided to give Kisha an emergency C-section.

Dr. Kluane, Chuck, his wife Lilly, and I waited well over two hours and there was still no news from the doctor.

"While I was a pastor in Guam, I was also a mid-wife," Dr. Kluane said. "There were times we needed a doctor to perform an emergency cesarean, it never took this long."

"Curtis's children were both born by C-section and we heard news quicker than this." I responded.

"They should send Carlton from the delivery room to tell us when we can see them," Chuck said.

I pointed down the hall. "Here comes the doctor, and Carlton's walking behind him."

"I know you've waited a long time to hear about your new granddaughter," the doctor said. "Overall she's a normal beautiful baby girl, but her lungs did not get the message that she is out of the womb. She's not breathing oxygen properly, so I had to rush her to the neonatal intensive care unit. I'm sorry to have to give you this news. This happens sometimes. It's not rare—but it is serious. Most babies make it, but some don't. I'll send the nurse to tell you when you can see her." He paused for a few seconds. "Kisha is doing fine. Ask at the nurse's station what room she's in."

I looked at the clock on the wall behind me and it was 2:20 a.m. I looked at Carlton and his face looked expressionless, numb.

Carlton, Dr. Kluane, Chuck, Lilly, and I entered Kisha's room. She was under anesthetic and groggy, but awake. We surrounded her bed with faces wet with tears of concern. One by one we prayed for baby Jeana's life, for her lungs to be healed, for her full recovery, and no residual damage to her lungs. We spoke against the death threat. We surrendered her body to the Lord and trusted God to bring her through.

Immediately I remembered painting baby Jeana's room on December 9th and the revelation I received about the word *death.* I reminded Carlton and Kisha about our warfare on that day and how we each took our authority over the spirit of death. They were encouraged how God through His grace and goodness warned us in advance.

I let them know, "The process for victory has started on Jeana's behalf. If nothing could be done to save baby Jeana from this assault against her body, then God would not have given us advanced warning. He's a good administrator, and He wastes nothing. He spoke concerning the Enemy's plan because we have an opportunity through the grace of God to reverse this crisis. We'll fight the good fight of faith. Each of us will fight as God directs us. I will add fasting to my fight."

Over the next few days, all of us declared the following statement several times a day: "We believe Jeana will live and not die. She'll declare the works of the Lord. She'll have healthy lungs."

Two at a time were allowed into neonatal intensive care for twenty minutes a visit. Carlton and I went in together. Baby Jeana had a tube in her mouth, an intravenous feeding tube in her arm, and monitors on her head, lungs, and feet. She looked so helpless, so lifeless. Our arms ached to hold her, and our lips longed to kiss her cheeks.

Carlton and I stared at Jeana for a while as our minds and emotions worked to comprehend what we saw. We clasped hands and prayed over her.

When the head nurse spotted us, she approached us. "We have her totally sedated because if she moves at all, she'll use oxygen, and her body needs all the oxygen it can take in. You cannot touch her because that would cause her to move and use oxygen. Even in a sedated state she might naturally respond."

Back in Kisha's room, the doctor returned with more news. "Some babies don't survive this for more than four days. Some who survive have permanent lung damage, and some come out with no problems at all. There is no way to tell in less than four days if a child will live, or not. Her response to the treatments within the first four days will show us what her chances are."

We called family and friends from across the nation to join us in prayer for our miracle.

Kisha's parents, Ruben and Helen, arrived at their scheduled time the next day, Saturday, March 1, from Tulsa, Oklahoma. We took shifts into the neonatal intensive care unit. What a torturous week. Each day, each hour, each moment we waited expectantly to hear that her body had responded to the treatments or there was some sign of improvement.

I chose not to eat one bite of food until I heard a good report. I drank water and one glass of juice each day. Helen was worried I might faint. But fasting food, television, sleep, social activities, is a regular part of my walk with Christ as I endeavor to live a fasted life. I sat at meals with them with no problem. I had the grace to do the warfare necessary, which, in this instance, included fasting.

On Sunday, the next day all grandparents and Carlton attended his home church and received corporate prayer for Jeana. I can't fully describe the comfort that came to us from the congregation's faith. I felt such confidence knowing his church, my church, and others across the nation were in agreement in prayer. I thank God for the Body of

Christ and especially for those who pray His Word in any storm—no matter the circumstances.

The doctor released Kisha to go home on Tuesday, which was Jeana's fourth day. Jeana's body still hadn't responded to any of their treatments. There was no improvement at all. On Wednesday they transferred her to a children's hospital which specialized in critical cases.

Chuck, Lilly, Ruben, Helen, Carlton, Kisha, and I alternated the overnight shift at the hospital. Kisha and I depended on others to drive us because both of us were recovering from abdominal surgery.

I cried out to the Lord on one of those shifts. "God, two months before Jeana was born You gave Kisha a dream about Jeana's name. In the dream someone told Kisha the name of the baby and even spelled it for her, Jeana instead of Gina. The name is a derivative of the name John. The Hebrew meaning is *Jehovah is gracious.* Hallelujah! You gave her a specific name because You have a specific purpose for her life. I declare and believe Jehovah will be gracious to baby Jeana!

"We refuse the threat of death. We believe she will live and not die. She will declare the works of the Lord according to Your Word in Psalm 118:17: *I shall not die, but live, And declare the works of the LORD.*

Carlton told us he made his own covenant with the Lord that Thursday morning. "I walked around the hospital crying. Then I prayed, 'God, I put my faith in You, and I ask for Jeana's full recovery and that I will be able to bring her home on Saturday *with no lung problems!*' I'm going to tell our doctor that everything is in God's hands, and I'm asking God for her to come home with us on Saturday. So when she is released on Saturday the doctor will know it was a miracle from God."

Thursday evening, to the doctor's amazement, baby Jeana's body began to respond to the treatments. Friday the doctor said she had completely recovered.

March 9, 2003

On Saturday, a *healthy* eight-day-old baby came home with joyful parents and grandparents. The death threat was over. Death was conquered, and the assault from the Enemy was cancelled. Since that time Jeana has never had any problems with her lungs. She is a normal active child today.

We overcame the assault from the Adversary through the wisdom of the Holy Spirit's leading. I thank God.

Throughout the Bible and history I've noticed that children who required extreme faith usually have a special calling on their lives. Somehow the Enemy sees God's special anointing on these children and tries to thwart their assignment. I call these children "Faith Child" because faith must prevail to cancel the Enemy's assignment. I believe that is true of Jeana.

God didn't make Jeana sick. The Bible is clear that He is our Healer. Jesus healed the sick in the Gospels we never see Him calling for sickness to come into anyone's body. Jesus said, *"The thief does not come except to steal, and to kill, and to destroy"* (John 10:10).

Carlton and Kisha trusted God and overcame the Adversary. They caused him to flee from their family. Our agreement and coming together in one accord can change the final outcome for our children and our children's children. Each generation has to learn to become warriors for the Lord.

The Israelites who were twenty years of age and older when they entered the wilderness died before entering the Promised Land because of their unbelief and refusal to trust God. Although the next generation came to the Promised Land, they still had to face giants.

Judges 3:1-4 (MSG) says: *These are the nations that GOD left there, using them to test the Israelites who had no experience in the Canaanite wars. He did it to train the descendents of Israel, the ones who had no battle experience, in the art of war . . . They were there to test Israel and see whether they would obey GOD's commands that were given to their parents through Moses.*

Carlton and Kisha now have their own battle experience in the art of spiritual warfare. They have firsthand testimony from a critical battle they overcame. They are warriors ready to come alongside others who need to fight the good fight of faith.

I shudder to think about the outcome of this testimony if we didn't know how to call upon the grace of God and obey His impressions.

Carlton doesn't usually write poetry. I know God gave him the grace to express himself in this way.

Here is the rest of the beautiful poem Carlton wrote:

Well, it's time to cut to the chase and list the things I admire.
These are priceless traits that all should acquire.
You are passionate and strong.
You don't back down from a spiritual fight, so you cannot go wrong.
You praise the King of Kings, who has risen.
You love and teach the Lord to those in prison.
You give the shirt off your back and advice with it.
The shirt will be nice and flashy, but may not fit it.
Giving a helping hand, you pleasantly choose to give.
It happens to all those around you, especially your kids.

I thank the Lord for my blessing, a mother who cares,
One who prays and cries, who gives God all her fears.

I should have seen. It was there all along and before.
Your love is unconditional; it comes more and more.

It was something special you said a long time ago,
That rings through my ears as the ages still grow:
"I love you, my Son. You are a gift to me.
God gave me a blessing the world will soon see.
You are a man of valor. Don't sell yourself short.
Hold onto your dignity, to God, and your shirt.
Do what is good for you along with others.
Give God your worries and all of your bothers.
"Pray and seek God to what you should do.
If that is done right, all will go through
With flying colors and abundant blessings alike.
So listen to this wisdom, Son, I love you, good night!"

PART III

Diane

Chapter 8

The Jinx

Then the seventy returned with joy, saying, "Lord, even the demons are subject to us in Your Name." And He said to them, "I saw Satan fall like lightning from heaven. Behold I give you the authority to trample on serpents and scorpions, and over all the power of the Enemy, and nothing shall by any means hurt you. (Luke 10:17-19)

A recurring dream haunted me from ages five to fifteen. My parents were arguing so loudly I woke up and went to see what was wrong. I entered the room in time to see Dad pick up the big, heavy, black telephone and hit Mom in the head with it. Blood squirted like a faucet. I let out a loud scream.

Dad snatched my arm. "Shut up! What's wrong with you?"

"I'm . . . scared."

Dad let go of my arm, and Mom grabbed the other arm. "Let's go!"

We got in the car, and Mom drove to the hospital to get stitches. She held a bloody towel to her head with one hand and drove with the other. I stared at her and the bloody towel in silence, afraid I would get in trouble if I said the wrong thing. I had never seen so much blood. The nightmare always ended as we entered the hospital doors.

Each time I awakened from this nightmare, I was shaking. *Stop shaking. It's only a dream. Mom and Dad argue a lot, but they never hit each other.*

Often I could hear their arguments behind their bedroom door. They took turns telling each other to *get out.* The other one would say, "I'm not leaving my kids, so *you* get out." No one ever left. But as a kid I lived under the emotional stress of an "impending" divorce that never happened.

One day, when I was fifteen, I was combing Mom's hair and I noticed an indentation under her hairline above her forehead. "Mom, how did you get this dent in your skull? Were you a little girl when it happened?"

"You *know* what happened. You were there and saw everything."

Unfortunately, I didn't have a clue. But I wanted her to tell me about the incident so I lied. "Oh . . . yeah. How old was I when that happened?"

"You were five. That was the night your Dad hit me in the head with the telephone. You came in the room screaming so I took you and drove myself to the hospital for stitches. Surely you remember that."

"I do . . . re . . . member." *Oh no, that recurring nightmare was real.* At the age of five, my parents didn't give me the opportunity to talk about my feelings. So my subconscious mind took that traumatic incident and buried it so deeply it only surfaced as a nightmare. For ten years I didn't realize this was an actual event. Once the truth brought light to what was hidden in darkness the recurring nightmares ended.

After this incident, my parents must have made an agreement to end physical violence in front of their children, since my siblings and I don't recall any additional physical altercations.

I was the oldest of four children raised in Los Angeles, California. My parents worked hard to give us the comfortable middle-class lifestyle. They owned most of the homes we lived in over the years along with a four-plex rental property. I think they were the average pseudo-Christian American couple of the 1950s. By pseudo-Christian I mean the Bible was their compass when deemed necessary, otherwise they lived by relative morality.

Both grew up in small towns in Texas and came to California for employment opportunities. John Gardner and Annie Gordon met in

L.A. and married after a short courtship. Dad was thirty-three and a landscape gardener in Beverly Hills—this was his first marriage. Mom twenty-seven and a few years after their marriage became a practical nurse—this was her third marriage. Mom worked the swing or night shift and Dad worked days. They saw each other in passing and argued over finances and kids.

Mom received Christ as a Methodist teenager and Dad as a Baptist kid of seven. Both committed many scripture passages to memory. They taught us all the basics of the faith: the Ten Commandments, Jesus is God, He died on the cross, He resurrected from the dead, and heaven and hell are real.

They lacked good communication skills. Their words were caustic to each other and to us. They spoke their version of "truth," often filled with criticism and seldom offered compliments to us. The following incident was typical example of my parents' brutal version of truth.

September 1966

One evening, when I was seventeen, I was lying on my bed while I finished my homework when a surprise visitor knocked on our front door.

Mom greeted him. "Hello, I assume you're one of Diane's friends from school."

"Yes, I'm Carlos from her senior class, Mrs. Gardner. I know it's a school night, and it's late, but I wanted to ask you and Diane a question."

Mom guided him the few steps to the living room couch.

I leaped from the bed and bounced down the hall, excited to greet my friend. "Hi, Carlos, I'm glad to see you. What's going on?"

Carlos nodded his head toward me with a big smile and then turned toward Mom. "Mrs. Gardner, I bought a car today—an English convertible sports car called an MG. My parents said I could show it off to a few friends. I wanted to know if I could take Diane for a ride. I'll have her back in no more than twenty minutes because I have to get home."

She wrinkled her forehead. "I don't know if you want to take Diane with you anywhere. *She's a jinx.* Cars and things break down when she's around. I don't think it's a good idea for you to chance your car with her in it."

"Are you joking? Why would you say that about your daughter?"

"Because it's true, and I'm concerned for you and your car. But if you want to chance it, then go ahead." She said as she threw her hands in the air.

"OK, we will be back in twenty minutes. Oh, I would also like to pick her up for school some mornings. Would that be OK?" He tried to look pleasant after her last statement.

Mom shrugged her shoulders. "It's up to you."

"I'll get a scarf, I like convertibles," I said. On the way to my bedroom I screamed on the inside. *I'm not a jinx! I'm not a jinx!*

We climbed into his car. "Your MG is so cute. Can you let me see how the top goes up and down?" He raised and lowered it a couple of times and we giggled.

We drove about two blocks, and the engine shut off. He tried everything, but couldn't get it re-started. Carlos stared at me, but didn't speak. We walked in silence back to my house.

He greeted Mom and asked to use the phone to call his father to pick him up. I was so glad she didn't say, "I told you so." Her look and our silence said it all. He and I sat motionless on the couch while we waited for his father.

Was I a jinx? If I was a jinx, how did I become one? Why had my life been marked with this curse? What had I done to cause this? How could I get rid of whatever caused this? Could Mom's words have played a part in this scenario?

Proverbs 18:21 states: *Death and life are in the power of the tongue.*

Later I wondered if the Enemy used what he knew about the bad condition of the car against me. If so, did he motivate Mom to speak a word curse about me being a jinx so I was blamed for the breakdown?

A mechanic came the next day and towed the car to his shop. Obviously, something was already seriously wrong with the car or it would've started when Carlos's father tried. Although that time it was not because of the harassing spirit on my life, the Enemy used this incident to shred my self-worth.

Carlos never did pick me up for school when he got his car running. In fact, he stayed far away from me after that fateful night—only an occasional hello. I lost a friend, and I didn't understand why.

This problem of mechanical breakdowns continued after I left my parents' home and married in 1968, and beyond. Two weeks into our marriage we purchased a used refrigerator. Within five days it stopped and we had to call a repairman. In 1970 we moved into our first home and purchased a new refrigerator. Within a few days it stopped running and needed repair.

I can't count the times my car stopped after doing errands. When that happened my preschool age sons and I walked or rode the bus home. When Chuck came home from work, we drove his car to where my car was parked, and of course, my car started immediately for him. He accused me countless times of mishandling my car. I didn't understand at the time how to express to Chuck that this was beyond my control. Neither of us understood the chaos and jinx-like incidents needed to be addressed through spiritual warfare. I didn't believe it was God doing this, but I also knew it was not natural.

One particular day sticks out in my mind. My children and I went grocery shopping, then stopped at the bank. When I got back in my station wagon it would not start. I went back inside the bank and called my church a few blocks away to see if someone could pick us up. My pastor came. We piled the groceries into his small Volkswagen. Curtis sat on top of the groceries in the back seat while Carlton sat on my lap in the front. We were cramped.

"Thank you, Pastor Rob for coming. Don't worry, Chuck and I will get my car."

"Diane, it looks like you are having a bad day today."

"No, not a bad day, Pastor Rob, I'm having a bad life." I choked back the tears. Self-pity had put a stranglehold on my emotions. Years of harassment had worn me down. What could I do?

At home that day, I put the groceries away and put my kids down for a nap. I got into bed also and pulled the covers over my head. The word *jinx* kept playing in my head and got louder until I had a splitting headache. What was wrong with me? Was I under a curse?

After attending Pastor Rob's church for over a year, I had enough faith to believe God could help me. Finally I got the courage to tell the children's director, Pastor Phil, about my jinx plight. I spoke of the mechanical breakdowns that happened in bizarre ways. Then I asked, "Why is this happening to me? Everyone has something break down occasionally, but mechanical things that work for someone else don't work for me. Is God punishing me? This has been happening since I was young. Do you believe people can be a *jinx* in one area and not be *jinxed* in another?" I began to cry. "I hope you don't think I'm making this up."

He answered with compassion and wisdom. "I don't believe you're making this up. And I know God is not punishing you. God has an enemy and so do you. Satan is real and has a kingdom of demonic spirits that do things like this. His name was Lucifer and he is a fallen archangel. He is not equal to God, but he was created by God, and so he is in the supernatural invisible realm. The Godhead, which consists of the Father, Jesus, and the Holy Spirit were not created. They are eternal—they have always existed.

"Revelation 12 tells us the Enemy was cast out of heaven when he tried to bring a coup against God. He convinced one-third of the angels to be on his side. These are now the demons that work under him to bring destruction to mankind. They hate God and us because we are made in God's image.

"Satan cannot violate our will. He has to use deception, fear, unbelief, and lust to get us to agree with his plan. In the Garden of Eden he used deception. Our will is the strongest part of us. We can resist the Devil's plans if we choose. He goes after our will when we are young.

"When there's a pattern of destructive activity like you have described, there is usually an entrance where he has deceived someone into giving him access to operate.

"God knows what started this harassment. You can pray and ask Him to show you *why* and *when* this started. You have been captive to Satan's assignment for years. This is not coincidental—this pattern shows Satan *is* at work. Jesus came to set captives like you free. There's a scripture in 1 John 3:8 which says: *...For this purpose the Son of God was manifested, that He might destroy the works of the devil.* The Devil is a spirit and a spirit never dies, so Jesus didn't come to *kill* the Devil, but to destroy the things he does, his works."

He reached over and patted my hand. "Let's ask God to reveal the open door that allowed this demonic spirit to enter and harass your life. I believe a good scripture passage to memorize that can help you is Luke 10:17-19. In verse 18, Jesus says He was there when Satan tried his coup in heaven and was cast out. He said, *I saw Satan fall like lightning from heaven.* Verse 19 says, *Behold, I give you* [that's you too, Diane] *the authority to trample on serpents and scorpions, and over all the power of the enemy, and nothing shall by any means hurt you.*

"Remember this, all evil spirits of darkness know you are addressing them when you say the name of their Master, Satan. You don't need to always call their names. But if you want, you can call this a harassing spirit because that's his assignment.

"Next time something breaks down or acts like there is trouble then you say, 'Satan, I resist and rebuke you, by the blood and in the name of Jesus! You harassing spirit leave now! You take your hands off of my car or anything else.

"Have faith and believe what the Word of God says. The Scripture is your weapon. The Bible says you have power over the Enemy in the name of Jesus. If it's a real demonic spirit causing the activity, then it will leave and the equipment will work right. If the equipment doesn't work, then your equipment is broken, so call the repairman." He chuckled.

He took my hand and we bowed our heads. "Lord, please reveal to Diane what is the root cause of this problem. Show her *how* and *when* this jinx-like problem started. We submit to the truth of Your Word. We call upon the blood of Jesus. For this cause You came to destroy the works of the Devil."

He raised his voice slightly. "In the name of Jesus we *break* the word curse that has been spoken over Diane! She is not a jinx! Satan, you will not harass, accuse, or deceive her with this label any longer. You foul harassing spirit that causes trouble with mechanical things, leave her now! Go!"

We raised our heads. "Diane, agreement prayer is so powerful. Keep fighting the good fight of faith and you will win."

I went home feeling much better. I had received prayer and felt like a tormenting fear had left me. I had hope.

One day I was in my kitchen as I washed dishes. My children were playing in the front yard. The inside door to the garage was only a couple feet from the sink. Suddenly, I heard the washing machine in the garage make strange loud noises like a motorcycle revving its engine. I opened the door and saw the washing machine spewing water from the top and underneath. It shook violently.

I put my hands on the washer top while it shook. I decided I would yell at the top of my lungs—not because I thought demons were hard of hearing, but because I was scared. I thought I might feel more powerful if I was loud and forceful. "No you don't! Your power over me is broken now that I have prayer agreement. I know I am not a jinx! It's you causing the problem, *not me*! Take your hands off of my washing machine. God blessed me with this washer only a year ago. So I know it's not broken. I rebuke and resist you. In the name of Jesus and by His blood, stop it now! Luke 10:19 says: *Behold, I give you the authority to trample on serpents and scorpions, and over all the power of the enemy, and nothing shall by any means hurt you.* In Jesus name I command my washer to be healed!"

While my hands were still on the top of the washer, it shook violently twice more. The water stopped spewing out, and it started to whirl like a normal washer. I crept back into the house, mesmerized by what had just happened. Once I reached the sink, I stood frozen and stared at the wall behind the dishes. I had knots in my stomach from fear.

"Whoa, Jesus, this stuff is real! Demons are real! Your name has *real* power! What just happened was scary. I just fought and won! I am not normally a fighter, but I just fought with my words and won. All I had to do was speak! Gee whiz."

There were several more instances similar to the washing machine incident, mostly with my car. When I prayed in faith and used the name of Jesus, I had the same results—suddenly they worked. Faith, in the authority of the name of Jesus, made them work.

I decided to speak the Word of God over my life instead of speaking about my circumstances. I used Psalm 23 as my antidote. "I will see Psalm 23 work for me because the Lord is my Shepherd. So I choose goodness and mercy to follow me all the days of my life. No more demonic harassment over mechanical things. No more chaos and confusion to follow me. Goodness, you will follow me. Mercy, you will follow me."

Gradually the jinxes happened less and less. One day, about two years after my prayer with Pastor Phil, I noticed nothing had mechanically gone wrong for several months. To follow the instructions Pastor Phil gave me, I asked the Holy Spirit several times to reveal the open door of access. My lingering question was: Why and when did this demonic assignment start? One day I had what I call a *Holy Spirit flashback* or a quick replay in my mind of the past. I saw myself in a conversation with Mom when I was eleven years old.

"Diane, I needed some answers to some problems in my life so I prayed and looked for answers," she said. "I started to study astrology and pay attention to my horoscope in the newspaper. I bought some pocket-sized astrology books. You can read them too. I consulted a couple of fortune tellers. I wasn't sure about them, but one told me a young man was coming to live with me for a few months, and today your Aunt Louise called to tell me your cousin Charles, who is your age, will come to spend the summer with us. I knew you'd like to hear that. Well, I believe in this stuff now."

I received the answer to both prayers—everything started at age eleven because of Mom's involvement with astrology and the occult. The doors of access for demonic activity were opened when Mom sought guidance apart from the Bible and God. This was idolatry.

Astrology and psychic fortune tellers operate under a spirit of divination and are influenced by demonic spirits called familiar spirits. These spirits are familiar with people and are able to tell the psychic what they know about a person. There is no time or distance in the spirit realm. God's angels and demonic spirits heard Aunt Louise in Texas talk to relatives there about her plans to send Charles to spend the summer with us before she called us.

This is the Enemy's counterfeit to the supernatural gifts of the Holy Spirit mentioned in 1 Corinthians 12:8: *For to one is given the word of wisdom through the Spirit, to another the word of knowledge through the same Spirit.* A word of wisdom is a word revealed from God about the future.

Mom could have asked God for His guidance through the Bible. Then God could have given her direction to call Aunt Louise. He would've been pleased with her faith. Then the door to goodness and mercy would have opened to her family instead of chaos, confusion, and demonic spirits.

Instead, she violated Leviticus 19:31: *"Give no regard to mediums and familiar spirits; do not seek after them, to be defiled by them: I am the LORD your God"* (Leviticus 19:31).

This Holy Spirit flashback healed me and brought me closer to Jesus. He longs to bring truth to us, but often we believe the lie of the Enemy that He's too busy to answer us. His purpose is to get us to remove our eyes from God.

My eyes were opened to the invisible war that required my participation to be an overcomer. I've never been in a fist fight—not with anyone, not even my siblings. I talked my way out of conflicts or I hid. I hated any form of confrontation.

I learned this was *not* God's way. He wanted me to fight back. He didn't want me to allow that bully, Satan, or his plan, to prevail over my life. It was kingdom against kingdom, and I was the deciding factor as to which prevailed in my life and family. I had to learn how to use the authority Christ gave me to overcome the kingdom of darkness.

Matthew 11:12 was a key: *And from the days of John the Baptist until now the kingdom of heaven suffers violence, and the violent take it by force.* The more I studied the Word, the more I saw how my fearful, non-confrontational victim's mentality was contrary to who God created me to be. It was certainly contrary to Jesus' example of how He dealt with His adversary.

The Bible often uses the phrase "Lord of Hosts," which is a warfare term. It means He is Lord of all the hosts of the armies of heaven and hell. Lord of Hosts, *Jehovah Sabaoth* is one of the covenant names of God when there is something to be conquered. Exodus 15:3 says: *The LORD is a man of war; the LORD is His name.*

I received a second *Holy Spirit flashback.* This time it was revealed like a video clip. I saw moving boxes stacked everywhere in our home. My siblings and I complained and whined to Mom about the move from our home into one of their rental apartments a few blocks away. We felt our 2,300 square foot two-story home with a large basement built in 1917 was perfect for us. We had a swing made of rope and an old car tire Dad had tied to our fig tree. The backyard was just right for softball. We didn't want to take down our elaborate model train layout built on a platform that covered half the basement floor. Each Christmas our parents bought us two boxcars, some scenery, and liquid for the locomotive to blow smoke when the horn blew. After the move, we never saw the train set again.

We moved in the summer of 1962, which was about two years after Mom visited the fortune teller. During those two years she began to regularly read her horoscope, faithfully read astrology booklets, and purchased a Ouija Board we occasionally played. I thought it was stupid to think God needed a piece of wood to talk to us. If we were made in His image, then He has a mouth to talk like we do I expressed each time we *played* with the board.

Mom had difficulty convincing us the move was in our best interest. In the flashback, she told us to sit down because she had something to tell us. "We don't have a choice. We have to move. I have to protect you from the evil that is in our house. We all know this house is haunted.

Our superstitious relatives think someone died in this house, and their ghost is still here and wants to reclaim the house. I don't know if that's what's going on or if it's something else. But I *do* know something or someone is here. I don't know how to get rid of him or her, so we're leaving. I don't have time to sell the house, so I'll rent it until I can sell it. I won't say anything to the renters. Maybe that ghost-like thing won't bother the next family. Believe me, they'll tell me if anything happens."

"We don't care if the house is haunted," we said. "Nothing has ever hurt us. We hear the footsteps in the attic and see the shadows move across the wall, but we're OK. We want to stay."

"The footsteps in the attic and the shadows on the walls and windows have happened for a while and we didn't move, but now I have to protect you from the latest development. I'm afraid for your safety." Mom rose from her chair and paced the floor. "The *final straw* was when I felt someone sit on my bed when I was asleep. I figured it was one of you. So I asked, 'What do you want?' There was no answer. 'If you don't want anything, then go back to bed.' Still there wasn't an answer. I opened my eyes and saw the corner of my bed was indented as if a large man had sat down, but no one was there. I don't know what or who it was. All I know is that I made my mind up *right then* that we were moving."

Finally, after seeing this flash back, I understood the big picture. The demonic activity in our home and the harassments that followed each of us were in *direct correlation* to my family's idolatry and open door into the occult. I saw the sneaky way the Enemy slithered his way into our lives through our ignorance. We were manipulated through our idolatry and deception. We sought guidance from other gods. I realized how much the Enemy hates children and takes advantage of them by deceiving their parents or loved ones.

Once my eyes were opened, I wanted to help others recognize and defeat the Enemy. But first I had to learn how to defeat his plans for myself. I studied the Bible about spiritual warfare and about our authority as believers. Teaching from 1 Timothy 6:12: *Fight the good fight of faith* helped me.

I asked my Helper, the Holy Spirit, to help me develop the mentality I needed to become an overcomer and fight the good fight of faith. I needed to fight for myself, my children, and my family who weren't saved and my community that was becoming plagued with violence.

I made my mind up to overcome every opposition that came against me. I discovered the awesome power we have through the name and the blood of Jesus. Demons must flee. I no longer looked like a jinx but looked like and talked like an overcomer!

Chapter 9

The Pictures

Deliver me from the guilt of bloodshed, O God, The God of my salvation, And my tongue shall sing aloud of Your righteousness. (Psalm 51:14)

May, 1999

"God has revealed to me at least one of you ministers in this room today had something traumatic happen to you at age eighteen," said Pastor Brent Douglas of Encounter Christian Centre, from Auckland, New Zealand—my guest speaker at a ministers' meeting I hosted at my church in Riverside.

He expanded on the revelation from God. "At eighteen some traumatic events took place, and they were a 'direct assault' from Satan. They were sent to stop your destiny. You have gotten free from most of the impact of these assaults. Through forgiveness and healing you've become strong and resistant to this spirit. But there are times it oppresses you, and for a short season you become paralyzed in your effectiveness concerning your calling. Eventually you fight your way to a breakthrough. You have asked God many times to send someone to agree with you in the spirit. God wants to release you totally today."

Age eighteen certainly was a traumatic and difficult time in my life, but to my surprise I was the only one who responded and came forward for prayer.

"There's an actual demonic spirit the Enemy assigned to you at eighteen," Pastor Douglas said. He paused and then added, "In fact, the Holy Spirit shows me that it's a *controlling spirit*. You felt trapped by the control of others who violated your will. He gained a door of access through a weakness in your emotions. His main goal was to kill you. When that didn't work, he sought to destroy your will, your character, and your ability to influence others for God."

Pastor Brent asked his wife, Pat, to pray with him as he ministered to me. He declared to the demonic spirit, "By the God-given authority in the name and by the blood of Jesus Christ I *break* the power of this controlling spirit off Diane—now! In the spirit realm, now! God has revealed your calculated assault and influence against her that started at eighteen. You foul controlling spirit, we agree with Diane that *today* your assignment is cancelled! Leave her!"

Then he spoke to the Lord. "I thank You Jesus, You alone will control her life. Amen."

Pastor Patricia Douglas concluded the prayer. "Lord Jesus, bring grace now and fill Diane through Your mighty name."

I felt a shock wave of electrifying energy run through my body. It was so powerful I dropped to the floor on my hands and knees. Suddenly I cried from the depths of my being. While down on all fours, I felt a shroud of darkness like the presence of a veil lift from my back. The demonic presence I fought for years was totally gone! When I finished crying, I had no strength to get up off the floor so I rolled over on my side and lay there taking deep breaths to regain my composure, but I remained on the floor.

Pastor Brent concluded his prophetic ministry to the pastors and ministers. I heard my assistant receive the offering for my guest speaker. I probably looked like I was unconscious, but I could hear everything. Yet, I was unable to move a muscle. I heard the ministers say goodbye to one another. Some stood by me and said, "Give her more, Lord. We agree with what You're doing in her." Then they left.

I'm in charge of this meeting and I can't get up to thank them for coming. I planned to take my guests to lunch. The power of God has me pinned to the floor. I won't attempt to get up anymore, but I'll trust God by His grace to finish what He started.

My two assistant pastors stayed in the building to wait until God was finished with me. I thanked God they didn't interrupt what He was doing, because they respect the Holy Spirit's work.

God exposed how the Enemy undermined my calling and my self-worth. I have never been the same since that day. His nature was exposed: a thief, an accuser, a destroyer, a deceiver, who had a calculated plan of assaults against my purpose. A direct hit at eighteen was designed to destroy my passion and hope to serve God.

I thought my problems came because I was a victim of circumstances, a victim of bad choices—mine and others. I never suspected the depth of the Enemy's calculated assaults directed against my will, my character, and my destiny.

I felt another wave of God's power wash over me as I lay on the floor. Then detailed pictures, like movie trailers, flooded my mind. They were Holy Spirit flashbacks primarily of a period in my life just after my eighteenth birthday in early 1967 to November 1968. The decisions I made during that time period has had lasting consequences.

The Enemy's assaults against my will were revealed, and with a shattered will, I made unhealthy decisions. My worst decision was to decide God was the source of the bad things that happened to me. I was taught God causes everything that happens, so naturally I blamed Him.

Through the flashback I saw how I unwittingly embraced Satan's plans by accepting the lies he said about me. Then I blamed God for the consequences. The pictures revealed how my parents and others followed the Adversary's diabolical strategy.

After I accepted the Lord, I found John 10:10 where Jesus said, *"The thief does not come except to still steal, and to kill, and to destroy. I have come that they may have life, and that they may have it more abundantly."*

God unlocked my emotional closet doors and revealed to me how He saw the Enemy take advantage of me and why. I learned how I developed wrong judgments about myself, God, and others.

First Picture: Church, 1961

I was in church at age twelve, shortly after we joined a wonderful Baptist church with my dad. Mom was at work that Sunday. In the picture, I prayed a prayer and made a vow that both God *and* the Enemy heard. "Lord Jesus, I want to be a good girl. I want You and my parents to be proud of me.

"I promise not to get drunk. I promise not to do drugs. I promise to stay a virgin and only be with whomever You want for my husband. I promise I will work to stop my lying and exaggerating, too. Please help me keep these promises, amen."

In my family, the adults often warned us as children to not *play* with God because He would punish us if we didn't keep our vows. Later I read this in Psalm 116:14: *I will pay my vows to the LORD now in the presence of all His people.*

I tried to keep my vows. I was afraid not to keep them. Some vows worked because I've never been drunk, never smoked a joint, and never taken illegal drugs. For years I kept my virginity vow (which was the hardest vow to keep because most of my friends were sexually active by fifteen or sooner).

At fourteen I tried to smoke a cigarette with my friends on the way home from school. Cigarettes were not included in my vow to God. Naturally my body rejected that first cigarette and I coughed for quite a while on the way home. When I walked into the house I must have smelled like smoke, because without a word from me, Mom talked about cigarettes.

"Diane, you already have problems breathing because of your adenoids. Your shortness of breath could get shorter if you smoke. You'll probably lose oxygen and you could even die."

The fear worked because I had a terrible fear of dying. From that day forth, I never touched another cigarette. Later that year my adenoids were removed, and I was able to breathe better.

Second Picture: February, 1967

In this picture I saw my attempts to keep my vow to God. Whenever I was approached on a date about sex, I gave him my standard answer. In the sixties "good girls" did not use the word sex. So, I said, "I'm *only* going to do *that* with my husband. I made a vow to God and to my mom. So, no, I'm not going to do that, and don't ask me again."

I had a couple of close calls, but I was determined to keep my vow and keep my virginity. No wonder by age eighteen I had received three marriage proposals from guys who wanted to become my husband. I had never been a victim of incest, so I had no sexual experience at all. I dated only basically nice guys who may have tried to talk me out of my vow but ultimately respected my boundaries. Consequently I was naïve about sexual things.

When I turned eighteen, I believed I didn't possess the intelligence to attend a four-year university, but I thought was mature enough to accomplish my goals: get a part-time job, go to Harbor Junior College, move out of my parents' home, get married by twenty-one, buy a house at twenty-two, get my bachelor degree at twenty-four, have my first child at twenty-five, and a millionaire by thirty-five.

Third Picture: March, 1967

Because I thought I was "in love" I gave up my plans to get married at twenty-one. I accepted a marriage proposal from my high school boyfriend, Larry. We set our wedding date for the end of June, two weeks after our high school graduation. My family was moving and I wanted to get married before they left L. A. We had fun at the beginning of the year as we each searched for a part-time job, registered for college, and looked for an apartment together. Of course, these were all *my* goals that he agreed to pursue. By the way, he never found a job, and never spoke of his own goals. Like many women, I discussed my goals and because he agreed and echoed what I said, I assumed he had the same goals. All he did was say, "Me too," when I told him mine.

Neither his family nor mine attended church. So our next goal was to find a minister. We planned a small ceremony with close family at my parents' home. Only a handful of people knew we were engaged. Two weeks after the wedding, my family planned to move to a small town in Riverside County. Larry and I were to stay in L.A. while we worked and attended college. My goals were coming together nicely, or so I assumed.

Fourth Picture: April, 1967

In the next picture, Larry sweet-talked me into having sex. This picture showed how I let my guard down when I overrode my vow to God. When I did this I inadvertently came into agreement with Satan's plan for my life. I allowed my fiancé to convince me it was alright in God's sight to become intimate because we were only a couple of months from our wedding day. It was OK because in God's sight he was already my husband. My heart knew it wasn't OK with God, but my head accepted the deception of the Enemy. *It wouldn't be too bad of a sin because I waited until eighteen, and I'm with my future husband.* Later, I admitted to myself I was also curious about sex, so I justified my decision to have it. I thought, *I'm only partially breaking my vow to God.*

Fifth Picture: April, 1967

In this picture I was praying a couple of days after I was intimate with Larry. I prayed a crucial prayer—one I should have prayed much earlier. "Jesus, please show me for sure if Larry is the husband You have for me. Mom told me the Bible says that if I am tempted to marry the wrong man, You will show me the way to escape by giving me a sign. If Larry is the right one, You will also give me a sign. I make a vow to listen and not ignore the sign You show me. I promise, amen."

I had no clue where the Bible said this, but at the time I had faith that it did. I also believed God heard me when I prayed. I know now that the prayer was based on 1 Corinthians 10:13: *No temptation has overtaken you except such as is common to man; but God is faithful, who will not allow you to be tempted beyond what you are able, but with the temptation will also make the way of escape, that you may be able to bear it.*

Unfortunately, I did things backward. I said yes to Larry's proposal, said yes to sex, and only *afterward* I prayed and asked Jesus if I should marry him. What a mess. James 1:5 says, *If any of you lacks wisdom, let him ask of God, who gives to all liberally and without reproach, and it will be given to him.* I certainly lacked wisdom and after the fact I did ask for wisdom. Still God honored my childlike faith, and through His grace answered my prayer about whether to marry Larry.

The Holy Spirit removed the blinders from my eyes. A couple of days after I prayed, I saw another person in my fiancé. Like Dr. Jekyll and Mr. Hyde, he exhibited a split personality. Suddenly he displayed extreme jealousy. I caught him in lies and found during our engagement he was unfaithful. One night at a party he got drunk, vomited on himself, and passed out. My friends helped me put him in the car, and I cried as I drove him to his house and helped him get in.

This is not at all who I want to marry. The next day I broke off our engagement. Immediately Larry started to stalk me.

Sixth Picture: May, 1967

My next picture was a conversation with Mom right after I broke off my engagement.

She stared into my eyes. "Are you pregnant?"

"No, I'm not."

"Have you started your period?"

"Not yet, but my breasts are sore like I'm going to start my period."

"Wasn't your period due to start four days ago? We have it marked on our calendars, and you haven't looked like you have had the cramps."

"Yes it was supposed to start then. Ah . . . ah, we only did something *one* time! It was on the spur of the moment. We only did a little bit because it hurt me so we stopped."

"You idiot! It only takes *one* time! Don't you know that is what happens? Your breasts get sore, and there's no period. I thought you said you changed your mind, and you're not marrying that lazy bum."

"I don't want to marry him!"

"Then you absolutely *cannot* have this baby, because no decent man will *ever* marry you if you have another man's child out of wedlock. If you change your mind and marry Larry, you cannot live here. Do you understand?"

"Yes." I cast my gaze downward.

Mom was right. My cycle was like clockwork. I had never been four days late in the past. So there was no need to guess any longer whether I was pregnant or not. Surely, I was.

Watching this picture being revealed to me by the Holy Spirit about how I opened the door to Satan's plan through my sin, I realized I had embraced self-condemning thought patterns of guilt, shame, and hopelessness. I saw how they replaced the passion to be a good girl. I saw how I felt trapped because I was pregnant. Therefore, I thought God was far away from me because of His disappointment with me.

We never talked about my mess up as a family, certainly not with my younger brothers—not even my sister, with whom I shared a room. No one said anything to me, and I said nothing to any of my friends. My parents didn't hug me, cry with me, or show compassion toward me. So I learned to stuff my pain behind an emotional closet door and ignore it.

I was stone faced when I approached Larry. "Larry, I'm pregnant."

"That's OK. We can still get married."

"No, I *don't* want to marry you. God showed me that you are not to be my husband and besides that I can't trust you. Mom said if I am not marrying you, then I cannot have the baby."

"What? You don't get to say anything about it? I don't get to say anything, either?"

"This is what Mom says I have to do. I'm very sorry. It will be done right after graduation."

"Your family is moving to Perris, California after you graduate. Are you staying here to go to college? What about the contract on the apartment?"

"I won't stay in L.A.," I said. "I cancelled the contract on our apartment. I also withdrew from college. I'll look for a job in Perris, and sign up for college in Riverside. Mom has been sick, so I'm going to help her move and set up the house in Perris. I told her I'll give it three months for me to get a good job. If I don't get one, I'll move back to L.A. into their rental property with Dad and Barbara, and then find a job here."

Seventh Picture: Early June, 1967

The next picture was a scene at home a few weeks before my high school graduation. I was the oldest of four and the first to graduate. But my family did not plan a party. My dad was not happy, my mom was not happy, and I was not happy. My grades weren't the problem. They were fine.

In the picture God showed me, I walked toward my dad in the hallway of our home in Los Angeles and smiled at him. He looked right past me. He had not spoken one word to me for a month. I knew he loved me, but I had become a disappointment to him, and he didn't know what to do with his emotions. So he refused to acknowledge my presence for three months.

Each day I cooked dinner for the family after school while my sister made the desserts, and I worked part-time three nights a week in the credit department of a downtown major retail store to earn money for my senior year expenses. What had this "good girl" done? I had lost my virginity and become pregnant.

Eighth Picture: June 19, 1967

The next picture was a few days after graduation, in the doctor's office, as we waited for him to perform the abortion. They called my name, and I went back to the private room while Mom waited with the other patients in the reception room. I was totally unaware of the next assault Satan planned.

As I got onto the table I wondered why it seemed lower than most doctors' tables. Suddenly I knew why, the doctor was on top of me. He put his hand over my mouth while he raped me. As suddenly as it started, it was over. He got up, zipped his pants, washed me off, and performed the abortion. I squeezed my eyes shut through the entire process. I was screaming on the inside, but could not find the strength to open my mouth or fight back on the outside.

The doctor was calm after the procedure, as if raping his patient was a part of the process. "You did fine. I have opened your womb and let air in. I've put gauze in there. Pull it out tomorrow morning, and you'll naturally lose the baby like a miscarriage by tomorrow night. No one will know you had an abortion."

He led me into the reception room. I must have looked pale because Mom jumped up immediately and began to comfort me.

She put her arm around me. "You'll be alright in a couple of days. Don't worry."

"She really did well," the doctor told Mom loud enough for everyone else to hear. "I gave her instructions. She'll recover by tomorrow evening, so no need to come back."

He kissed me on the cheek, then shook Mom's hand, and disappeared down the hallway. I felt like I would throw up.

The trip home was long and I didn't say a word. Neither did Mom. In fact, I didn't talk to anyone in my family for quite a while. I felt dirty and worthless. *The best thing to do is pretend the rape never happened. Then no one will make a scene and take me back to that doctor's office to confront him. I never want to see him again. I already don't remember his name. Dad or Mom would probably try to kill him if they knew what happened, and it would be my fault.*

I pulled out the gauze the next morning while I prayed. *God, I know you see me even if You don't like me. Please forgive me. Help me. I'm so sorry. I'm so scared. Mom said I had no choice because I had already messed up. I know You didn't want me to be with Larry or have an abortion. Please help me.*

The abortion did not go well. I didn't pass the baby that day or the next. Instead I developed severe cramps.

Ninth Picture: Late June, 1967

The next picture was when Mom drove me to a different clinic for examination. "Don't tell the doctor what we've done. Just let him see if you're OK."

After the doctor was finished, he had Mom come to his office. With a wrinkled brow he said. "Mrs. Gardner, I don't know if you knew your daughter is pregnant. It looks like she is threatening a miscarriage, so I gave her a shot to help her keep the baby, if possible. Take her to the hospital if she starts bleeding or keeps cramping."

"Thank you, doctor," Mom said.

As soon as we got into the car, Mom interrogated me. "Why did you let him give you a shot to *keep* the baby when we don't *want* the baby?"

"I didn't know what to say, so I said nothing. How could I refuse the shot and tell him I don't want to keep the baby? I didn't know what to do."

Tenth Picture: June, 1967

My body didn't know whether to abort or to keep the baby. I ran a high fever and changed clothes three times from perspiration. That night I became delirious and hallucinated. The cramps went into full labor contractions. The next morning Mom rushed me to the hospital.

Three nurses surrounded my bed. One held my hand and coached me through labor. One had her hand on my stomach as she told the other nurses how to help me. One of them held the bedpan to catch the baby. After several hours of labor, the process was finally over.

The three nurses walked toward the door. I called out to the nurse with the bedpan. "Could you please tell me if it is a boy or a girl?"

She spun around. "What the heck do you care? You didn't want the baby anyway! We know what you did! We see people all the time who want children so badly and can't have them. You had another choice. You could have put the baby up for adoption for someone who wanted it. Whores and sluts like you are having sex and then killing their babies as a form of birth control because they're selfish and don't want to be inconvenienced. You don't deserve to know the answer!" She stormed out of the room and the door slammed behind her.

My baby died that day, and so did a part of me.

This picture revealed Satan's desire to *kill* me, physically, spiritually, and emotionally. He did kill my desire to be a "good girl." I died many deaths during those three months—the girl who often told her friends to do right because of God, was gone.

Eleventh Picture: June, 1967

Satan's next assault was when he became my Accuser who filled my mind with tormenting accusations. Over the years I figured the thoughts originated with me, but through these pictures I saw they didn't. Some of my accusatory thoughts were:

God has given up on me. He doesn't want someone like me to serve Him. Mom is angry with me. Dad is so disappointed he can't talk or look at me. All three nurses hate me. I picked a sick guy to marry who God didn't want to be my husband. The doctor raped me, and I said nothing. I'm a terrible person because I aborted my baby. God gave us the ability to bring life into the world and I took that life away. There's no use in attempting to be good anymore.

Because I believed the accusations, I didn't talk to God. Satan's assault against my will worked. Even though I was a church member from ages eleven to sixteen, I was not born again. I was God-fearing, but I had not received the life of God in my spirit by confessing Jesus as my Savior. I thought I had to handle these storms alone. I didn't receive any grace because I didn't exhibit any faith in God. For the next month before we moved I became promiscuous with two guys who were my friends and used protection.

I also didn't know the truth found in Revelation 12:10: *For the Accuser of our brethren, who accused them before our God day and night, has been cast down.* Since I didn't know this, I didn't know God's grace was available to me. I didn't have a clue how to receive healing from these traumas. Consequently, I continued to make shamed-based bad decisions.

When I saw this picture I understood that predators have their own pain from childhood. They have chosen to shut God out of their lives and therefore become tools of Satan. They have a keen "spiritual perception" that is totally demonic. They know "nice kids" make good victims because they rarely fight back.

The shame I carried into the room to have the abortion was obvious. As a predator, that doctor believed I wouldn't report him because I would be too ashamed to tell anyone I had an abortion. He recognized my victim mentality as someone who became helpless when controlled by others. If I reported him to the police, my abortion would become exposed. He felt safe. I felt trapped.

Twelfth Picture: June 27, 1967

Mom came into the bedroom my sister Barbara and I shared. Barbara was outside in the back yard. "I told everyone you had a very severe kidney infection, and that's why you needed to be hospitalized, so remember—a *severe kidney infection.* One of your friends is here to see you. He called two days ago, and I told him you could see him today. I neglected to tell you."

"Who is it, Mom?"

"It's the guy who goes to the university in Northern California. He comes to see you when he's on school break. He must be home for summer. I can't think of his name."

"Oh, you mean Mason."

I met Mason two years earlier as we practiced our routines for the debutante ball, which is a social event that introduces a young lady usually sixteen to society. He was an escort of another debutante who was a relative of his, he and I exchanged numbers. We dated a couple of times when he came home on break. I had not seen him since I got engaged to Larry five months earlier.

Mom walked into the hallway and entered the living room. "Mason, she'll be out in a few minutes. It's nice of you to come by to see her. I mentioned to you when you called that she would be home from the hospital yesterday. She is doing much better, but can only visit for a short while.

"We're moving from Los Angeles within the next month, so get our new address and phone number from Diane before you go."

"Thank you, Mrs. Gardner, I'll be sure and do that."

He and I sat on the couch. "We're moving almost two hours away. I'll lose contact with all my friends because it's too far to drive. But I'll give you our information anyway."

"I'll drive out there to see you this summer while I'm home," he said. "We'll do something fun. Speaking of fun, I have two tickets to hear a jazz band next Saturday. That's what I called about when your mom told me you had a severe kidney infection and were in the hospital. Will you feel up to going?"

"That's groovy. I'll be OK by Saturday."

In July my family and I moved to where my cousins lived, Perris, California—a town of 3,600 people. I reminded Mom that there were 3,600 students in my high school.

"Mom, this whole town could fit in my high school. People come here to die or retire and I'm too young for either one of those." I was not happy about the move.

Mason drove to Perris twice that summer before he returned to the university. We made a promise to write to each other and a commitment to spend time together during his Thanksgiving and Christmas breaks.

Four months after we moved to Perris, I attended a teen dance in town and met the two chaperones—Judith who worked at the Teen

Outpost, and Chuck, her brother. After a short courtship, Chuck and I were married in March 1968. Our first child was a beautiful baby boy who Chuck named Curtis.

Thirteenth Picture: November 19, 1968

This next picture was when Curtis was nine days old. Chuck rushed me to the doctor's office because I vacillated between a high fever and chills.

"You've got to stop breastfeeding immediately," the doctor said. "Your fever is so high that it could cause problems with the baby's milk. You have a severe kidney infection."

When we got home Chuck sat in the living room and rocked baby Curtis to sleep. I lay in bed in my own perspiration, waiting for the pain medicine to kick in. Because Mom was a nurse and a grandmother, she insisted that she come over to help take care of me and the baby. She sat on a chair next to my bed and placed a cool damp cloth on my forehead and another on my neck.

"Isn't it an ironic cruel twist of fate that you have a severe kidney infection?" she whispered so Chuck couldn't hear her. "You know why this happened, don't you? This is not a coincidence."

I sighed. "No, I don't know why."

"Well, this is God punishing us for what we did when you had an abortion last year. Remember we told people you were in the hospital with a severe kidney infection? See, God is punishing us by giving us exactly what we lied about to cover up the abortion. We need to ask Him to forgive us because He's mad at us."

"Mom, I already asked God to forgive me many times."

"Well, I'm saying that you are sick for a reason. God's trying to tell us something by giving you this severe kidney infection. Think about it."

My heart sank as she gave me her doctrinal view of my kidney infection and God. I felt hopeless and confused. My response was internal because I dared not say it out loud. *Yes it is "ironic" that this is the same thing you lied about to people. I was in the hospital and had nothing to do with that lie you made up, Mom! If God is going to punish me, it should be for having an abortion, and punish "you" with the severe kidney infection because it was your lie.*

Mom, I don't like your God anymore. I already asked Him to forgive me many times, but from what you are telling me, I guess He didn't do it. How do I know when I'm forgiven? Why am I sick with the same thing we lied about? Did God really make me sick because He's mad at me? If He did, then I want Him to leave me alone. I don't want anything to do with Him.

As I looked at this picture, I understood how the Enemy influenced me to embrace the lie which said *God was my problem and not my answer.*

For the next fourteen years I suffered with chronic kidney and bladder infections. For seven years I vacillated between a belief that I was being punished and wondering if there was another explanation for this *irony.* Then I studied the Word of God about Jesus being our Healer and how He carried our sicknesses to the cross and that changed everything.

First, I changed my belief system. God was no longer the cause of this ironic problem. My breakthrough came when I renounced the lie Mom told me about God punishing me with this sickness.

Second, I forgave Mom for telling me this untruth even though she sincerely believed it. My sickness was from the Enemy, not God.

Third, I changed some eating habits to foods more easily processed through my kidneys, drank more liquids, and flushed my system with water throughout the day instead of just quenching my thirst.

Fourth, for the next seven years I fought this problem by reciting scripture verses about God's healing power. I gradually got better until I had no more kidney infections.

Overcoming the Picture of Shame: January, 1978

Over ten years after the abortion and rape, I had a life-changing encounter with God. One night, Chuck was at night school and the kids were asleep when I flipped on a Christian television program. The host interviewed Rev. Dr. Evelyn Carter Spencer, whose nickname was

Rev. Ev. She spoke about how shame can consume us, and how we fail to recognize what the problem is. If we don't determine to get rid of shame, it hinders our lives and we take it to our grave. She testified about the shame she carried as the oldest of five illegitimate children. She quoted Psalm 25:2: *Let me not be ashamed; Let not my enemies triumph over me.*

Unexpectedly, tears flooded my face like someone had turned on a facet inside my head. Yet I felt nothing and didn't know I was about to cry. The program went off, and I decided the Holy Spirit was up to something and I should cooperate with whatever He was cleansing. I had the feeling that if I went to bed and shut my emotions down, God would not be pleased.

Although I had no clue what was going on, I wanted God to complete whatever He started. So I knelt in front of my chair. "Lord, I don't know why I'm crying. Rev. Ev talked about the shame of an illegitimate child. I know I'm not illegitimate. So why am I crying? I trust You and surrender to allow You to finish whatever You're doing."

He spoke to me. *You have shame over circumstances you've never brought to Me or told anyone. It's still hidden in darkness, and Satan has power over darkness. You have shame about the abortion and shame about the rape. You have shame about your unmet expectations about your goals in life. And you have shame about not completing your education. Your life is filled with shame, and many of your decisions are shame-based. I want you free from shame. I carried your shame to the cross and left it there. I want you to see your shame nailed to My cross.*

I asked forgiveness for holding onto shame since Jesus came to take away my shame. Hebrews 12:2b says: *Who for the joy that was set before Him endured the cross, despising the shame.*

Then I renounced the shame from the abortion, the shame from the rape, and the shame from unmet expectations about my life. Each category carried its own set of tears, fears, and disappointments. It was gut-wrenching. Ten years worth of shame hidden in darkness was brought to God and put into His light. I commanded shame to go from my emotions and my life.

Shame had covered me like a blanket and distorted how I saw myself and my God. Unhealthy shame tainted my conversations, it left me feeling unworthy. Immediately after I let go of shame I recalled the details of the rape and the name of the doctor. Facts I had buried. I forgave him for yielding his will to the Enemy to become a predator. I prayed for his salvation in case he was alive, and if he was not alive I prayed for his family's salvation.

I rebuked the shame associated with my lack of education. I canceled the shame I carried about my fear of the future. Shame had been my companion, but now it had become the enemy I hated and was determined to squash.

I clung to Isaiah 61:7: *Instead of your shame you shall have double honor, And instead of confusion they shall rejoice in their portion. Therefore in their land they shall possess double; Everlasting joy shall be theirs.*

Each time I share any part of my testimony about how I overcame the shame of rape, the shame of abortion, and the shame of failed educational goals, I tell the audience I now have double honor and double joy, as this passage says. I'm not ashamed to share my testimony. I've continued my education later in life and earned my degrees.

My past no longer defines my future.

Chapter 10

Our Secret

So the great dragon was cast out, that serpent of old, called the Devil and Satan, who deceives the whole world; he was cast to the earth, and his angels were cast out with him. (Revelation 12:9)

February, 1968

In my excitement I snatched the envelope from the dining room table where Mom usually put my mail. She was in the kitchen cooking dinner for Kenneth and me. I grabbed a knife from the kitchen and ripped the envelope open. "Mom, you saw I got a letter from Mason. He kept his word about my gift! It's already the 15th of February, and my nineteenth birthday is only three-days away. See, here it is!" I waved the airplane ticket over her head. "This'll be my first airplane ride, and the first time I'll be going anywhere by myself. I'm frightened, but *excited*!

"That's great. When do you leave?"

"Let's see." Because I had never seen an airplane ticket I read carefully every detail then shouted. "Oh, it's for next week! I leave on George Washington's birthday, Thursday the 22nd in the evening and return on Sunday evening. That's the three day presidents' holiday weekend. Great, I only need to take off work on Friday. His letter says we'll be going to his college football game and a house party he and his friend will have. I'm going to have so much fun! I'll be staying with his classmate and her roommate."

"That's good. I'll take you and pick you up from the airport."

"Thanks, Mom."

Still in my work clothes, I threw myself onto my bed. I stared at the ticket, then read and reread the letter. I opened the drawer to my nightstand and picked up the last letter he had written me dated November 1.

Dear Diane,

My classes are much harder this semester so it's taken me a month to write you back. I had fun with you too this past summer when we were together. I need to let you know that I won't be home for the holidays because I have an engineering intern job.

My letter will be short because I have a study group in a bit. I've been thinking about your last letter in which you asked me what it's like to be on an airplane. When I saw you this summer you told me how bored you are, living in that small town.

I decided I'll make enough money this winter at my intern job to solve your two problems. I'm sending you an airplane ticket to fly up here and hang out for a few days. You'll receive it before your birthday in February. This will be a combined Christmas and birthday gift. This will give you flying experience and cure your boredom for a few days. We'll have fun and you can meet my friends.

Because of my work and my difficult classes you won't hear back from me until then.

Write me soon and let me know if you want to do this, and I'll take care of it in February.

I'll miss seeing you for the holidays,
Mason

The closer I got to the day of departure the more excited and hesitant I got at the same time. This confused me. By this point in my life I had learned to notice my inward warnings. But I didn't understand sometimes it was God warning me. According to 1 Corinthians 10:13c: *but with the temptation will also make the way of escape, that you may be able to bear it.* That hesitation I was experiencing was God giving me a red light on the inside, but Mom and I overrode the warning.

The feeling became so strong that I expressed my hesitation about three days before my departure. "Mom, I'm feeling 'weird' about my trip to see Mason. I don't know why. Should I still go, or should I return the ticket to him so he can get his money back? You know I met Chuck in November after I wrote Mason to accept his invitation. I like Chuck more each time I'm with him. I don't know what to do about my feelings for him. Mason and I are what I call dating friends. We date, we kiss sometimes, but we date other people, too. We're not going steady.

"I'm still excited about going on an airplane. And it'll be good to see Mason. I miss his friendship. I'm excited about going until I think of missing Chuck and that confuses me."

"It'll be fine," Mom said. "Maybe you're just a little afraid of flying. You always get afraid when you do something new."

"Yeah, you're right."

"Remember this, if you and Mason do anything, be *sure* and use condoms for protection."

I took a couple of steps back and threw my arms in the air. "What? We don't have a relationship like that! I told you we've kissed, but not even passionately. I've known him three years, and we've never done anything, and we're not going to do anything! I told you, I'm staying with one of his female friends."

For years, Mom had not been sexually faithful to Dad, so she had no concept about how to help me be true to my own heart. She didn't understand how I was crying out for the needed help to make the hard choice to stay home and pursue my relationship with Chuck.

God knows how to protect our hearts. He continually provides that way to escape from sin and the trials that cause heartache, but we don't recognize the warnings or we dismiss or override the impressions He gives us. The Holy Spirit always does His job to warn us that Satan has a trap.

Mom picked me up when I returned on Sunday evening. I talked about the trip, the football game, and the party, but I wasn't my usual hyper self after I've done something exciting. I told her I had a wonderful time, but she could tell something was wrong.

"You said you had a good time, but something isn't right with you."

"I, I . . . well. Mason and I *did* do something one time, and I feel bad about it. I think it's going to mess up our friendship. We were stupid." I let out a big sigh. "I mentioned I was going to stay with one of his girl classmates. Remember?"

"Yes, you told me. What about it?" Mom asked as she took her eyes off the road to look at me with wrinkled eyebrows.

"Well, it didn't work out. After he picked me up, he took me to lunch, and we went to her place. Her roommate was there and made it clear she didn't want any stranger staying at their apartment. Mason was embarrassed and took me back to the house that he and two other guys rent. He gave me his room and he slept on the couch. Everything was fine until yesterday.

"Then when his roommates were gone, he asked me to be with him, and I said OK. I don't know why. I guess I felt obligated to say yes because he had given me so much. I know it doesn't make any sense to feel that way—it was his choice to pay for the trip. I didn't owe him anything. I should have said no. He would've respected my decision."

"Don't worry about it. If you used protection it is no big deal."

"We did."

"What did you use?"

"Well, I told Mason to use a condom. He went to the store. When he came back he told me he didn't like the feel of condoms. So he bought something I had never heard of before called Norforms Suppositories."

"That's not for protection! That's feminine hygiene deodorant! That isn't going to stop someone from getting pregnant! You've really messed up!"

I was in shock. When we got home, I went to my room. Thoughts swirled in my head. *I feel bad enough to know that Mason and I may have ruined a wonderful friendship. Now I have to deal with the horrible news Mom just dropped on me. I can't be pregnant again! It's only been eight months since I had the abortion and almost died. Never mind, I don't want to think about it. Other people do this all the time and don't get pregnant. I'll be alright.*

Later, as I loaded my dirty clothes into the washer, Mom called me into her bedroom. My thirteen-year-old brother Kenneth, was in his room doing homework, so she motioned for me to close the door.

"What are you going to do if you *are* pregnant?"

"I don't want to think about that. We only did something yesterday. I guess I'll know in a week if my period doesn't come. It's always on time."

"What about Chuck?

"I guess if my period doesn't come, I'll tell him I'm pregnant by Mason."

"No, I mean what are your feelings toward him?"

"The whole time I was up north I kept thinking about Chuck. I realized I love Chuck more than I thought, and I missed him."

"Even though you guys only met three months ago, he has been here most nights after work and almost every weekend. He seems serious about you. He and I have had two serious conversations about what he wants out of life, and what he wants in a wife and family. He's the one who brought up the subjects. A man only talks like that with the parent of the woman he's dating because he's thinking about marrying their daughter."

"You didn't tell me about those conversations."

"I believe he is the man for you. You'll ruin things if you're pregnant. I told you last year that a good man does not want to marry a woman with someone else's baby."

"Mom, if I am pregnant, you know I will *never* have another abortion! I'll take care of my baby without a husband if I have to. I have a good job at the telephone company."

"No, we will never do an abortion again. But we must fix this problem because we can't wait until next week to see if there really is a problem. If Chuck asked you to marry him, would you?"

"I know for sure that I love him very much. But I want to work, save money, get my own place, and continue with my junior college night classes. But, if I married anyone, I could see myself with Chuck."

"You pray and ask God if he's the one for you. I believe he's the one. Everything you said about college and your own place before marriage is fine *if* you are not pregnant. But if you are, there is no time for college and saving money. If you're going to get married, you want to do it immediately after you know you're pregnant. You need to keep people guessing and protect your reputation. I don't want you to put the stigma of illegitimacy on my first grandchild."

She sat up in bed and beckoned me to come closer. "Chuck is here most week nights. When is he due to come over again?"

"Tomorrow night. I'm preparing dinner for all of us. Then we'll sit on the couch and talk awhile, until about 10:00 p.m. or until we hear you yell goodnight from your bedroom. Then, as always, he'll take that as his cue to leave." I smiled at Mom as I recalled our routine, and I tried to lighten the atmosphere, but I wasn't successful.

"When is the next time you guys are going somewhere?"

"We decided last week we weren't going anywhere until we both get paid next week."

"I told you next week is too late! When he comes over tomorrow night, after dinner tell him you want to go somewhere. Listen to me carefully! I want you to have unprotected sex with Chuck."

I took a couple of steps backward. Her words felt like a slap to my face. "What? I can't do that."

She stared at me. "Look, if you are not pregnant, then no big deal. But if you and Chuck have sex, and you get pregnant by him, then that's OK. You guys were going to get married eventually anyway. If you are pregnant already, it won't matter whether Mason is the father or Chuck is the father, because you will still be married to the *right* man. And we will have fixed the problem.

"This will be our secret. Only you and I will ever know that there may be a question about who the birth father is. If you are not pregnant and you don't get pregnant, then life goes on. You continue with work and college, and one day when you and Chuck are ready, you'll get married."

She gave me a moment to think about *our secret* plan. "In a week, if you are pregnant, then you tell Chuck, but you never tell Mason because that would just complicate things. When you and Chuck get married, Mason does not need to be in the picture. Chuck will be your husband and the father of the baby, and that's that. If you are pregnant, or get pregnant, the sooner you get married, the better for both of your reputations."

I stared at her with a scowl, attempting to show her I didn't want the deceptive "wisdom" she had given me. We stared at each other until my eyes began to well up with tears, but I knew I couldn't cry in front of her. "OK Mom," I whispered.

I didn't think to ask God for a plan to circumvent what I had been handed. My victim mentality caused me to shut down when I was backed into an emotional corner. So I bought into Satan's right sounding lie. The lie that made sense to my carnal mind said I had no other choice.

I walked slowly back to my room with a big lump in my throat that felt as if I would choke. I closed the door and dove onto my bed as I buried my face in my pillow. I prayed. "God, please forgive me. Have mercy on me. You're probably mad at me and I don't blame You. Tonight You may not want to hear from me, but I don't have anyone else to talk to. Forgive me for being with Mason, I know it was wrong. Show Chuck and show me if we should marry. I'll obey what You show me."

I neglected to ask God what I should do about Mom's secret that was soon to become our secret. I wanted to ignore the fact that God sees and knows *all* secrets.

The next day, Chuck came to dinner. Mom and Kenneth laughed and talked with him during the meal. I was too nervous to say much. I kept myself busy in the kitchen and only sat down briefly.

Mom glanced my way a few times when there was a lull in the conversation. Finally I got up enough nerve to say, "Chuck, instead of staying in tonight, let's go out."

"Sure Diane, if that's what you want to do. I only have enough money to buy us soda pops. What do you want to do? You know in Perris everything closes at 6:00 p.m. So what's open and doesn't cost money?" He laughed.

"We can ride around and talk and drink our soda pops."

"Hey, that sounds good. I'll wait for you to get your coat."

Mom smiled at us both. "You guys have a good time. See you again soon, Chuck."

We drove around for a while and talked. Strangely Chuck asked me what I wanted in a family—how many children I wanted and what my life goals were. Chuck wanted to show me this beautiful scenery overlooking a lake, so he found a nice spot on a hill and parked. I laid my head on his shoulder, but didn't say much because I had a lump in my throat. *I have already done wrong. Now I'm doing wrong to "fix" the wrong, but it doesn't feel like I am fixing anything.*

Until now, Chuck and I had been on about six official dates. His family or mine accompanied us on three of those dates. We had not kissed passionately before that night. We had a respectful relationship that was comfortable, fun, and with no regrets.

Only one good thing happened that night. I never had to ask Chuck to have sex. I kissed him passionately a few times and I told him I loved him. I think he felt my sincerity and gave me a big hug and passionate kiss in response. Because he was a twenty-three-year-old young man, he took over from there.

When I came home, I'd hoped Mom was asleep so I didn't have to say anything to her. But Mom called my name as I walked past her bedroom at 11:00 p.m. "Did you do it?"

I dropped my gaze. "Yes."

"OK, we'll wait until next week and see what the results are. It'll be our secret. Good night."

I felt emotionally sick. I threw myself across my bed and sobbed into my pillow so I wouldn't be heard. *I hate deceptive secrets. Mom always has some secret plan to fix life's problems. Yet, these seem to cause more problems for me. But, I know I'll get into trouble if I resist her plans. I don't want to be pregnant! I can't be pregnant! I feel dirty!*

One of Mom's favorite sayings to her children was, "Two wrongs don't make a right." It would've been nice if she followed her own advice. I had done wrong. Mom tried to help me fix my wrong with another wrong. Our two wrongs surely did not make anything right.

As I reflect back on that time, I can imagine God asking Mom and me the same question He asked Eve in Genesis 3:13: *And the LORD God said to the woman, "What is this you have done?" The woman said, "The serpent deceived me, and I ate."*

The serpent (Satan) deceived Mom and me with his lie as our solution to a perceived problem. He offered us sin to fix the problem. We listened to him instead of obeying God's Word.

Many nights I tossed and turned as I replayed both sexual encounters. My insomnia grew worse. The next week came, and my worst nightmare came true—no period, I knew I was pregnant, *again.*

I convinced myself the only way to get through this horrible process was to totally shut down emotionally. *I've cried in private enough, so I won't let anyone see me cry. I'll make a list of everything I want to say to each one and handle things like business. Without emotion, I'll tell Mason, Mom, and Chuck that I'm pregnant. I'll tell Chuck and Mason that abortion is not an option. I'll tell everyone that if it comes to it, I can take care of my baby alone. I'll just have to live with my parents longer than I wanted.*

If I do marry Chuck, and the baby looks exactly like Mason, I couldn't live with that—I don't know what I could say—I guess we will have to tell Mason. I'll tell Chuck up front that there is another guy. Mason deserves to know in case it's his child. I'll never tell Mom I spoke with Mason. If Chuck wants to marry me, then I'll make a list of things to tell him.

First Week of March, 1968

The next week I told both men I was pregnant. I called Mason first. He wanted me to take more time to make sure I was pregnant. He said he'd call back later. A few days later Chuck came over to the house. We sat on the couch and made small talk before I told him I was pregnant.

"I thought you might be. I don't know why, but I had a feeling." We sat silent for a moment. "I told you a couple of times already that one day we were going to get married. I knew the first day I met you we were supposed to get married. When you walked toward me before you ever said a word I heard God's voice say to me, *This is your wife.* I told you about two months ago and you didn't believe me. That's why I asked you all those serious questions about what you wanted in life." He paused a moment. "Diane, I have always been serious about our marriage. It's only been three months since we started dating, so it'll be fun getting to know each other better. We'll get married sooner than I thought, without a big ceremony."

"I don't care about a wedding ceremony. All I know is that I love you and would love to be your wife, but it's not that simple. I'm so sorry. I am *really* sorry." I looked down, gathered my courage, and made eye contact with him again. "We need not to see or talk to each other for three or four days.

"Please have a talk with God and ask Him if He *still* wants me to be the one you are to marry after I tell you something. He could change His mind or you could change yours. I don't want us to marry just because I'm pregnant. I want to get married because we love each other. We feel we are right for each other, but I don't want you to feel trapped, and I don't want to feel trapped."

"I don't feel trapped. I know what I want," he said. "I don't need any more time. I know you're the one for me and I want to marry you, pregnant or not."

I looked away from him. "That's good. I'm glad to hear that, but you *will* need some time after I tell you this next part. Before I left for Northern California I told you my friend sent me a plane ticket." I was quiet for a moment before I continued. "My friend is a guy I met when I was a debutante three years ago. His name is Mason. He's in college up there. He comes to L.A. to see his family on holidays and school breaks. We dated when he visited, but were never serious or intimate."

I looked in Chuck's face. "We are not in love with each other and we dated other people. In fact, he arranged for me to stay with one of his female friends while I was there, but it didn't work out. So I stayed with him and his roommates. I slept in his room alone. I didn't sleep with Mason."

"So what's the problem, then?" he asked.

"Mason and I *were intimate* once before I left. Then you and I were together only two days later. So I am not sure who the father is."

Chuck jumped off the couch and paced the floor.

"This is why you need to take time to see what you really want to do."

He continued to pace. "Did you tell him you were pregnant?"

"Yes, I told him first because I was with him first. He was understandably upset. He said he has to finish his education and can't handle something like this at this time. I told him I was only informing him about the pregnancy, that I wasn't expecting anything from him. I was naïve, and I let us ruin a good friendship. Then I told him about you. And I said I'm not sure who the father is."

"Is that where you left the conversation? What did he want to do next?"

"Mason said he'll call me later to give me time to see if I'm really pregnant. I haven't seen a doctor yet, but there's no doubt because I've missed my period, and I'm always on time."

I stood up and took a couple of steps toward Chuck, who had stopped pacing. "I'm going to tell you exactly what I told Mason. I can raise my baby by myself. I will *not* have an abortion, but I also won't get married simply because I'm pregnant."

I paused to let it all sink in. I had determined not to cry. I didn't know what to do with the emotions I felt, so I showed almost none. From April 1967 to February 1968, my life had totally changed from that innocent virgin full of hope.

A few minutes of silence passed. "I have a decent job at General Telephone Company," I said. "I'll stay at my parents' home until I can afford my own place for me and the baby. I do love you, but I don't have to marry you."

I stopped and thought about how I would phrase my next sentence. "I have a list of major points I want you to think about. May I read it to you?"

"Sure, go ahead."

"If we do marry, you can never throw this in my face when you get angry with me, nor hold the circumstances of conception over this child's head. You can never tell the child that you only married his or her mom because she was pregnant. What I did was wrong, but this child is innocent and must know love no matter what. I'll never marry anyone who would treat me or my child like that.

"Next, there can never be any physical abuse. I'll never hit you, and you can never hit me or threaten to do so. If you do, we're done. I'll never tell you to get out of the house or the bedroom and you can't tell me to get out. It'll be *our* home and *our* bed. I want to stay home with the baby for the first year, and then I'll go back to work. You'd need to let me know if this would be a problem.

"You don't have to respond to any of this yet."

I reached out took his hand. "Now, do you see why you need some time to think? If you still want to marry me, then you'll have a child who may not be yours. I know I have hurt you. I'm so sorry. I've hurt myself, too. I make a vow to you. If we get married, no matter who the father is, the child will be ours, not Mason's, and my heart will be only yours."

"Alright, that's good. Who else knows about this?"

"Mom does."

"How does she feel about it?"

Once again, I covered Mom's wrongdoing and took the total blame. "She's heartbroken that I'm pregnant. She only wanted me to tell you about the pregnancy and not Mason. She doesn't know I've told you both. That's the only way I could be fair to Mason and you. She thinks you and I should get married."

I walked him to the door. "Please don't call me until you have made your decision. Hopefully, it will only take a few days. I'll respect your decision, either way it goes."

I got little sleep over the next few days and wasn't my usual joyful self at work.

Three days later Chuck called and came over to the house. We sat on my parents' couch, and he shared his heart. "Nothing has changed. I knew you were to be my wife from the first time we met when my cousin brought you over to introduce you to me and my sister at the dance. I told you God said to me before either of us said a word to each other, *This is your wife."* Chuck took my hand and stared into my eyes.

"All this other stuff certainly complicates things, but it doesn't change anything. As far as I'm concerned, the true father of a child is the one who raises it, protects it, provides for it, and loves it. That's what makes a man a father. It's not just because he had sex with the mother."

He paused took a deep breath and asked, "Diane, will you marry me? I love you, and I want to marry you because I love you. I know to be married is the right thing for us, even if we went about it the wrong way. Also, I'll never bring this up to you or to the child. I will never physically abuse you or our child. You can stay home with the baby until you want to go back to work. Did I cover you concerns on your list?"

"Yes, you did. And yes, I'll marry you. I love you, too."

We held each other's hands and waited for one of us to say something.

Chuck broke the silence. "We'll get married as soon as we can. No sense in waiting. We don't have much money so we can shop for some simple wedding bands next week."

"OK. I love you." I hugged him and gave him a passionate kiss.

Dad worked at his landscape gardening job in Beverly Hills during the week and stayed at one of the four-plex apartments my parents owned. Barbara stayed with Dad while she finished her last year of high school in L.A. Some weekends, Mom, Kenneth, and I went to

L.A. Other weekends, Dad and Barbara traveled to Perris to spend time with us. Occasionally on a weekend we visited my brother Johnny in juvenile detention camp in the San Bernardino Mountains.

Dad saw Chuck only three times before I told him Chuck and I were getting married. We had an awkward conversation. "Dad, I'm getting married in two weeks."

"Which guy do you want to marry? I've seen three guys around there the last several months. There's the guy in the Navy who drives out from Long Beach, and the guy in college up north that you knew from L.A. Then there's one who has a Firebird, who just got out of the Navy, and lives in Perris. I don't remember any of their names."

"Dad, I'm marrying the one who drives the Firebird. His name is Chuck. We've dated for three months."

"Oh good, I like him."

I couldn't bring myself to tell Dad I was pregnant *again*. I left that for Mom to do. I couldn't bear the thought of loosing relationship with him again.

Chuck told his parents around the breakfast table that he was getting married in two weeks. They had only seen me twice. It was unsettling for them. His mother took the news the hardest—especially after she learned I was pregnant.

March 23, 1968

March 23, was a beautiful typical sunny spring California Saturday. In the late morning I received a call from Mason.

"How are you doing, Diane? How are you feeling? Are you definitely pregnant?"

"Yes I am. Thanks for asking. I'm sleepy all the time. OK otherwise."

We had a moment of awkward silence. "I told you I can't let anything interfere with my schooling. What do you want me to do?"

I thought to myself, *Hold it together. Don't show any emotion and this conversation will be over quickly.*

"I don't want you to do anything. Mason, I told you I don't know who the father of the baby is, but you don't need to worry. I love Chuck, and he loves me, and we'll be married soon. He knows about you, but he will raise the child as his own—no matter who is the father."

"If you're absolutely positive this is what you want to do, then I'll respect your decision."

"Yes, I'm positive. Thank you for being a wonderful friend. I think you'll be an important person one day. That's all I have to say, so if you have nothing else to say, then good-bye."

I couldn't bring myself to tell Mason that Chuck and I were getting married only *seven* hours after our conversation. Our wedding at my parents' home was set for that evening with about twenty relatives, half of them children.

Chuck's Dad was a Baptist minister who formerly pastored a church in L.A. His protégé, who now pastored the church his father retired from, performed the wedding. I wore a dress I recently purchased for work. We bought each other $35 gold wedding bands. Our honeymoon consisted of one night in a motel in downtown Riverside, but we were happy. We stayed with my mom until our apartment was ready four days later. We moved in with nothing but a bed and a few kitchen items his mom gave us.

Throughout my pregnancy I prayed the baby would look like me or exactly like Chuck and nothing like Mason. A futile prayer because by the time I prayed this the baby was forming to be whoever he was. When our beautiful baby boy was born in November, he had his own unique features. So Chuck and I still were not sure who the father was. DNA tests had not been invented, but I'm not sure if we wanted to know. We were a family and we enjoyed our baby. Chuck was a good hands-on father.

A week after Curtis was born, around Thanksgiving, Mason called. I guess he had counted the months and wondered if he had a child or not. He phoned my parents' rental apartment in L.A., and my sister Barbara answered.

A week later, she told me about their conversation. "I told Mason you were married now and had a baby. He asked if it was a boy or a girl and I told him it was a boy. I wouldn't give him your number. I made it clear to him you didn't need any calls from an old boyfriend. He said he understood and wouldn't call again."

Mason deserved better closure than that empty conversation, or the way I left things back in March. I never told my sister the truth about Mason's involvement. I don't know if Mom told her. I always wished Barbara would've given me the choice to talk to him or not and given me his number.

My emotional healing concerning Curtis's conception was like peeling away layers of an onion. Layer upon layer was removed over the years as I used the Word of God as my Sword. I peeled back layers of shame, grief, deception, pain, guilt, and pride. The Holy Spirit consistently convicted my heart to take the Word of God and cut off another layer.

Each time I had an encounter with the Holy Spirit, I had a conversation with Chuck. "The Lord has dealt with me concerning Curtis's conception. He has healed me, and I want us all healed. Can we talk about it with Curtis now? I know we don't have the skills to walk him through this complex issue. I want us to find a counselor who can help us."

Chuck's response was always the same. "Absolutely not! Curtis struggles with his self-esteem enough already. To tell him we're not sure if I'm his biological father will devastate him. We won't be doing him any favor—we'll only hurt him. I told you I'd never bring that subject up, so you don't bring it up either."

God revealed some of Chuck's feelings to me. Although when I took my original trip to Northern California to see Mason at the time there had been no commitment between Chuck and me, Chuck had embraced me as his wife-to-be from the moment God spoke to him. Therefore, he felt betrayed because to talk about this subject was to uncover my secret affair in his mind. His pain went deeper than he ever wanted to examine. I was his wife and Curtis was his child. Period.

One of the times God healed me I was convicted to tell Chuck about Mom's involvement with our secret. That was extremely hard to do, but I knew whatever I kept hidden could not be totally healed.

"Chuck, Mom's been dead since 1977, but there's something I've not told you. She told me to have sex with you because she believed you were to be my husband and not Mason. She didn't want you to reject me in case I was pregnant. Can we talk about how we both feel about all this?"

"That's over and done with, so there's nothing to talk about."

The door to his heart never opened for me to tell him how much I respected him for his strength of character. I honored him for his obedience to God's voice to take me as his wife—even with my baggage. I believed that any counselor who heard the whole story would've commended Chuck for embracing Curtis and me.

So I kept the secret for far too long. That backfired on me many years later. The Enemy possessed control of what was hidden in darkness and brought it out when it could do damage to my relationship with my children.

June, 2001

Chuck, Carlton, and Kisha flew from Atlanta to California to visit Curtis in prison. On their visit Chuck finally came clean with Curtis. "Carlton is getting married and will start a family. There's been a secret your mom has kept from you and Carlton for years. Curtis, we're not exactly sure if I'm your biological father. Carlton, Curtis might be your half brother."

Carlton and Kisha told me later that everything went downhill from there.

Because Chuck's pain was never brought into the light of Jesus to be healed, his story was filled with pain, bitterness, unforgiveness, and falsehood. It painted an evil picture of me as a mom and wife. He insisted I never told him about the secret until after our twenty-four-year marriage fell apart. Our sons have always teased him about his inaccurate memory. This was no different, his story was filled with inaccuracies, except the stakes were higher—the acceptance and identity of our son.

The Enemy waits for the most opportune time to expose a hidden painful issue—when it can do the most damage. Unfortunately, Curtis and Carlton believed their dad's distorted story. Because of the years of silence from me, there was no other story to compare his with. They individually told me what Chuck said and asked me for my side of the story, but by then their emotions had already embraced Chuck's story.

To this day they have bitterness concerning this issue, and this has put a strain on our relationship. Chuck presented this to them as evidence women cannot be trusted. They were defiled by Chuck's bitterness.

Looking carefully lest anyone fall short of the grace of God; lest any root of bitterness springing up cause trouble, and by this many become defiled (Hebrews 12:15).

I pray God will show them how to open their hearts to be healed, and overcome any hardness of heart toward women.

I believe they will allow God into this painful place and destroy the root of bitterness. In Jesus name they will talk this through with the right person and not hold this against me or other women. I decree the Enemy shall no longer bind them to their pain. They shall be overcomers whom the Son sets free and be used of God to set other men free.

Chapter 11

My Search

But what does it (Deuteronomy 30:14) *say? "The word is near you; it is in your mouth and in your heart," that is, the message concerning faith that we proclaim: If you declare with your mouth, "Jesus is Lord," and believe in your heart that God raised Him from the dead, you will be saved. For it is with your heart that you believe and are justified, and it is with your mouth that you profess your faith and are saved* (Romans 10:8-10 NIV).

January, 1961

I never doubted God's existence. Early in my childhood we didn't attend church, but my parents told us God the Father, Jesus the Son, and the Holy Spirit formed the Godhead and they told us they know everything and hear every conversation. I hungered to know God personally.

My parents sent my siblings and me to Sunday school at the Presbyterian church across the street from our home when I entered the fifth grade. Miss McFarland my Sunday school teacher gave me my first Bible. I regularly read parts of it, but didn't understand much. No one instructed me, and I didn't think to ask for help.

At the age of eleven I intensified my search. On Sundays before my Sunday school class at the Presbyterian church I walked to mass at the

Catholic church with my neighbors, a family of ten. Around this same time period, Dad found a church home for our family at a Baptist church. So for a year on Sundays I attended early morning mass at the Catholic Church, sixth grade Sunday school class at the Presbyterian church, and 11:00 a.m. worship service with Dad and my siblings at the Baptist church. Mom only attended with us about three times a year because of work or because she was asleep after working at night. That was OK with us because she always had a hot meal waiting when we came home.

Each church experience was entirely different, which confused me. Eventually Dad decided the family should attend Sunday school also at the Baptist church so this became our church home.

During this time I noticed a spiritual hunger that stirred in my parents. I saw them individually read the Bible in their bedroom or at the kitchen table, but I don't remember if we read as a family. Soon Dad encouraged us to quote the scripture passages we learned in Sunday school at the dinner table every evening. It seems families are doing this less and less these days. That's sad.

My curiosity grew about spiritual things. *When I sinned, did an angel mark a check after my name on the big chalkboard in heaven? Did that angel erase the mark when I remembered to ask forgiveness? Does God love me because He has too or because He chooses to?*

As I reflect back, I know the Holy Spirit wooed me toward God. Because of this I decided I wanted to be a *good girl*, live for God, and tell others to live for Him. So three years after we joined the church, at fourteen, I became curious about how people, and especially women, served God. I took mental note of the women in my church. They served as Sunday school teachers and ushers. They also led the choir, led the youth group, and cooked meals. Although I noticed that women were not allowed to stand behind the pulpit, but spoke from a microphone used by the choir.

I decided I would serve God as a missionary and go to Outer Mongolia. I had no clue where Outer Mongolia was located, but it sounded like the ends of the earth. I heard there was a scripture that said God wanted people to go to the ends of the earth.

As new church members, Dad volunteered his children to be baptized in water. When it was my turn, Rev. Jones asked, "Do you believe Jesus is God?"

"Yes, I do." He baptized me, but I didn't get born-again.

I thought water baptism that was all there was to salvation—to *acknowledge* Jesus as God instead of other gods or no god. I received church membership, water baptism, choir membership, and a job assignment, but I still wasn't born-again. None of these things gave me access into heaven. As Rev. Jones taught about Jesus from the Gospels, the convicting power of the Holy Spirit caused tears to fill my eyes. As a teenager this made me uncomfortable. Crying was a sign of weakness in my family, so to release my emotions in church was out of the question. Whenever he talked about Jesus, I wanted to cry, so I distracted myself by passing gum and candy to the other teens with me on the back row. I joined the youth department and we were required to memorize every Psalm with twenty verses or less. This foundation kept me from joining a cult later in life.

I searched the television for programs about God. At home, in our upstairs den, I secretly watched Billy Graham, Oral Roberts, and Kathryn Kuhlman. Since I didn't understand biblical terminology, I mocked their words, and their personalities. Eventually I believed some of what they said and hoped the healing in people's bodies and lives were real. These programs spoke about and appeared to demonstrate the real possibility that Jesus could heal today like He did in the Bible.

The Enemy opposed the spiritual hunger in my family. He knew if Jesus was first, then we could influence others. He offered my parents pride-filled counterfeit spirituality and they followed his plans.

Dad made a bad decision when he joined the Masonic Lodge. He became distracted from his pursuit of God. The oaths he took are horrible confessions of death and destruction to the candidate and his family if you betray the lodge. He eventually became the potentate which is like the president of a Masonic chapter. Years later I had to renounce the influence of those words spoken over my life. I knew something broke off of me.

Mom became distracted with a bi-monthly Jehovah's Witness Bible study. Mom, Barbara, and I studied with a lady and her two daughters. They presented a Jesus who was not Deity, but a high archangel. We studied the book, *Paradise Lost,* for a year. This led to more spiritual confusion on my part.

Mom wasn't satisfied with the Jehovah's Witness Bible study. In her spiritual quest for answers, she turned to astrology, a fortune teller, and bought an Ouija Board. The spiritual climate in our home changed from spiritual hunger to demonic activity and confusion.

We moved in July, 1967 from Los Angeles to Perris, California shortly after my high school graduation. In March, 1968 Chuck and I married, and my spiritual hunger resurfaced. Thoughts haunted me. *Who is God? What about life and death? How can I pray for my husband and myself to be better people and have a good marriage? If God is in charge of everything, why are things so messed up? What is truth? Can human beings really know for sure what truth is?*

A co-worker asked if I wanted to study the Bible with her. I was hungry for truth. She was a Jehovah's Witness who was a sincere, lovely person. The God she and her partner presented to me was not a God of love or mercy, only rules. I needed practical answers from the Bible for everyday life, not readings about the end times from the books of Daniel and Revelation. They also told me I was *not* one of the chosen 144,000 worldwide listed in the book of the Revelation, therefore I could not receive communion. I searched the Bible to find the criteria to become "chosen" by God. This made no sense to me since I had received communion once a month for five years from ages eleven to sixteen at the Baptist church. All of this confusion without any clarity in sight prompted me to stop my search. Apparently, nobody had the answers to my questions.

August, 1968

The flu was going around like it did every year, but Mom's flu lingered. One night at bedtime, Dad called me. "I'm taking your mom to the hospital. She can't stop coughing and can't catch her breath. Meet us at the hospital."

Although Mom was not a smoker, she was diagnosed with lung cancer. She received aggressive radiation and then chemotherapy. Over the next two years, she lost all her hair, lost a lot of weight, and was sick most days. Countless times she seemed to be at death's door. Often her violent coughing made us think she would not catch her next breath.

Finally her doctor approached Dad and me. "Although one lung is destroyed, the other lung functions at almost eighty percent capacity. This is good. She can live with this. As far as we can tell, she is now cancer free."

We were ecstatic and called relatives and friends with the news. During her illness, Mom and Dad moved from Perris to Pomona. The shorter drive allowed Dad to be home every night to help take care of Mom, but my drive time doubled to an hour and a half roundtrip in good traffic and three hours roundtrip if she needed to see a doctor in Riverside.

August, 1971

About six months after Mom was declared cancer free, her legs became weak and at times gave way, causing her to fall. Gradually, she developed a limp and needed to use a walker. Her doctor gave her a series of tests with no conclusive diagnosis.

January, 1972

Mom's physician sent her to a neurologist. The neurologist gave us a hopeless report. Oddly, he seemed to be disgusted with Mom and offended with her doctor. "Lady, you've got to stop going from doctor to doctor! The cancer from your lungs is now eating away at the nerves in your spinal cord. There is nothing anyone can do for you! My examination shows you have no normal reflexes.

"You're dying! You'll probably be dead in a year. Go home and get your house in order. You're wasting your money, and wasting doctors' time! I'm angry at your doctor for sending you to me and I'm going to tell him he was giving you false hope!"

He stormed out of the room and left us sitting there in shock.

We stared at one another and then embraced each other, but there were no tears, only moans. Then, in a quiet solemn disgusted tone Mom spoke. "He's not God. He can't tell people when they're going to die. I'm *not* going to be dead in a year. He's wrong.

"Get the car, I'll get my walker and meet you out front. Look in my bag and get out the antidepressant pills. They're the ones I told you I would never take—but I need one now."

I took Mom home and fixed dinner for her and Dad. On my drive home the doctor's words pierced my mind like needles stabbing me. "There's nothing anyone can do . . . the cancer is eating the nerves . . . you're dying." *Mom was told she was cancer free. Now she's not. Who's going to give me antidepressant pills to put me to sleep so I won't hear his words? I have to get my kids from the babysitter, cook my family's dinner, and go on with life. Who do I talk to? Who do I yell at and blame for this tragedy? What do I say?* I could feel bitterness rising inside me. I wanted to scream at someone, but whom?

I arrived home before time to pick up my kids, so I ran to my bedroom, stomped around, and took my frustration out on God. I saw Him as part of the problem and yet part of the answer. "God, are *You* the cause of all the mess going on in mine and my family's life? Everything is going wrong. Big and little things are horrible. I'm only going to mention the big stuff to You.

"First, that mean doctor said Mom is dying with cancer of the spine. Second, every month Curtis has an asthma attack. Third, every other month I have a kidney and bladder infection. Fourth, Chuck received first and second degree burns at work thirteen months ago when I was seven months pregnant with Carlton. I could've been a widow at twenty one! The doctors had to take skin from his thigh and perform a skin graft on Chuck's back, they also had to rebuild his eardrum. Everything was successful, but that was horrible to go through.

"Life is miserable. I heard You're the One who causes everything. If You're the cause of these sicknesses and problems—*leave us alone.* If everything that happens in life is exactly what *You want* to happen, then You're doing a lousy job of taking care of your children! I think we would be better off without You! Why would you treat us this way when we are supposed to be Your creation. I would treat my kids better than You treat Yours."

I paused to wait for lightning to strike me or the roof to cave in. Nothing happened so I continued. "If You're *not* the problem and what I have been told is *not* the whole truth, then show me the truth and show it to me now! In fact, I'm not going to pray to You again until You can convince me that what I see and hear is the *real* truth. Everyone says they have the truth, but all I see is emptiness. I don't want religion, rules, or superstition, I want the real truth!"

I was afraid God would punish me for screaming at Him, but I was angry enough not to care. How could God love my family and try to destroy it at the same time? How could I trust Him when I didn't know whether He was trying to hurt me or heal me?

So I refused to pray. I was silent, but He wasn't. My life became flooded with the *truth* about Him—in undeniable ways. That's called grace by divine providence. I meant what I said when I told God to leave me and my family alone. But conversely, I actually opened the door to the grace of God, by saying, "If what I believe is not right, then I want to know the truth, and I want to know it now!" That was faith. I didn't know it was faith, but it was.

Six providential encounters led to me to acknowledge God had revealed the truth to me. They all happened from January to March, 1972.

First Providential Encounter

Chuck and I wanted to improve our lives as a couple. We decided to let go of all our friends who were unfaithful to their mates, those experimenting with marijuana, and those who had no vision for their future. We established a closer bond to some former neighbors and their friends who were all more than ten years older. They were on the fast track to wealth and all had education and successful careers. Among them were doctors, university professors, community leaders, and other career professionals. They called us "the babies" and invited us to some of their social functions. I was twenty-three and Chuck was twenty-six. We attended our first formal Black and White Ball held on the university campus.

As I got dressed the night of the ball I had many happy thoughts. *We've finally got it made. Our lives are going to change in the right direction. We're going to learn from these professional people how to have monetary success, be faithful to our spouse, and get well connected socially. Chuck and I always have said we will be millionaires by thirty-five.*

At the ball, I became concerned with the number of married men who flirted with me when my husband was at the bar or talking with someone else. I was appalled at the conversations I overheard as men talked to each other about how they took their mistresses on their business trips. After the ball we were invited to a home to hang out all night. They set up the reel to reel projector and their wives left the room.

"Diane, do you want to go to the bedroom with us?" the women asked.

"No thanks, I want to see the movie."

I thought we were going to watch family vacation films and the women wanted to visit with one another instead. Suddenly hard-core pornography glared in my face. Chuck was passed out drunk on the couch with his head on my shoulder. I pushed his head to wake him up, but he didn't budge.

I jumped up and Chuck's head hit the couch, still he didn't wake up. "I don't want to see this! I've got to go right now! Help me get Chuck in the car!"

Two men lifted Chuck's 6'4" frame from the couch and dragged him to our car as they laughed at my naïveté and embarrassment. Once in the car tears ran down my face as I drove home with my drunken husband. My head swam with thoughts I couldn't shut off.

Where are the people who want to do right? I thought they were our key to a better life. These people are no better than our other friends. Instead of having an affair at the motel down the street, they get on a plane and have an affair in Mexico at a fancy hotel. More money, more education, and a successful career hasn't made them better people. They're empty and searching, too, like the rest of us. There's nothing that group can teach me about life. I'm done with them, forever!

I didn't know it, but God opened my eyes that night. I saw my worldly search for truth, money, education, and connections could lead me to a dead end.

Second Providential Encounter

While living in our apartment in Perris, California, Chuck and I agreed to buy a home in Riverside before we had our second child. He was in construction and had no medical insurance, so I applied exclusively for jobs with medical benefits. In July, 1969, when Curtis was eight months old I started work as a clerk typist at the Riverside public library. After our medical benefits were secured it took me three more months to get the nerve to stop my birth control pills. We figured we would be pregnant in a few months so we had time to prepare for our next child. To my astonishment I became pregnant the same week. By this time I figured I must have the reproductive genes of a rabbit.

We saved a portion of my salary for the down payment on our home and planned to continue saving as I worked to the end of my seventh month. But at the end of my third month of pregnancy my supervisor called me into his office.

"Diane, you're a good employee and I appreciate your work. As you know you've used up all your sick leave and although you show up for work we've sent you home a few times because you were too sick to stay. On other occasions even though you've stayed to the end of the day you've had too much pain to complete your work. I have your doctor's notes but I'm concerned because you don't seem to be getting any better. You've told me the doctor said you're suffering from chronic kidney infections and it's complicated by your pregnancy. This has been going on for three months.

"You can't miss any more days from work without it affecting your next evaluation. As you know the City of Riverside's employee pregnancy policy is that you must resign when you reach seven and a half months pregnancy, anyway. I suggest you resign now while you still have a good work record and we can give you a good reference. If you miss many more days I may be asked to fire you and neither of us wants that. Go home and get well and take care of that son of yours."

Around the time I quit the library my mom, who had been told she was cancer free, developed a limp and needed more doctor's care. So I became her caregiver.

Before I got pregnant Chuck and I joined a multilevel marketing business. Our plan, if we became successful, was for me to stay home after our second child and develop a home-based business. This would also free more time to help my mom.

We started off with a bang! In three months we recruited six couples in our "down-line." We were at meetings most nights and I was on the phone or delivering product daily. We were excited about our small commission checks in addition to our product sales.

We bought a home in a new subdivision in Riverside with many other young couples. Across the street was a couple our age, Gary and Judy, who were also expecting their second child. We quickly discovered they belonged to the same multilevel marking business and had the same desire for her to be a stay-at-home mom with a home-based business.

One-by-one our down-line couples dropped out as quickly as they had joined us. Chuck was recovering from work related injuries and I was home with our new baby, Carlton. So it was next to impossible for us to recruit. Our neighbors lost their down-line people also. Gary and Chuck lost interest in the business, but Judy and I were determined to be successful. When our babies were a few months old we came up with a plan to build our businesses.

Twice a month Judy and I sold our products door-to-door to build our customer base. Then once a month our husbands babysat as we sought to gain down-line recruits in the evenings. On one of these recruitment evenings in February, 1972, around 10:00 p.m., after two hours at three department stores with no success, we made the Denny's Restaurant near our homes our last target. We wanted to recruit a waitress or a business person.

Judy wore a dress that reminded me of *Little House on the Prairie.* I wore a puffy big hair wig, red, white, and blue stripped gaucho pants, and laced up white go-go boots like Cher on *The Sonny and Cher Comedy Show.* We were an unforgettable pair.

We laughed and talked with our waitress and then Judy gave our bait line to her, but she didn't bite. We stared into our glasses as we sipped on our shakes in silent disappointment over our unsuccessful evening efforts. We put our money and tip on the table and stood to leave. The older of the two men in a business suit at the adjacent booth stopped us. "You ladies came in smiling. Now you're leaving with frowns on your faces. Why so sad?"

I quickly changed my expression to a pleasant smile. "We won't be sad if you give us your business card. My friend and I are in the same business, and we are offering opportunities for success. One of us would love to share with you our business opportunity."

"I am certainly curious. Here's my business card. Be sure and give me a call."

I took his card. "Thank you. You'll hear from one of us soon."

We were anxious to see what kind of business he was in. We stood next to my car under the street light and giggled at each other with delight. And then we both stared at his card, and then looked at each with our mouths wide open in shock. His card identified him as Pastor Rob and it listed a church name.

I shoved the card at Judy. "Here, I don't want to talk to any pastor!"

She withdrew her hands by putting them behind her and refused to take the card. "I don't either. Remember our agreement is whoever talks to the person gets to recruit them. You opened your mouth, so you have to call him."

"OK. I'll make an appointment with him. In fact, I'll take my directors who can win anyone. If he's not interested in the business, then I'm not interested in him. It'll do no good for him to invite us to church because my directors are Jewish and I'm not interested."

The next week my directors and I met with Pastor Rob. He was familiar with the products and used them regularly. Sadly, he wasn't interested in being recruited. Just as I suspected, he invited us to his church. My directors told him they were Jewish and politely declined his offer. I politely said I was not interested. I walked away thinking I would never see him again.

Third Providential Encounter

Judy was a serious person who showed little emotion. I was hyper and exactly the opposite. A week after our evening at Denny's Judy had a providential encounter that spilled over into my life.

We went door-to-door on an unfamiliar street to do our product demonstrations to find potential customers. We pushed our strollers with one hand, held our toddlers hand with the other, and stored our products under the strollers. She took one side of the street and I took the other. Each time we walked home we shared our successes. On this particular day we each made two sales and gained at least one new regular customer.

Judy expressed one of her sales was to a minister's wife. "The lady bought two products and while she wrote her check for them I noticed a book about the baptism of the Holy Spirit on her table," she said. "So I said, 'I see you're Christians,' I pointed at the book. You'll never guess what she said next."

"What'd she say?"

"She said her husband was the author of the book! Imagine that! After we talked a bit, she asked if they could come over and teach me what the book says about the Holy Spirit."

"What'd you tell her?" I asked.

"I made an appointment for a couple days from now. Do you want to come?"

"No, I don't. You be careful. I'll babysit your kids so you can talk to them in peace."

Two days later, *after* Judy's appointment with the minister and his wife, she uncharacteristically bounced through my door. She was talking so fast I had to slow her down. "Diane, Jesus loves you, and Jesus loves me! I feel His love in my heart more than I ever have! Give me the card from the pastor we met two weeks ago."

I opened my kitchen drawer, pulled out the card, and handed it to her. "Why do you need it?"

"The minister, Rev. Joe Jordan, said he holds monthly healing meetings at that pastor's church. He also suggested I make that my home church. That's amazing! We just met the pastor two weeks ago at Denny's. That's neeto! Hey, you want to go to church with me this Sunday?"

"No, thanks. You're talking so fast and smiling so much, you're making me nervous. Did those ministers put a whammy on you?"

"I don't know what you're talking about. All I know is although I received Christ when I was a kid at the Baptist Church I grew up in, I surrendered my life *totally* to Jesus today! He loves me! They taught me how to pray in a new prayer language.

"Diane, we've known each other a year, and the whole time I've told you about my shoulder trouble how painful and stiff it was and it affected my back. Well, Rev. Joe and Barbara prayed for me and my shoulder was healed on the spot. Look!" She started swinging her arm around in my kitchen.

"My shoulder doesn't hurt anymore! The doctor had said it would never get better. Rev. Joe elevated my arms and put them side-by-side to measure them and one was shorter than the other. He prayed and the short one grew past the other one then came back into perfect alignment. Wow! He said these things happen at his healing meetings at that pastor's church all the time!" She grabbed my arm and shook it.

I snatched my arm from her and jumped back in shock. "I don't know what they've done to you, but whatever it is, it's driving you crazy. So if you want to go crazy, then do it on your *own* property. Here are your kids. I'll talk to you later when you are not under some spell."

"No, I'm OK. I'm just excited. My shoulder is healed, and now I can pray to God stuff I didn't even know I needed to pray about and . . ."

"Judy, go home!" I opened the door and escorted her and the kids out.

I fell back against the door and slapped both my hands on my forehead. *I know she doesn't have any reason to lie to me. I know her arm is noticeably better, but how can I wrap my mind around what just happened? Why is she so weird?*

Fourth Providential Encounter

The next couple of days Judy canvassed the neighborhood to show anyone who would watch her swing her arm and tell them she was healed. She'd end with announcing that Jesus loved them. We all whispered to each other about the change in her and were frightened by it.

One day she asked me, "Diane, I'm inviting everyone I know to come to my house this Thursday night to watch a video of Rev. Joe Jordan. His assistant, Rev. Bob will show the video. Promise me you'll come."

"I'll come as long as this is the only time you ask me to something like this."

Only two of us showed up. The other person was an elderly lady from her former neighborhood. We watched the video and afterward Rev. Bob, asked if we had any questions or wanted prayer for anything. The older lady asked a couple of questions, and he graciously showed her a couple of scripture passages. He prayed for her then she left.

"I'm going to go now, thank you," I said.

"Diane, you are always full of questions, so ask Rev. Bob your questions," Judy said as she pointed at me.

"He doesn't want to hear my questions. No one has ever answered my questions about God." I said as I folded my arms across my chest in disgust. "They say they have the truth, but they don't. They give the same four scriptures to me no matter what question I ask. Well, that doesn't fly where I'm concerned. I'm searching for real truth no a pacifier!"

"I'll do my best to show you the truth and show you Scripture to back up what I'm saying," Rev. Bob said. "If it's not in the Bible, then it isn't truth. In John 14:6, Jesus said, '*I am the way, the truth, and the life. No one comes to the Father except through Me.*'"

I poured out my bitterness toward God, my disappointment with people, and my frustration at life, and how hard it's been to find the truth. He listened and was gracious with his responses.

Finally he said, "Let me show you how loving God is. Rev. Joe and I had a healing meeting at a church recently, and a teenage girl came forward for prayer. She was born with only the first joint of her little finger on her right hand. We prayed, and before the meeting was over the second joint had grown out, and the finger was still growing. What do you think of that?"

"I think that's good. But I would want to see her finger and feel it before you prayed. Then I want to watch as you pray. Then six months later I want to feel her finger to see if the healing is still intact."

He smiled. "You sound like doubting Thomas who said he would not believe Jesus was raised from the dead unless he saw and felt him for himself. Do you mind if I call you Doubting Diane?"

I smiled back at him. "Sure you can call me what you like. I believe God created the body so I'm sure He can fix what He made, but I don't want to be fooled by anyone. Years ago on television I watched Oral Roberts and Kathryn Kuhlman, and some people were undeniably healed, I could tell. But I also think they paid others to bring crutches onstage so they could throw them away hoping to convince the audience that they were healed. But it was probably the power of suggestion, like mob psychology."

"How can *you* be the judge of what is a real healing and what is a fake?" he said. "Why don't you come to our next healing service with

Rev. Joe? He prayed for your friend Judy, and you know her healing is real. Judy told me you met Pastor Rob from the church that hosts our local meetings."

"Yeah, Judy's healing is real. Her shoulder has bothered her the whole year I've known her. OK. I'll try to come. Thanks for your time."

I couldn't sleep that night because of the conviction of the Holy Spirit and my mind which didn't want to believe the things he said. Finally I said to myself *Why would he come over to her house just to lie to me? He had nothing to gain. What if everything He said is true, what should I do with that information?*

On Saturday Judy convinced Chuck and me to take our children to church to learn about God. Although we had never heard of an Assemblies of God church, we took our children on Sunday. It was filled with people in their sixties and seventies with only two young couples with preschool children. The music was nice but boring; the preaching was clear but monotone so that made it boring also. It was good the people were friendly. There was around one hundred and fifty people.

It felt awkward, and at the same time good to be in church. After we returned home, Chuck and I discussed our need to raise our children to know God. We decided we would definitely go to church regularly, but we wanted a lively Baptist church with more young people our age for our social needs.

Fifth Providential Encounter

Two weeks after we attended his Assemblies of God church Pastor Rob knocked on our door on Friday night.

"I hope I'm not disturbing you," he said. "I remembered you were neighbors of Gary and Judy. I just left their home, but they weren't there. I left a note on their door. I asked their neighbor if they knew where you lived, and they directed me to your home. May I come in? I have something on my heart to share with you."

Our visit was uncomfortable, at least for me, but pleasant. He said to express to him any questions we had. We asked him about his church, what he believed about the Bible, and why there were only two young couples. Although the average age was sixty-five to seventy to our surprise he said he was only thirty-five and his wife was twenty-nine. He told us he was prematurely gray. He didn't mention our multilevel business encounter and neither did I.

"I've been in Riverside and pastored this church for one year. I want vibrant young families like yours. Please come at least for a month or two and consider becoming part of us. Gary and Judy and you two are the type of people I've asked God to send to our church and help us grow."

We promised to come for at least a couple more visits.

Sixth Providential Encounter

The following Sunday after Pastor Rob's visit I couldn't find my glasses anywhere and this was making us late. So I grabbed my prescription shades as we grabbed our children and ran out the door. We sat on the last row. I wore a fluffy wig and a bright orange and white mini-dress. To be modest I had hot pants on under the dress, in case I needed to bend over to pick up my kids.

As the worship service began, I felt that same conviction I experienced as a kid when I felt I would cry in church. I held back the tears and didn't cry. Near the close of the service I felt compelled to answer Pastor Rob's invitation to come forward for prayer, but I didn't know what kind of prayer. So I decided to ask for prayer for my children who were extremely active and strong-willed.

When I reached the front he directed me toward his wife Sister Ann, who stood in front of the first pew. She asked me to kneel next to her. I was thankful for my hot pants. She turned in her Bible to Romans 8:8-10 and asked me to repeat the scripture with her in a prayer of salvation. Because I had been baptized in water at thirteen and sang in the choir until sixteen, I thought I was already "saved" so I said, "I don't know about your salvation prayer, all I know is I want God to help me raise my kids. I don't want them to become juvenile delinquents or end up in jail like my brother.

"I've talked to God all my life and He's answered my prayers, but if you think praying *your* prayer will get *God* to do what I want Him to do, then I'll pray *your* prayer." I wondered why she didn't ask me what I wanted her to pray about. Weeks later as I heard a few similar alter calls I understood the invitation was for salvation not general prayer requests.

She answered, "This prayer will work. The criterion is for you to mean it from your heart. Pray these words out loud after me as I lead you in the scripture that tells us how to become born-again." She opened her Bible and showed me Romans 10:8-10: *"The word is near you, in your mouth and in your heart . . . that if you confess with your mouth the Lord Jesus and believe in your heart that God has raised Him from the dead, you will be saved. For with the heart one believes unto righteousness, and with the mouth confession is made unto salvation."*

I bowed my head in reverence and followed her as she prayed. "Father God, I come to You in the name of Your Son Jesus. I believe Jesus died on the cross and shed His blood for me. Forgive me of my sins and cleanse me by the blood of Jesus. I renounce every work of Satan in my life. I submit my pride, rebellion, and fear to You, Lord. I believe in my heart and confess with my mouth that Jesus Christ is God and was raised from the dead for me as it says in Romans 10:8-10. I believe Jesus is seated in heaven next to You and my salvation is found in no other name but the name of Christ as the Bible says in Acts 4:12."

I believe this in my heart and I said this with my mouth like the Bible says. Am I supposed to feel something? I feel nothing. I felt like a parrot repeating sounds. Although I was sincere, I felt no emotions. I lifted my head and stared at Sister Ann.

She paused, and then continued. "Repeat this conclusion please. I receive You Jesus as my Lord and Savior. You gave Your life for me, now I give my life to You. I give my children to You also. I'm now born-again, Amen." I repeated after her and received the grace to be saved because my faith was real and my feelings had nothing to do with my faith.

Sister Ann grabbed me and hugged me. "Praise the Lord! You're born-again!"

OK. Why is she hugging me? She didn't ask permission to touch me. My family doesn't even hug me.

People in the church wanted to hug me as I left. This was a strange group of old people.

To my surprise, as I picked up the Bible that week and read it, I understood it. I listened as Pastor Rob gave the invitation for salvation to others over the next two months. I realized I truly had become born-again. As a teenager I was a God-fearing religious, baptized in water, church attending choir member. But I wasn't born-again and did not have the Holy Spirit resident within me.

The spiritual confusion left my mind as I received the assurance of my salvation, just as it says in Romans 8:16: *The Spirit Himself bears witness with our spirit that we are children of God.* I knew, that I knew, that I knew, that Jesus was the truth.

I embraced the inward knowing that I belonged to God and He belonged to me. The more I surrendered my life to Christ the less passion I had for my multilevel marketing business. I finally realized it was in my life for a season and God used it twice to bring about His providential encounters.

The Holy Spirit confirmed to my spirit that an authentic relationship with Jesus was what I had searched for. I knew I found the truth, and my search was over.

One year later, God had a surprise for me that altered the trajectory of my life.

PART IV

Ministry

Chapter 12

The Calling

Cry aloud, spare not; Lift up your voice like a trumpet;
Tell My people their transgression, And the house of Jacob
their sins (Isaiah 58:1).

April, 1973

Chuck and I sat wide-eyed in a Sunday evening service as we watched Prophet Flynn prophesy to individuals in our home church congregation. This was one year after I was born-again. We were familiar with a person who would speak what God wanted to say to someone. Chuck grew up with his father giving him or someone else what the Holy Spirit had spoken to him in prayer. My mother often said God revealed something to her that was about to happen and often it did.

This was different. Person after person received what God had spoken. We'd never seen this kind of ministry before. Chuck leaned over to me and whispered, "Diane, I asked God if Prophet Flynn's words are accurate could he please speak to us. We need God to give us some direction about our callings."

As soon as the last word left Chuck's lips, Prophet Flynn pointed our way. "I want this young couple to come up here, please. God has given me something for you both."

He turned toward Chuck. "You are called to be a prophet, a pastor, and a teacher who takes difficult passages of God's Word and breaks it down to feed God's people."

Chuck went down under the power of God on his back and was out cold for several minutes. God dealt deeply with Chuck's willingness to surrender to the call of God on his life to preach, pastor, and become a prophet, while he was on the floor.

I stood in amazement as I watched what happened to my husband. Prophet Flynn turned in my direction. For a moment he was quiet, I assumed he was listening to God speak to him about me. Then he put one hand lightly on my forehead and the other at the nape of the back of my neck. His voice was deep and sounded authoritative as he prophesied to me. "Sister, God says you are to go and witness for Him. Go and *preach*, and He'll preach through you. Go and believe the Word, and the Word will flow through you.

"God has given you the gifts of healings mentioned in 1 Corinthians 12:9 and 28. These gifts will cause miracles to flow through your words and through your hands. People will receive emotional and physical healings. Use this power in Jesus' name and you'll experience the power of the Most High God. Amen, Sister."

> *And to another faith by the same Spirit, to another gifts of healings by the same Spirit to another working of miracles, to another prophecy, to another discerning of spirits, to another different kinds of tongues, to another interpretation of tongues. . . . And God has appointed these in the church: first apostles, second prophets, third teachers, after that miracles, then gifts of healings, helps, administrations, varieties of tongues (1 Corinthians 12:9-10, 28).*

The power of God picked me up a few inches off the floor (a week later a lady confirmed to me that she saw my feet dangling—she said they didn't touch the carpet until he was done speaking). He removed his hands, and I slid to the floor.

A few months later, Dr. Dick Mills came to our church to prophesy, and he had a message for me as well. "God has given you a keen discernment of spirits. You can discern whether God or the Enemy is influencing a person. God will use you to warn people and expose the Enemy's plans. Don't judge people or situations and don't come to a conclusion about a person or circumstances without consulting the Holy Spirit first. Many times the Holy Spirit speaks to you, and you ignore that inward 'impression.' Don't ignore what you sense anymore. You are very sensitive to the Holy Spirit. Ask Him if He wants to show or tell you something about a situation or a person."

Prior to this day I had a calloused heart because of the pain I had stuffed down. In many areas my emotions were locked up. I didn't know how to surrender my emotions to Christ, but right then I understood that God touched my life in a deep way. I believe He softened my hardened heart that day, and unlocked my emotions to allow me to feel good or bad emotions deeper than I had in years. The first thing I felt was His love for me. For the first time I realized God has an individual love and purpose for *every* "whosoever." *God has something He wants me to do. He has purpose for my life. Wow!*

John 3:16 became a reality to me: *For God so loved the world that He gave His only begotten Son, that whoever believes in Him should not perish but have everlasting life.*

I decided I wanted to do His will no matter what it took, but I needed clarification. Chuck's dad was a Baptist minister so I figured Chuck knew more than I did. "I didn't think God had a purpose for my life. What does God mean when He said, "He will preach through me?" And what kind of healing are gifts of healings? I read the scriptures several times, but I don't see an explanation."

"I've known God had a purpose for my life since I was eight years old when God gave me a dream," Chuck said. "In the dream I joined the military, and as you know I completed that part of the dream by serving in the Navy for four years. Then, in the dream when I left the military, I became a Bible teacher and pastor. I traveled places as I taught the Word. When I woke up, I went into the kitchen and said to my parents,

'If you think I'm going to preach and pastor a church, then you're crazy! I don't want to teach the Bible!' They asked me why I said that, and I told them about the dream. They looked at each other and smiled.

"They explained that this was my purpose and God would lead me to do His will. At eight I had the assurance that God had a purpose for my life. I don't know how to help you though with your questions, so make an appointment with pastor to get more understanding."

When I met with the pastor, I was full of questions. "Pastor Rob, when God spoke to me through Prophet Flynn, He said for me to *preach* and God would *preach* through me. He said believe the Word and the Word will flow through me. What does that mean? Am I supposed to preach like you behind a pulpit and tell what the scriptures mean?"

Pastor Rob smiled. "Yes, that's exactly what it means. God has placed a *calling* on your life for you to become a minister. To be called of God means you have an invitation to a specific thing God created you to do—a purpose. He has called you to tell others His will and His Word."

"That's really neat! To think God has a purpose for me excites me!"

"We belong to the Assemblies of God denomination, and A/G believes God calls women as well as men to minster and preach His Word," he said. "There are women in the Bible who led churches and groups of people. Dr. Flynn is a prophet who speaks on God's behalf. The Bible mentions many prophetesses who spoke on God's behalf: Miriam, Deborah, Huldah, Anna, and the Prophet Isaiah's wife. Lydia was a successful business woman who helped the Apostle Paul start and oversee the church that met in her home in Philippi. Priscilla taught the Word alongside her husband Aquila.

"I'm going to give you a quick Bible study. There were two ladies who were teachers and possibly pastors in 2 John, one is referred to as the Elect Lady, the other is simply called 'your sister' and 'her children.' We know God's not talking about two natural sisters and their five children because they are being given instructions for leaders. Also you need to know the Bible interprets itself. Jesus referred to His disciples and Israel as 'children.'

He raised his eyebrows and with an excitement in his voice said, "Diane, the Apostle Paul by the Holy Spirit wrote 1st John through 3rd John."

Pastor Rob turned his Bible around and slid it across his desk while flipping the pages he said, "Look here in 1st John and other places he calls those whom God has given him to disciple as 'my little children.' The terminology in 1st and 2nd John is consistent. So we can see these women's 'children' are those God has given them spiritual oversight and are their disciples."

"I mentioned Deborah in the book of Judges counseled men and women, was a prophetess and judge over the whole nation of Israel."

I grew even more excited. "Oh boy! That's great! I'll study the women in the Bible. Thank you for helping me to understand. You've opened my eyes to things I have never seen before. But Pastor, since the A/Gs believe women can be called to preach, how come I've been here over a year and I've never seen a woman preacher? Sister Ann, your wife, and the wives of the missionaries have stood behind the pulpit to sing, or give testimonies, but have never taught the Bible.

"When we first started attending this church, Chuck used to say, 'In my dad's church, the women stood at the soloist's microphone. They *never* stood behind the pulpit. It bothers me when Pastor Rob invites Sister Ann to stand behind the pulpit.' He was angry about that issue. But I think Chuck's getting over it now, he hasn't complained about women in the pulpit for more than two months!

"Pastor, will I ever see a woman preach here?"

"Oh, we haven't taken the opportunity to have a woman preacher yet, but we will."

"Pastor Rob, the other thing God said to me was He had given me the gifts of healings—for emotional and physical healings. What does that mean?"

"These are different categories of healings," he said. "Some have a special gift for those who are hurting emotionally. This may be the gift He's saying you have. God gives whatever gifts He chooses. He administrates our callings. He calls some to become specialists in certain areas of healing rather than general practitioners. Some may have lots of people with back trouble get healed and not as much healing in other areas. Some may see deaf healed."

Pastor Rob's clarification helped me have the determination to grow and fulfill God's call. I wanted an education, but I had small children and served as a caregiver for Mom. So Chuck and I enrolled in the Assemblies of God correspondence course called Berean School of the Bible. We studied together most evenings. I discovered my Bible stories were mixed up. For instance, I thought David the shepherd boy and David the king were two different guys named David. And I had no clue why four different people wrote about Jesus' time here on earth called the Gospels. I had a lot to learn and Chuck was a wonderful mentor.

Prophet Flynn was a frequent guest speaker at our church. The third time I saw him I wanted to know his secret about how to help people hear from God. I knew my life was changed in a significant way through his ministry and I was hungry to touch people the way he did. After the meeting, I trembled as I approached him. "Dr. Flynn, may I ask you a question, please?"

"Sure I'll be glad to answer it if I can," he said.

I spoke a little louder over all the talking around us. "I want God to use me to touch people's lives in a permanent way like you do. My life was changed forever through the words God gave you to speak to me. What's your secret?" *This is probably one of the best kept secrets in the world. Only a few people probably know the answer, and here is one of them standing in front of me. One of God's generals in the faith is about to share with me what he may have only told a few people in the world.* As my head swelled with pride, I leaned closer so I could hear clearly every word.

He paused, and then let out a robust laugh. "Oh Sister, that's an easy one. Love the Lord with everything in you and don't try to be like anyone else. Just be yourself in the Lord. That's it, be yourself in the Lord. God bless you."

As he walked away, I felt slighted. I realize now that I was immature in the faith and my emotions, but I didn't know that at the time. The next day as I sat on my couch and talked to the Lord I got even angrier.

What a brush-off. He knew the secret to God's power and didn't want to tell me. I guess, if I were a man, he would have given me a better answer and taken me more seriously. Man or woman, his answer didn't make sense. How can I "be myself" when I don't like myself and I don't know myself?

Last week Pastor Rob taught on fears, and I had every fear he mentioned—fear of man, fear of success, fear of failure, fear of death, fear of rejection, and more. God revealed to me I also have rebellion that needs to be destroyed. How can I be "myself in the Lord" with all this junk?

I sensed the Holy Spirit was grieved with my response of self-pity instead of faith. So a few days later I repented. "Father, forgive me. I didn't choose to allow You to show me who I am and how to be myself in the Lord. Holy Spirit, You're my teacher. Please teach me who the Father wants me to be."

As I matured, I realized Prophet Flynn's advice was good—just what I needed to search for my identity in the Bible. I had such a deep fear of rejection and I allowed others to shape who they thought I should be. Every few months I chose to conquer a new fear and defeat it. I didn't stop until the Holy Spirit revealed I could move to the next fear. Also every few months I chose to conquer another root of rebellion in me.

My key verse to jump start my new identity came as I realized this passage is how Jesus announced His identity in Luke 4 by reading Isaiah 61:1-2 in the synagogue: *"The Spirit of the Lord GOD is upon Me, Because the LORD has anointed Me To preach good tidings to the poor; He has sent Me to heal the brokenhearted, To proclaim liberty to the captives, And the opening of the prison to those who are bound; To proclaim the acceptable year of the LORD, And the day of vengeance of our God; To comfort all who mourn."*

As I quoted the passage, I imagined myself doing the works of Jesus. I saw myself preaching the gospel to the financially, physically, and emotionally poor. Casting out demons, healing the sick, setting the captives free, and recovering the sight of the emotionally, spiritually, and physically blind.

As time went by, people gradually recognized the anointing on my life and dedication to the Word of God. Invitations to speak at home

Bible studies started coming. I joined Women's Aglow as a hostess to learn how to serve women and work behind the scenes. In my mid-twenties, I joined two Lutheran senior citizens who ministered one Sunday afternoon a month at the Riverside County Jail. I did this for around three years. This was great training. I became a speaker at Aglow meetings, seminars, churches, and women's retreats.

Coming up with a good title for my messages was difficult for me. So to eliminate stress for the first three years all my messages had the same great title: *Steps to Maturity*. I figured everything I taught was leading us to a step toward our maturity. Finally, the Holy Spirit put pressure on me to take my own step to maturity and title my messages.

I asked the Lord to show me what He had called me to do. The passage that stood out to me was from Isaiah 58:1: *Cry aloud, spare not; Lift up your voice like a trumpet; Tell My people their transgression, And the house of Jacob their sins.*

This was the core of what I was called to preach. This meant if I preach on peace, the first thing I'll say is to look for the sins that rob us of our peace. My title might be *7 Things That Rob You of Peace*. Point number one would be unforgiveness, point number two might be fear, and so on. I would not speak on the sweet benefits of peace and everyone leave peaceful. My message will send you home with a challenge and an assignment of self discovery and repentance to help you get rid of the enemies of peace.

At first, Chuck was excited about the call of God for my life, and was my biggest supporter. I encouraged and supported him as he taught Bible studies at church to the youth, and he did the same for me as I ministered at home Bible studies and women's meetings. God used him to petition Southern California College (SCC), now Vanguard in Costa Mesa, to allow our church to become a satellite campus for the school so he could work full-time and attend the Assemblies of God Bible College. Permission was granted for a satellite campus in Riverside. After my correspondence courses I attended the Bible School. We studied for tests together.

On the other hand, I noticed Chuck withdrew his support concerning listening to the tapes from my speaking engagements. I brought home the cassettes of my teachings and asked him to listen and give me feedback. After he told me he would get to it when he had time, I noticed my cassettes sat on his desk, and he never chose to listen. I was deeply disappointed. This continued for years.

He supported me with my message preparation as I shared my points with him. He shared additional Scriptures and gave me spiritual insight. We prayed together before either of us spoke. But he couldn't bring himself to listen to my messages. As assistant pastor and Christian education director he asked me to leave teaching children's church and teach an adult Sunday school class, I realized Chuck believed in me and my gifts and knew God wanted to use me.

We were invited by Rev. Ev to speak at a four-day conference in Oakland, California in 1982. Rev. Ev noticed when I spoke, Chuck stayed in the break room of the church in deep discussion with a fellow minister. After the second day, she left my session and approached Chuck. "Chuck, your wife is highly anointed. Have you *ever* listened to her preach?"

"No, I haven't. Honestly, I never wanted a minister for a wife."

"I can understand how you feel, but who she becomes is not for you to judge. That's God's choice, not yours or hers. Maybe Diane never thought she would be married to a minister, either. I suggest you start listening to her. Start today." He followed her to the sanctuary where I was speaking.

Once again he became my biggest supporter. A year later, Rev. Don had a daily radio program and invited us to be his guests. Chuck declined but I accepted. After doing a week of broadcasts, he said he received more responses from that week than any other time. Rev. Don asked mutual friends to pledge a small amount monthly for six months for me to have my own program. He received sufficient pledges before he ever told me about it. He offered his equipment and said he would help me.

I made arrangements with the radio station for a time slot that would soon be available. Chuck and I went to Rev. Don's studio and I recorded half of a program. Suddenly, I was overcome with a tormenting fear and I burst into tears.

"I can't do this! I'm going to say something wrong and someone's life is going to be messed up forever because of me!" I took off the headphones, grabbed my notes and purse, apologized to Rev. Don, and got in our car.

When Chuck and I arrived home I ran into our bedroom and sat on the floor with my back resting against our bed. He sat down on the floor next to me and let me finish crying. "Chuck, I prayed for years that God would give *you* a radio program. You're a good teacher, better than a lot of the one's I hear. I was never thinking He would tell me to do it. I'm afraid."

"I rarely listen to the radio. It's not something I enjoy like you do. Diane, you have the confidence to speak at retreats, churches, seminars, and Aglow meetings, so how is this different? The only difference is that you can't see your audience."

"You're right. My mind was tormented this whole week because it's the next step in my ministry and I allowed the Enemy access to my insecurities. I realize that now. Let's pray and then I'll call Rev. Don and ask if I can come back in today and finish my programs."

I finished two weeks' worth of programs before we left the studio later that afternoon.

In ministry, there are always various persecutions against being a woman leader. I've had visitors walk out of the church when they recognized a woman was going to teach. I could hear them say to each other, "The preacher is a woman, let's leave." Sometimes, when I officiate at a wedding or funeral, family members refuse to attend. My publicity has been changed to call me an evangelist, missionary, or no title so I could speak and not be referred to as being a pastor.

There's no worries, mate, because I will share the same word and the anointing is the same whether I'm allowed in the pulpit or not, or whether I am referred to by a title or not. In our early days of pastoring, our new members would approach me or Pastor Chuck and say, "We don't want a pastor's wife who preaches. We are only familiar with a pastor's wife who sings, plays the piano, teaches kids, or cooks." Our response was "It's certainly fun breaking tradition, isn't it?"

I cooked often because hospitality is a part of my calling also. I entertained groups or families in our home almost every week. But singing or playing an instrument was not my calling.

I heard a well-known minister say that persecution is a key to the anointing. Persecution sends us to our knees and destroys any self-willed motives and pride. Therefore we are led to a greater anointing.

I've experienced family persecution. Chuck's family blamed me for the suicide of a family member. At a holiday gathering I counseled his wife not to leave, but she left that same night. Months later he killed himself while begging her to come back. His family was convinced I counseled her to leave him. This is how the Enemy is the Accuser. He plants the seed of a lie and we take it from there. They ostracized me for two years. I forgave them and tried to treat them with unconditional love so I could do what the Bible says and not act like the world. But they ignored me. I cried in private at night. Eventually I got over the tears and released the care completely.

God dealt with their hearts and we were restored. How did that happen? Suddenly they acted like nothing happened.

Because my lifestyle was so different from my own family, at times they alienated me from family gatherings, and refused my invitations to any milestones in my life for twenty-five years. God restored my relationship with my family at my fiftieth birthday celebration at my church. My cousin Peggy, motivated many of them to come to my church for the first time.

The guest minister Rev. Raul asked my family to come forward and hug me then he said, "I sense God is doing some kind of healing here tonight in this family." Wow was he right on!

My mother-in-law's nickname was Mother Dear (she was from Oklahoma and preferred this southern term instead of grandmother). She loved me, but she was adamantly opposed to my call to ministry.

Below is an actual example of the types of conversations that took place at family gatherings after a meal. Chuck was usually watching football or asleep when this dialog occurred.

"Diane, someone told me you have a daily radio program where you teach the Bible," one relative said.

"Yes, I do." I cringed on the inside knowing what might come next.

"That's great, you're spreading the gospel. I'm proud of you."

Mother Dear wasn't as supportive and expressed this to her relatives. "Diane no longer wants to be a woman. I've told her to let me raise her boys because she's trying to be a man by doing a man's job. God never called a woman to teach from her own radio program."

At this point in the conversation, I excused myself to the kitchen to do dishes until the subject changed.

But Mother Dear wouldn't quit. "You know that women cannot teach men on the radio or under any circumstances."

The supportive relative disagreed. "Why shouldn't she be able to do what she feels God wants her to do? You're acting like she's doing something terrible. It's good to tell people about Jesus, no matter who does it."

The debate about my calling would last anywhere from a few minutes to a few hours.

For years I asked God to reveal to me why I received such persecution from my mother-in-law about my calling. I knew it was not personal, although it took me many years before I finally quit taking the verbal assault personally. In 1994, two years after Chuck and my divorce, I discovered the source of Mother Dear's attack on the call on my life. She had been ill so Carlton and I went to her home to help her around the house. She asked me to sit and visit with her and she told me something she had never shared with me in the twenty-six years I knew her.

She began her story by talking about Chuck's father, whom she called Pap. "As you already know, Pap and I were married nine years before we had our first child, Eunice. Eighteen months later, we had

Judith, and then a year and a half later, we had Chuck. I wanted nine boys and three girls."

"Mother Dear, God loved you, so that's why He didn't answer *that* prayer," I joked.

"You're probably right." She smiled then continued. "There was a well-known Bible scholar who has written many commentaries. His material is read even today. He started several Bible colleges for the Baptist denomination throughout the country. He wanted to start one in Texas and he asked us to assist him. Pap and I received scholarships for our help and attended as students also. As you know, Pap flew to England to receive his doctoral degree diploma. This Bible scholar was instrumental in all of that.

"Some time before graduation he called me into his office. He told me I was an excellent student. I was great at my speeches and should go far in life. Then he said, 'Almer, you have all the academic qualifications to become a licensed minister, but we cannot license you because we would be going against the Bible. The Bible does not tell us to ordain women. You will be out of the will of God and so would we. You can go through the rest of the classes, but we cannot give you a Bible degree or license when we license your husband. I'm telling you this so you'll be in the will of God.' I was so disappointed, but if that's what the Bible says, then that settles it. So I learned women are never to do a man's job when it comes to teaching men."

Suddenly the light went on in my head. For her to admit that God called me to teach and preach she would have to admit that she may have had a call to ministry on her life over sixty years earlier. She either had to defend her stand or admit that she may have put man's doctrine before God's will for her life. It seemed that would be too much for her to embrace.

A few years later, when she was in her eighties and had relocated to Texas with her daughter, she was in California on vacation visiting her other daughter. Judith brought her by my home for a short visit. She didn't waste any time in broaching the subject again. "I hear you're still preaching and helping people get saved."

"Yes I am, Mother Dear." I braced myself for the inevitable assault on my calling because now I was a senior pastor with many men in my church.

"Well, keep up the good work for the Lord!"

I hesitated a moment. *Did I hear her correctly?* "I certainly will do that—until the day I die."

We smiled at one another. I'm glad I had forgiven her years earlier so I could embrace the miracle of this moment. If Mother Dear believed my ministry was a sin against God she would have taken that belief to the grave.

Instead I don't know how she resolved her inner conflict with God that she took out on me for twenty years, but she must have released it to the Lord somehow. The following year at Christmas, she sent me a card with a similar message.

I'm so glad I accepted the call of God on my life because nothing is more fulfilling. Countless people have received salvation and others have been spiritually, emotionally and physically healed. Many mentioned that through my ministry they were spiritually awakened. They said as I ministered the Word and prayed for them they encountered the Holy Spirit's presence and power on a level they didn't know existed. The gratification that comes from fulfilling God's purpose is priceless. Neither fame nor fortune can compare. I've influenced people that have made a difference in many parts of the globe. I'm forever grateful that I surrendered to His call.

The first scripture I was directed to concerning my calling was Isaiah 58:1 as I mentioned. Later God expanded my calling by adding another passage: Hebrews 12:1b-2a. *Let us lay aside every weight, and the sin which so easily ensnares us, and let us run with endurance the race that is set before us, looking unto Jesus, the author and finisher of our faith.*

A few years later this passage was added as my calling unfolded: 1 Corinthians 2:4-5

And my speech and my preaching were not with persuasive words of mans wisdom, but in demonstration of the Spirit and of power, that your faith should not be in the wisdom of men but in the power of God.

I needed God to give me something concise to hang onto. So I asked Him to make my calling clearer by giving me *one key phrase*. And this is the phrase: I'm called to bring healing to hurting humanity, spiritually, emotionally, and physically, through the power of the Holy Spirit.

As I ran the race God set before me there were times I felt I was mortally wounded on the track and lay there in hopes that God would change His mind and use someone else. He didn't, so I got up and kept going. I may have fainted at times when I should have crawled, and crawled when I should have walked. Perhaps I walked when I should have sprinted, and sprinted when I should have run. But *I've never left the track*, and I make it my goal to run with endurance (patience) the race set before me. I desire to run by the guidelines expressed in the Word so the Lord will see me as an overcomer and eventually say, "Well done good and faithful servant."

I have a passion to reveal not only God but His nature as our loving, gracious, heavenly Father. I have an equal desire to expose the nature of the Enemy who devises plans to kill, steal, and destroy, everything God has given us in Christ. I want people to know the Bible so they don't blame God for what Satan does.

My goal is to help many find their track and others get back in the race for the kingdom of God.

When the Apostle Paul knew his race was coming to a close he said, *"I have fought a good fight, I have finished my race, I have kept the faith"* (2 Timothy 4:7). He must have known what he was called to do, what race he was to run, or he would never have known when he was finished.

When I still had a victim's mentality I decided the best way to glorify God with my life was to have the mentality of an overcomer. This means I must do what the Word of God says and not what I want. I can't look for excuses *not* to do the Word, but look instead to the answers in the Bible on how I'm to respond to everything in life. Therefore, I set my will to run my race and not back down from living His Word. I will fight a good fight of faith. I will finish my course, and I will keep the faith, no matter what has happened or what will happen. I will keep moving forward because faith pleases God. He has no pleasure when I draw back.

I'll bring many more to the saving knowledge of Christ. I'll write books and articles about His grace. I'll preach in prisons and pulpits, I'll coach marketplace leaders to embrace the Holy Spirit (their Helper). I'll be a chaplain to politicians and business developers. I'll lay foundations of truth for the next generations to build upon.

I'll awaken women and young girls spiritually and emotionally to their *value* in the kingdom of God through my Beautiful Women of God Seminars and marketplace Holy Spirit Encounters for businesswomen.

Like Jesus, I want to bring love, truth, authority, and power to heal everywhere I go. I want my calling to be expressed through every sphere of influence God will give me.

Chapter 13

The Betrayal

But behold, the hand of My betrayer is with me on the table (Luke 22:21).

March, 1990

I answered the knock on our front door around 1:00 p.m. and yelled, "Chuck, drop what you're doing and come to the front door quickly, please!"

Chuck's mom and step dad stood on our porch on either side of Curtis. They held him under each arm because he was barely able to stand.

"Curtis is sick with asthma, and we've done everything we can for him," Mother Dear said. "We're too old to take care of him when he's this sick. You need to take care of him, and he needs to live with you guys now."

With his other hand, Pops gave Chuck a large trash bag full of clothes. "Here's some of his stuff. You can get the rest later."

Chuck and I put Curtis's arms around our necks and our arms around his waist and led him to our spare bedroom. Chuck helped him get undressed and into bed while I looked for our old humidifier and a jar of Vicks Vapor Rub. I took Curtis water and apple juice so he wouldn't get dehydrated.

I asked Curtis, "Do you have any pain?"

He shook his head.

"Have you used your inhaler and do you have enough medication to last at least a couple of days?"

Between coughs and wheezes he said, "Yeah Mom, I have." Then he started to doze off.

Curtis was twenty-years old and had not lived with us since he abruptly moved out at seventeen—just two months after he graduated from high school. He made it clear at the time that he wanted to run his own life without parental influence. He wasn't doing drugs or alcohol. Instead, he simply wanted to rebel and it broke our hearts. He bounced around from friend to friend until his grandparents realized he had no permanent place to live and invited him to rent the attached two-room apartment they sometimes rented for extra income.

With holidays usually at his grandparents' home we saw Curtis on most holidays. Our subsequent contact with Curtis was strictly on his terms, and he came by our home when he wanted to see us. Curtis made it clear he did not want to live with us so we were curious why the sudden change of heart. After Curtis fell asleep, we sat in the family room to talk.

"You guys already know the company Curtis worked for went out of business," Mother Dear said. "You may not know that his new truck was repossessed last week. Now he has no job and no transportation to look for work. I think it's too much stress on him because last week he started to wheeze and become lethargic. He needs to humble himself and start over.

"He's too proud to ask you to help him, but when he got sick I told him he doesn't have a choice. So Pops and I gathered his stuff and brought him home so you can help him get back on his feet."

It took him three weeks to fully recover physically. Our time of bonding with Curtis those first couple of months was good for all of us. Carlton was away at college so Curtis had all our attention. After almost a year, he had not found a steady job. He worked for temporary agencies, and earned enough money for activities he wanted to do and to buy a used car. He only looked for a job when he ran out of money. He reconnected with high school friends who came by to play basketball, play video games, go to night clubs, or go to church.

Our guidelines were that he needed to attend church on Saturday or Sunday with us or with friends. Curtis did just that. I encouraged him to grow in his relationship with Christ through personal Bible devotion and study. He enjoyed church, but was reluctant to study the Bible and grow in his faith. *How much guidance do I give a reluctant grown child?* I suggested he find a group of Christian peers who have a Bible study, and group activities.

Gradually he became rebellious, disrespectful, and moody. At times he ignored me, and other times he was critical of me. Peaceful discussions with him seemed fruitless. Chuck didn't seem to care how Curtis treated me. I petitioned Chuck many times for us to get family counseling. If I had it to do over, I would have invited Chuck but not waited on him. I would have asked Curtis to go with me, and God would have provided the right person, the finances, and the Lord would have had an opportunity to move on Curtis's heart. The rest would have been up to Curtis.

Chuck and I disagreed on how Curtis should be handled. I wanted to give him two months notice to get a job and move out. I knew with some pressure he would find a job and become more responsible. Chuck thought I was too strict with that ultimatum. We agreed to let a third party help us with many decisions concerning Curtis.

We agreed to see a gifted counselor Dr. Dianne McIntosh who held doctorate degrees both in psychology and theology, who we met two years earlier at a minister's retreat held by Dr. Iverna Tompkins in Phoenix, Arizona. Dr. Dianne prayed and did brief counseling with each couple who signed up for it at the retreat. She was sensitive to the Holy Spirit and a great counselor.

March, 1991

Chuck and I arrived at her office in Arizona in March, I don't know why we didn't take Curtis. I think we wanted to get some direction as parents first. Looking back we could have had him meet with her after we met.

She shared wisdom with us on how to help Curtis move forward. Then she showed us both areas in which we needed to apologize to each other. She agreed Curtis should move soon.

"Give Curtis measurable instructions with reasonable timelines," she said. "He's grown so have him sign an agreement and you two sign it also. Put in what you expect him to do and what you are willing to do for him after he takes some steps. Go over the instructions bi-weekly. You two must agree which part you will focus on for that week and what the expectations are.

"Chuck, I want you to be aware of something. When you discuss these issues with Curtis watch out for making Diane the bad-guy."

In our counseling sessions Curtis was our center focus, but Chuck and I never mentioned *our secret*. This would have been a good time to bring it out in the open, but it was buried so deep we never thought about bringing it up.

"How have you felt betrayed by one another?" Dr. Dianne asked. "Say the first thing that comes to your mind."

Chuck admitted that although my mom died in 1977, he still harbored resentment toward me and her for the nine years I was her primary caregiver when she had cancer. "I feel betrayed by Diane and her mom. For years Mrs. Gardner had unreasonable demands on Diane to take care of her and all her affairs. The drive was an hour and a half round trip, and Diane made that round trip four and sometimes five times a week because the doctors were in Riverside near us and Mrs. Gardner lived in Pomona, near LA. That's a lot of gas money and wear and tear on our car. Because of this, for years we weren't able to save or have any extra money."

He let out a sigh and continued. "Diane was always tired and often was short with me and our kids. Our family was robbed of time, money, and a quality of life I expected to have for the first few years of our marriage. We never got a chance to be newlyweds because the cancer was discovered when we were only married a few months. Mrs. Gardner had three other children, who lived nearby her, but she wanted Diane to do the cooking, cleaning, banking, and doctor visits."

"Chuck, I apologized many times years ago. I didn't know this still bothered you." I turned slightly in my chair to face him. "Please forgive me for the times I put Mom's needs before the needs of our family. Some of your concerns are just life issues, and I cannot apologize for the wear and tear on the car and our not being able to save money. But you know I grew in Christ Mom's last couple of years. So she had to adjust to our family's priorities as I began to put some healthy boundaries on Mom's requests."

Dr. Dianne looked at me. "Diane, what is the first thing that comes to your mind when I mention the word *betrayal?*"

"I feel betrayed by Chuck because he undermines my authority with our kids. He talks about my faults with them and teaches them to be critical of me. He does the same thing with our executive board and staff at church. I made a covenant with God not to talk about his faults with our children or anyone else. I have kept that covenant for years."

She gave us wisdom and assignments to do when we returned home. We met with her two hours a day on two consecutive days. At the end of the second day, we spent some time in prayer.

When she finished her prayer she directed her attention to Chuck. "Pastor Chuck, I know your main concern in coming to see me was your son Curtis, but the Lord's shown me something He wants you to know.

"God says, *You have a tight fist around your family, your ministry, and yourself. You are trying to make everyone fit your mold.* He says, *Humble yourself and open your hand so He can take control. You are trying to control your ministry and your wife's ministry. Let go. If not, God says He will have to pry your hand open.*

"You are more intelligent, more gifted, and more educated than your wife. She has a bachelor degree, and like me, you have two doctorate degrees. Although all that is true, Diane is more obedient and flexible in God's hand—more humble to His will. If you don't make some changes, your wife will be in on the next move of God, and you'll miss out. You'll be stuck in time and miss where God is headed next. God's not looking so much for the talented, but for the pliable. God resists the proud and gives grace to the humble.

"I see your foot in the Enemy's mouth. He's trying to devour you entirely. It's up to you to pull your foot out of his mouth."

On the airplane trip home, I was curious to know what Chuck was thinking. "What do you think about what Dr. Dianne said about missing the next move of God? Didn't that put a knot in your stomach and frighten you a bit?"

"No, it didn't."

"I felt what the Lord said through her was a serious warning and it put a knot in my stomach. Didn't it feel like a warning?"

"Yeah, I guess so."

I became more concerned for Chuck because I saw indifference in him that was frightening. Had he lost all his passion to pursue obedience? I thought about Hebrews 3:7-8: *Therefore as the Holy Spirit says: "Today, if you will hear His voice, Do not harden your hearts as in the rebellion, In the day of trial in the wilderness."*

When we returned home we addressed our issues. Carlton came home on spring break, and Chuck apologized to me in front of Curtis and Carlton. He admitted he was wrong to undermine my authority and God-given position as a mother. He apologized to the congregation for undermining my authority with them. I'm not sure whether our sons or the congregation got the point, but it was his attempt to obey that portion of his instructions from Dr. Dianne. I was thankful. I hoped this was the beginning of a new start for us as a couple, a family, and a congregation. I knew our healing had to go much deeper than an apology, but it looked like a significant start.

I changed my demands and gave Curtis three months to get a job and an apartment. We spelled out clearly our expectations of him and what we were willing to do to help him if he followed through. Within thirty days Curtis had a good job, and at the end of three months he was able to move to an apartment. Soon thereafter he purchased a better used car.

After Curtis moved out, a thirty-something year-old-woman named Ruth moved in. We had mentored her when she was a student at California Baptist University (CBU). She wanted to relocate back to Riverside after living in Louisiana for a few years. We offered our home to help her with the transition. She quickly reunited with us as a part of our family. Ruth noticed the indifference in Chuck and without my knowledge began to warn him about his growing lack of integrity.

Chuck was losing his grip on his reverential fear of the Lord. He was indifferent to the crucial warnings God sent his way, so my prayers for him became more desperate. From 1991to 1992 God sent Chuck warning after warning. God showed Himself as his loving Father and also a Righteous Judge. Here are some of the warnings he received after the warning through Dr. Dianne:

Summer 1991

It was a beautiful warm summer day, when Kathy, our church prayer coordinator, rushed into our Industrial Suite offices almost out of breath. She stormed into the secretary's office. "Betty, I need to see Pastors Chuck and Diane right away. It's important! I'd like to see them both in Pastor Chuck's office."

"OK, I'll see if they are both available." Betty called us on the intercom. "Pastor Chuck, Kathy is here to see you in your office. Pastor Diane, Kathy wanted to know if you would come into Pastor Chuck's office. She says it's important."

Kathy and her husband were one of our founding church leaders in 1983. She had an excitable temperament, but she was not a person to rush in and want your attention.

Chuck sat behind his desk. I walked across the hall to his office and stood in front of the loveseat until Kathy came in and I gave her a quick hug and a big smile.

"Good morning Kathy, it's good to see you this beautiful morning," Chuck said. "What's on your mind? Have a seat."

"No thank you. I'm too nervous to sit down. Thanks for seeing me right away. I didn't want to wait to tell you about this because I believe it will require immediate prayer." She paced back and forth between the door and Pastor Chuck's desk. "This morning as I prayed for you and the church God showed me something that disturbed me. It was an ugly demonic spirit with a big sword in his hand." She pointed at Chuck, then me. "You two were standing side-by-side, and he was facing you. He had the sword raised up over your heads and his intent was to bring it down between you. Satan wants to use that demonic spirit and his sword to divide you two."

She walked over to Pastor Chuck. "God impressed me that *you* have put the sword in the Enemy's hands, and only *you* can take it out."

"Oh that's horrible," I said.

Chuck's jaws became tight and he had a piercing stare at Kathy. "Well, that was quite some revelation. Thanks for sharing it. Diane and I will take this into consideration." He stood and extended his hand for Kathy to shake. "Keep praying for us, and thanks for taking the time to come."

"Pastor Chuck, may I take a moment to pray right now? I feel we should pray together."

He nodded at her.

"Lord Jesus, You know what You showed me this morning. You know what the Enemy has planned and what that sword represents. Give us wisdom to make the right decisions. Show Pastor Chuck what to do to take the sword out of the hand of that demonic spirit. Show him how to destroy that evil plan.

"I come against the Enemy's assignment against my pastors. God has exposed your plans today. In the name of Jesus, I stand against you!

"Ok, I feel better. I delivered what the Lord wanted me to say. I know He will show you what to do and how to destroy that evil assignment against you guys. I love you both, goodbye."

I was stunned and thankful at the same time. God exposed the assault of the Enemy. *Maybe we should go into the sanctuary and pray together and see if God gives us any instructions on how to take that sword out of the hand of that evil spirit. I hope Chuck embraces what was said and doesn't resist it through pride. There is no way possible Kathy could know some of the divisive things Chuck has said to me in private. I know this was God.*

Chuck and I stared at each other.

"God sure loves us a lot to expose the assault of the Enemy to Kathy like that," I said. "What do you want us to do?"

"Yeah, He sure does. I need to do some work right now, so we'll discuss this later."

I stood up. "I know you want to process what Kathy said. Let me know when you want us to pray together about it. I'm ready whenever you are." I returned to my office.

Chuck never mentioned Kathy's revelation again. After a week, I knew he had chosen not to resist the Enemy's plan. I felt frustrated and hurt by his decision.

September, 1991

Chuck and I attended a meeting near Los Angeles where a prophetic minister friend of ours, Rev. Carol, was speaking. When the meeting concluded and others had finished talking with her, we talked to her about the details of her upcoming speaking engagement at our church. Shortly after we approached her, she said. "Pastor Chuck, it's imperative that I speak to you in private." She pulled him off to the side and shared what was on her heart. He didn't tell me what she said. Two years later, she revealed to me that quick conversation.

"Pastor, I don't know if you know this or not but there's a lady in your congregation who has fantasized about being with you," Rev. Cartwright told him. "Don't give in to that deception. I know you're a man of integrity, so this is a warning. God says, *You're at a vulnerable place in your personal life so be careful.*"

October, 1991

Chuck and I were invited to be a part of a prophetic team to prophesy over ministers at Pastor Garnett's seminar. Dr. Jason and

Pastor Cathy were on the ministry team, and although we had several mutual friends, we had never met before that day.

Dr. Jason was led by the Holy Spirit to say, "Pastor Chuck, you and your wife have waited years for the promises of God to be fulfilled. You're like Abraham and Sarah who waited twenty-five years for Isaac. God says to you, *Isaac is almost here. You have both done well in your walk of faith. Diane is pregnant with the promised child—the next phase of ministry for your future. You cannot have the promised child without Diane. For you to enjoy the fruit of your labors, you must bring forth the promise of God's will with Pastor Diane.*"

November, 1991

In November, I received a warning for myself from the Lord about an upcoming attack from the Enemy. He said, *In February, 1992 you will see another level of Satan's assault on women. It's imperative you fast the entire month to be sensitive to the Holy Spirit, so He can help you overcome whatever battle you will face.* This revelation rocked my world.

December, 1991

At our pre-Christmas ladies meeting I asked them to pray for me. "Ladies, I need you to cover me in prayer. The Lord revealed to me last month that I will see another level of Satan's assault on women in February. I don't know what kind of assault it will be, but I know it will be something I've never experienced. I want to be fortified with your prayers. I'm determined to be an overcomer and walk by faith no matter what happens. Faith is what pleases God."

January, 1992

With the moonlight shining through the window above our bed, I noticed Chuck's face was wet with tears. He was usually the picture of strength and determination, but things had been changing.

"What's wrong, honey?" I asked. "The kids are alright, our church is going well, and we have our health. So I can't see any big problem. What's bothering you?"

"I don't want to be a spiritual father to anyone anymore. We lay down our lives to counsel and be available to those we mentor. We give financially to help some get their ministries started. After we make many personal sacrifices and host training meetings at our expense, then in private they say they respect us, but publically they don't show it. I'm going to shut them out so they can't hurt and disappointment me anymore."

"What do you mean, 'They don't respect us?' Everyone respects you a lot. You're well educated, you're prophetic, you have wisdom, and you're a great Bible teacher. People continually ask you to share your wisdom. In what way are they disrespecting us?"

"Take for instance the ministry trip I did last November. I counseled Pastor Kelsey by phone for months while I helped him put out fires in his ministry. Then I went back East to minster for him for two weeks while he was preaching for Dr. Myles in the Bahamas. I spoke Sunday and both mid-week services. I taught in the Bible school and trained his leaders. I also had training meetings with his employees.

"Pastor Kelsey admittedly came home to a more organized and healthier church. At the end of my stay, I was one of the speakers for his big conference. He had a well-known speaker come who only spoke once at the close of the conference. Pastor gave that speaker an honorarium that was three times the amount he gave me for my two weeks of hard work *and* my speaking at the conference. I've laid down my life for Pastor Kelsey and his ministry. I call that a betrayal!"

Chuck flipped onto his back in bed. "Yeah, I've been betrayed! That's what I feel. So many people have betrayed us. We've been betrayed by our former pastor who betrayed us to cover his wrongdoing. We've been betrayed by others we helped. As soon as numerically they increased larger than our congregation they ignore us. Now they never have us come and speak."

"You're right. Many people have betrayed and taken advantage of us. I was thinking the other day how many broken financial promises we've had in only one two-year period alone. In that time period, several members of our congregation have had lawsuits and God has settled and won every case. God has been faithful every time, but people have not. These are the ones I remember.

"The young single guy in his twenties was awarded $100,000. He called you and said, 'Pastor Chuck, I told you I would tithe on the money when I received it. After taxes I have $80,000, but $8,000 is a lot to give a church.' We never saw him after that call.

"We had a couple receive their inheritance after a sticky case concerning her mother's will. We prayed with them for a long time for closure. They cleared $350,000. They bought you a new computer and printer for $2,500, and then they left.

"One couple had a wrongful death suit pending for three years from her first husband's death. They were in the middle of all this when they came to our church. We held prayer meetings for them, and the suit was settled for two million. After all the expenses, including medical and attorney fees, the family cleared $800,000. Invited us over and made it clear what they wanted to give you, me, and the ministry. When the money came they didn't give a dime, and left soon after they received the money. I thought they would be different, I was disappointed with them. Remember she called me a couple of years later to ask me about giving her advice on a project. I'm glad my heart was clear of any offense. She told me they were divorced and she had no money left."

We were silent for a while then I brought up yet another incident that happened within that two year span of time. "Remember the guy who got hepatitis on his job when he worked in an infirmary? While he was going through his lawsuit he believed he would live with hepatitis the rest of his life. He became despondent and tried to commit suicide on his motorcycle."

Chuck said, "Oh, yeah. He said he saw an angel who caught him in the air and that's why he only suffered a broken leg even though his bike was totaled."

"He decided to come by the church to tell us what happened to him. The day he visited I was having a prayer meeting for my upcoming Beautiful Women of God Seminar. The ladies and I prayed for his healing. He went to the doctor the next day and insisted on new X-rays. Reluctantly, the doctor complied and verified his leg was completely healed and took the cast off."

Chuck added, "Then shortly before his lawsuit was settled, he asked for prayer concerning the hepatitis and God healed him miraculously of that also!"

"That's right, honey. I almost forgot about his healing. The other day I thought about how much he cleared after doctors and lawyers, it was over $360, 000," I said. "But he moved to Los Angeles before he received his settlement money. Then, five months later, he came one Wednesday night to Bible study in his new Italian sports car. After class he told us God had put pressure on him several times and told him he had not done right by us or our ministry.

"He said, 'I receive my money bi-monthly and I told you I will mail the ministry a check once or twice a month, but I didn't follow through. Forgive me for not keeping my word to you and to the Lord.' He took several church envelopes.

"We had forgiven him, and even then we didn't ask him for anything—only that he follows through on what God placed on his heart. We never saw one envelope or heard from him again. God always does His part, but people don't obey him."

I let out a big sigh, "One by one they left after they received their money. That's like hiring a consultant or a lawyer who guided you through your case the whole time, and you walk away without paying him a dime."

"That's the kind of betrayal I'm talking about, along with what ministers have done!" Chuck said.

"Jesus healed ten lepers in his ministry, and only one came back to thank Him. But in our case, none of our members came back to give what they pledged before God and to say thank you. That could make anyone feel unappreciated and betrayed, but we know ultimately it's between them and God. Their pledge was to Him." I said then continued.

"Our members were taught better, but they allowed the Enemy to influence their greedy side. I'm sure we would not be struggling financially today if only two of them had done what was right. We have both forgiven all of these people, but we need to make sure we let go of the hurt and disappointment also."

Neither of us said anything for a while.

"What are you going to do with the betrayals you feel?" I asked. "You don't want that pain to become a root of bitterness. It's sad, but human nature has always acted like that. Many want prayer, counseling, advice, teaching, and want someone else to pay the pastor's salary and money for the building so they can get their needs met. I call that welfare Christian. Someone else works and pays for the privileges they enjoy. Why is it bothering you now more than before?"

"I'm not sure yet. I know I don't want God or anyone else to tell me I need to keep doing what I'm doing. I'm tired. We hold nothing against any of them. In fact, we saw a couple of them this year, and I checked my heart to make sure I had completely forgiven them and I was fine. It's time I had a job where people pay me for sure for my services. I'm sick of this pattern of working and not getting paid fully for what I do. I want to do something different and do ministry also. I just don't want to pastor or mentor other pastors. I want to earn more money for my degrees and my time. I want to be more appreciated and respected for all my hard work."

"I hear you." I said not knowing what else to say. Then I had an idea. "Honey, we had a discussion two months ago when you shared similar concerns. Did you have a chance to read that book we talked about—the one we ordered from Dr. Dobson's Focus on the Family radio program last year to help some of our men, called *Men in Midlife Crisis?*

"Yeah, I read it. There were three important points that didn't apply to me, so I decided I'm not having a midlife crisis."

I raised my eyebrows in disbelief.

The moonlight had moved, so our room now was filled with darkness, but I could hear his sniffles. "Honey, I can feel the pain in your heart. I know you're hurting. My heart is hurting too, but I've been talking to the Lord about it. I'm working through my disappointments and hurts so I can be healed. I believe God wants us to come to another level of surrender. Give up our expectations of people and let Him prune our dead branches. I think I'll start a fast to see if I can get more answers."

"You can do that, but that's not what I want to do."

"Chuck, I have another thought. You probably need a break. We rarely go on vacations or take time off. Let's take three days off around Valentine's Day before the prophetic conference you're hosting in Los Angeles. You've been working hard. Would you like me to make reservations for a Valentine dinner and a hotel?"

"That's good," he said. "But I only want to be gone one night. Make dinner and overnight reservations for Valentines' Day only."

Chuck decided he was going to take my suggestion and take three days off, but he would do this alone before our Valentine's getaway. He chose the weekend before Valentine's Day because we had previously scheduled Dr. Valerie to speak on Sunday, February, 9th and at our prophetic school on Monday the 10th.

I was encouraged by something he said before he left. "Diane, I'm going away to reevaluate my priorities and purpose for everything I'm doing."

Maybe he'll talk to God about the betrayals that are hurting him and making him angry. Maybe he'll have a God encounter that will lead him to surrender his will and let God heal him on a deeper level.

February, 1992

Our services with Dr. Valerie on Sunday permanently altered the direction and anointing of our church. Chuck returned home on Tuesday, February 11. He didn't say or do anything out of the ordinary. He saved his reevaluation discussion for our Valentine's Day date night.

On Valentine's Day Chuck had a nice meal and, because I was fasting, I had juice and water.

We changed into our lounge clothes and then sat on the couch in our beautiful Old English style bed and breakfast room. He pulled out of his briefcase a yellow legal pad filled with dates on the first page—no writing, just dates.

"I've reevaluated my priorities and my purpose. I've come to some conclusions. First off, this entire page represents dates our marriage took a turn for the worse. Each date reflects a specific incident. Second, I know that I love you, but I am no longer *in love* with you. I know this may come as a shock, but that's how I feel. I'm letting you know today that I will be moving out when it's convenient for me."

I swallowed hard. *I'm hurt and disappointed. We've been together twenty-four years. God, please give me the grace to remain calm.*

Chuck scooted farther away from me to the end of the couch, probably expecting me to become hysterical after hearing such devastating news. He hadn't planned a Valentine's Day celebration at all. On the contrary, he planned for us to have this horrible discussion in our hotel room so I wouldn't yell at him or become frantic. As a perfectionist, he had planned the perfect setting—a public place so there could be no argument or hysteria. Fortunately, God warned me Chuck wanted to leave the Sunday before this conversation.

Tears rolled down my face at the gravity of our conversation, but I found the courage to ask a question that had never come up in our twenty-four years of marriage. "Are you going to file for divorce?"

"I don't know yet. I'll let you know when I make up my mind."

"Am I supposed to sit around waiting for the next shoe to drop?"

"It looks that way." He shrugged.

"To me, Chuck, every one of those dates mean a time you chose not to forgive me for something I did or something I didn't do that I was supposed to do. Or something you perceived I did to hurt you on purpose. If the Bible says to forgive because Christ has forgiven us then it looks like these passages don't apply to your wife. How is that right?"

"Doesn't matter whether you see it as right or not, these are the facts."

The list consisted of things he had said before, but what was surprising to me was how he felt justified to keep his unforgiveness and bitterness toward me and not feel convicted before God.

Some of his dates reflected how he attributed the natural ways of a woman to me being like his mother and trying to emotionally castrate him. When I was a teenager I watched Mom handle Dad with disrespect and attack his manhood. I decided at that young age with God's help I will not do the same to my husband. I worked hard to show him respect and honor as a man and a husband. I didn't criticize him to our children or anyone else. When my pride or stubbornness reared its ugly head, the Holy Spirit was quick to notify me so I could repent and forgive.

I realized Chuck never asked God to teach him how to respect and honor me. He didn't like certain aspects of my personality therefore; he chose only to respect me when I acted the way he wanted me to. He never learned to appreciate the women in his life. As such, he resented the nature God created in me and the basic temperament and personality God gave me.

I said, "Last year you counseled with a friend twice, and you said it helped you when they gave you Pastor Jack Hayford's book warning Christians against having an emotional affair. The book showed how that could lead to a sexual affair. You bought several copies of the book and gave them to different people. If that helped you, maybe we need to revisit the talk we had last year about getting counseling for ourselves this time. Unless you have someone else in mind, maybe we can start with Dr. Dianne. You said you respect her."

"You're right, let's go to counseling. The counselor can help us with all the decisions we need to make concerning our transition with you becoming the senior pastor. With me moving out, we need to discuss many things in front of a third party. You'll also have someone to confide in."

He paused, took on a stern look, and turned to face me squarely. "Let's go see Dr. Dianne, that's a good idea. If we wind up getting a divorce, the Body of Christ will be more forgiving of us if they *think* we went to counseling to try to fix our marriage. But get this straight Diane; I'm not going to counseling to *fix* anything."

Chapter 14

Divinely Positioned

Be strong and of good courage, for to this people you shall divide as an inheritance the land which I swore to their fathers to give them. (Joshua 1:6)

January, 1992

Rev. Ev called us and her words sent me to my knees in prayer. Chuck answered the call. They had a short conversation about her ministry's next board meeting. He was on her executive board and the annual meeting would be in a couple of weeks. After they finished talking about board business, I overheard Chuck refer to me. Curious, I stopped drying the dishes and walked toward his office.

"You're absolutely right! I've told her the same thing a few times this last year, but she doesn't want to hear it." He spoke with enough volume for me to hear.

I entered the room and chuckled slightly. "What is it you've been telling me that I don't want to hear? Don't you two gang up on me."

"I think she may hear it from you because you're one of her mentors."

There was a slight pause as he listened. I was getting more curious.

"Ok, I'll see you at the annual board meeting. I'll expect my ticket in the mail . . . Love you, too. Hold on, I'm giving the phone to Diane so you can tell her yourself."

I took the phone and went back into the kitchen to finish the dishes. "Hey Rev. Ev, what are you and Chuck discussing about me that he thinks I don't want to hear?"

"You are to become the senior pastor of the church right away and release Chuck from that responsibility because he will be doing more traveling."

I dropped the dishtowel on the floor. "What?" I shouted, and then took a deep breath and toned down my voice. "With all due respect, I want to know why you're saying this to me. Are you trying to help him because you can see he has gotten burned out in the last couple years? You may not know this, but he has been trying to unload the church onto me or our assistant pastors. Instead of doing the things you have taught us, like pressing into God, getting healed and getting direction, he has started to shut down. I think he might be going through a midlife crisis. He has not been himself in a long time. It seems he wants to be free of all responsibilities. He's self absorbed and prideful. I'm really concerned about him."

"Everything you said may well be true, but that is not why I said that to you," Rev. Ev said. "I haven't talked to Chuck in a few months. This morning I knew I would be calling my board members. So I prayed for each board member and the Lord clearly spoke to me to say to you both, *Diane is to become the senior pastor right away.*"

"Oh, umm, I guess I better go pray and see what God wants to say to me."

"I guess you *better* go pray. You might want to ask the Lord why you didn't want to hear it when Pastor Chuck spoke to you earlier."

"Thank you, I'll go pray right now."

I went directly to our spare bedroom, fell on my knees, and began to pray. "Father, You heard what Rev. Ev said, that I should immediately become the senior pastor of the church. What do You have to say about that? You know I don't want to be the main person in charge. I have never envisioned myself as a senior pastor. I recognize you have increased the anointing on my life to help the people of the church more. You've changed my schedule and I'm not traveling to speak as often. But I thought all of this was so I could help Chuck more with the church. Not for me to be in charge."

I paused to take inventory of what I had spoken. Then, slowly and purposefully I said, "Nevertheless, not my will, but Your will be done. I submit to hearing whatever You want to say."

The Father God spoke firmly to my heart. *You must start with repentance for not bringing to Me what you heard long ago from your pastor. Chuck spoke what he heard from Me. He spoke as the head of your church, not as your frustrated husband. You've been stubborn because of fear. You know I've increased your pastoral anointing and given you more favor with the people.*

I wanted to start the process almost a year ago, but you wouldn't listen. Now I must do a quick work. I want you to announce to the people at the end of February and step into the senior pastor position by the end of March. You will have the grace and the anointing for the position by the time you tell the people.

I felt to look up Joshua 3:7 and accept it as a verse for me to hold onto, *And the* LORD *said to Joshua, "This day I will begin to exalt you in the sight of all Israel, that they may know that, as I was with Moses, so I will be with you."*

The Lord said, *Diane, just as I gave Chuck the grace to lead my people, I will do the same with you.*

"Lord, please forgive me. I repent of my stubbornness, which is idolatry. I repent of my fear and how I didn't choose to trust you. I will become the senior pastor and obey you.

"Lord, I still believe Chuck quit on the inside a couple of years ago and has abandoned his responsibilities, one at a time. Our house is falling apart and the church equipment is also. And for the first time, we are $5,500 behind in our rent. I feel like the church is being dumped on me."

He answered my lack of understanding. *You don't see the bigger picture. Part of your frustration is because you are pregnant with my next move in your life. I need you to be aware of the times and seasons you're living in. This year, 1992, I've put out the call from heaven worldwide for women to become heads of churches, denominations, organizations, governments, political parties, and nations.*

You're not receiving this position because of Chuck's state of mind as the senior pastor. Instead, you're a part of My next move on the Earth. No matter what is going on with Chuck, you will be the senior pastor of the church before Easter this year because this is My timing. This is one of my divinely appointed positions for you and other positions will come later.

I came out of my place of prayer with a solemn demeanor. I repented to Pastor Chuck for not praying about what he told me almost a year ago. I told him I would accept the position of senior pastor.

"Good. Now let's sit in the living room and discuss the mechanics of the transition." He said as he motioned for me to follow him.

We were sitting on the living room couch, still discussing the ends and outs of the transition when our spiritual daughter and house guest, Ruth came in. She had been here several months and recently landed a good paying job.

"Ruth, get yourself something to eat, then bring your plate in here. We want to discuss something important with you."

"Sure Pastor Chuck, I'll be there soon as I can."

She adored Pastor Chuck, but had become concerned with the changes she had seen. When Ruth sat down, Chuck told her about Rev. Ev's word from the Lord. He expressed some things he had wanted to say over the last year since he first heard from the Lord about me becoming the senior pastor.

I spoke to Ruth about some of the things God had said to me about His move with women in the earth.

"Ruth, how do you feel about Diane becoming your senior pastor?" Chuck asked.

Although she loved me, she was candid with her response. "Well, I'm not sure. I love Diane and trust her implicitly. She is a real woman of moral and spiritual integrity. But I never thought I would sit under a female senior pastor." She looked at me, feeling a little sheepish.

"It's OK to feel strange Ruth, I totally understand. I have ministered at seminars with other women who were senior pastors and I respect them highly, but I never thought I would be one. To lead people from the position of the ultimate authority scares me. So we'll feel uncomfortable together. You probably reflect the sentiments the majority of our people will have."

"You live with us, so you get to be our guinea pig when we need to express something new," Chuck said. "Thanks for your honesty. It will be interesting watching the will of God unfold."

Two weeks later Chuck left for his few days at the timeshare of one of our members. We had a lot of decisions to be made. I thought time away was a good idea. I wanted us to go together to seek God's wisdom about this transition, we had a guest speaker the people knew well and we could trust her with the church. But I felt the Holy Spirit urge me not to suggest we go together.

February, 1992

Dr. Valerie DePastino was scheduled to speak Sunday morning, Sunday night and at our Prophetic School on Monday night. She has a degree in education, is a prophetess, and a teacher.

I sat in our Sunday church service listening to Dr. Valerie who spoke about our need to "take the next step" into the will of God for our lives. "Stop hesitating," she said. "As soon as you take the next step, then you are already into your future. Watch me." As she stood on the bottom step of our platform she held her right foot in the air then put it back on the step. She did this a few times. *OK, make the step and stop hesitating!*

She finally took the next step onto the floor.

"Now I've stepped into the future. Where you're standing is the present, but to move into your future, you take one step—then the next one."

My heart was racing. "Yes, Lord, I will take the next step, no matter how scared I am," I whispered, and then again I said, "Not my will, but Yours, Lord."

I no sooner got those words out of my mouth when I felt as though a warm ball of pressure was shoved into my chest. It entered my chest so forcefully that it took my breath away for a moment. I gasped for air and struggled to regain normal breathing. "What was that?" I asked God. "And why did it happen?"

This is the senior pastor anointing. I gave the fullness of this anointing to you all at once. You were not open to receiving it before. I've started a new dimension today that I will finish at the service tonight. Fully embrace what I'm doing whether you understand or not—trust Me. Your spirit can receive what your head is still struggling to accept. This is the grace you need for your next step.

As pastors, Chuck and I discussed a formal installation service on Sunday evening, May 3, we planned on inviting other ministers to participate, along with one of our mentors, Rev. Joe and Barbara Jordan. I thought our plans were organized and manageable. I comforted myself with the notion I had from January to May to get used to the idea of becoming a senior pastor. But today there wasn't a ceremony; there were no lay on of the hands of the presbytery. But God wanted me to be divinely positioned—today—by Him.

At the end of that Sunday morning service, Dr. Valerie said God revealed to her He wanted to finish in the evening service what He started in the morning. That was the same thing He told me. My stomach was tied in knots.

When I took Dr. Valerie to lunch, I didn't mention my experience with the senior pastor anointing ball of pressure God imparted to me while she ministered. I wanted God to reveal the senior pastor calling His way when He was ready. I was on my extended fast so I had one glass of juice and water. Afterwards I dropped her off at the hotel.

Then I drove to a secluded hilly area. I jumped out of my car and ran up and down the hill screaming at the top of my lungs and crying. I was crying because somehow I knew in my heart that Pastor Chuck was not going to fully support me as the senior pastor like I had supported him. I could feel this breach deep down inside of me. I felt abandoned and uncovered. This was something I didn't understand. I felt a unique kind of grief.

"I feel I'll have to do this alone?" I shouted to the Lord.

Yes, he'll not support you because of his jealousy and pride. You'll feel alone, but you'll not be alone because the Holy Spirit, your Helper, is with you.

At the evening service, God showed Dr. Valerie a prophetic picture that the congregation and I were to act out. This was a prophetic demonstration by the Holy Spirit. The picture was found in Scripture in Joshua 8:1, 18-19:

> *Now the LORD said to Joshua: "Do not be afraid, nor be dismayed; take all the people of war with you, and arise, go up to Ai . . ." Then the LORD said to Joshua, "Stretch out the spear that is in your hand toward Ai, for I will give it into your hand." And Joshua stretched out the spear that was in his hand toward the city. So those in ambush arose quickly out of their place; they ran as soon as he had stretched out his hand, and they entered the city and took it, and hurried to set the city on fire.*

We opened the emergency door to the sanctuary which led outdoors. Dr. Valerie handed me an ink pen that was to represent a spear.

My instructions were to stand two feet away from the open door and point the spear toward the door. I was to give the charge to the troops. "God has appointed me to win the city for Christ! Get into your positions! Warriors advance, decoys divert the attention of the Enemy outside, and intercessors stay in the sanctuary and cover everything in prayer! God will reveal your position to you. Don't break rank! Let's defeat the Enemy in unity! Charge!"

Before the decoys and ground troops took their places, Dr. Valerie instructed several of my key men to surround me like a shield of protection. She asked them to speak whatever the Lord told them. The power we all felt that night was electrifying.

By the Holy Spirit, they spoke powerful words over me which was captured on cassette that I cherish to this day. "Lord, You will establish the authority of God within this vessel. She will not wax or wane, but she will go forward. Pastor Diane will be even more determined to do Your will. We contend for the strength of God to be developed and perfected in her life."

One of the leaders exposed the Enemy's strategy. "I see demonic spirits at her ankles trying to drag her down." He glanced at the others. "Men, let's take care of this." He led them in a declaration to resist the Enemy. "We agree together in corporate authority that the demons will *not* have dominion, but *we* will have dominion! We come *against* those spirits as one body. We say *yes* to the plan of God! We say *no* to the Adversary's plan!"

Another man spoke next. "As one body, we will bind together to do the will of God, and the victory will come to pass. We decree together that we will support, stand with, walk with, and work with our leader. In Jesus' name, we thank You in advance for what You will accomplish through Pastor Diane and through us."

The various men spoke powerful words over the congregation: "Expand our vision, God. We aren't playing games anymore. We call those on the periphery to come forth. We command fears, inhibitions, and insecurities to be broken and banished through grace. God has appointed and anointed many here to see over His affairs on this earth."

When the men finished, Dr. Valerie prayed to seal this prophetic demonstration of divine positioning. "Father, by the authority invested in me by Jesus Christ, the Head of the Church, I say this according to the mandates that have been acted out and performed by Your instructions. By the declarations of the people, they will stand, they will go, and they will possess the land. By their spoken word, they pledge to the allegiance to the call that You have given to this church. This house is not divided. They are in one accord—to stand before You."

She laid her hand on my forehead. "I lay my hand on this vessel and seal that which has been spoken. I declare to the demonic realm, Satan, you shall not destroy that which God has brought forth this night! You shall not succeed in your plots! You cannot conquer because this house is *not* divided. You have seen the evidence this night of the congregation gathered as one—to stand behind the purpose and the vision. Take your notice this night that war is declared. The Word and strategy from the throne room of God brings victory! In the name of Jesus, let it be established now! Amen."

She had the congregation sit down and then instructed us. "I believe the Holy Spirit is finished with the will of the Father for tonight. If we go beyond the anointing, we will be talking from our flesh and not from God. When we add what God is not saying we may even open the door to deception. We must recognize the anointing to speak and to know when that anointing is over. Even if we still feel pulled in one direction or another to do more, we need to stop. When God moves so powerfully it is imperative to understand when He is done. I believe He's done."

She handed the microphone to me. My knees were so weak that a couple of the men had to support me on each side. Ruth and I were the only ones who knew this was about my senior pastor position.

I exhorted the people. "The significance of tonight will be known and felt over the next few months. I thank God for your obedience, your love, and your willingness to let the Holy Spirit use you to perform His will. Jesus *is* the Head of the church, it's not Pastor Chuck, nor is it me. It's Jesus. Tonight, He has established what He wants.

"I call upon all of you to begin a twenty-one day fast in whatever way God leads you to fast. I was instructed by the Lord to take only water and one glass of juice a day for the entire month of February. He revealed that the Enemy will expose his plan this month, and I must be spiritually ready to walk through the assault God's way. You may fast one meal a day, two meals a day, get up early to pray, or turn the television off for an hour each evening or two days a week.

"I call for a solemn assembly as the Bible teaches. This is for the transitions of God we are going through. By all means, do effective warfare as you have done tonight.

"We will be going through some major changes going forward, some good and some not so good. I don't know what they all are, but I believe that at the end of twenty-one days, we all will know more than we know now. The Enemy plans to assault our future. His wickedness will be exposed before the twenty-one days are up. We'll also know about the times and the seasons of God and what we ought to do. Cover Pastor Chuck and me in prayer diligently. Thank you."

The things that happened that night were awe-inspiring. And God did more as people prepared to leave. They had no knowledge I received the *senior pastor anointing* in the morning service. At least half the congregation of men and women cried as they stood in a long line to give me a hug.

One by one, each whispered in my ear basically the same words. "God told me to repent to you. Please forgive me because I have not respected you like I should. Forgive me for any stubbornness and rebellion."

"I'm here to serve you in any way you need me. I pledge my loyalty to you as a part of God's army. We'll win the war and win the city together. You taught us recently from Joel 2 that we should be in position and not break rank. I'll be in my divinely appointed position and I'll do whatever God shows me, and whatever you instruct me."

To each one I said, "I forgive you. Thank you. I receive your pledge, and I love you."

I understood how well God laid the foundation at the beginning of the year. He instructed me to teach from Joel 2:7-8 and this was the groundwork for what was taking place now.

They run like mighty men, They climb the wall like men of war; Every one marches in formation, And they do not break ranks. They do not push one another; Every one marches in his own column.

I was awestruck by the sovereignty of God. I hugged each one, and about halfway through the group I realized I didn't want to weep with them—I felt totally different toward them. I didn't feel like the nurturing motherly pastor's wife I had been to them for nine years. I felt more like a military leader with an assignment from headquarters. I felt I was carrying out orders, and this was a needed exercise for the troops to prepare themselves for their next assignment. *So this is how the senior pastor's anointing feels. God truly knew how to speak to our hearts, including mine, to accomplish His will.*

Ruth and I drove home in silence. The presence of God was so strong on Ruth and me when we returned home that we barely said a few words to each other and retired to our bedrooms. We were in awe of what God had accomplished, but we were also emotionally drained. It seemed disrespectful to make small talk when God's presence was so tangible.

On the drive home after that powerful church service Sunday night and God used Dr. Valerie to give direction about leading the troops to win the city for Christ, I thought back to the word the Lord shared with me three years earlier. *Diane, I want you to think about Riverside as a place I may call you to live for the rest of your life. Take spiritual ownership and authority over this city, the Inland Empire, and the State of California. In days to come, I will position you by My favor and give you unusual governmental influence. One day, you will be one of the most spiritually influential persons in this region with politicians and marketplace leaders. Plant your roots deep and get involved in the community where and when I direct you.*

I know we are always at war with the Enemy, so when God spoke this to me I knew it was imperative that I not expose God's strategy to the Enemy before it was time. If I were premature to reveal God's secret, then I knew the Enemy would stir up jealousy or unbelief in others.

I was not expecting such a high level of responsibility for my region. But I knew I had heard from God. I made up my mind to be patient with myself, silent before others, and pray to God in a way that did not divulge what He had given me. I regularly said simply, "I agree with Your purpose for my future and I will be obedient. Your will be done Your kingdom come through me as it is in heaven."

I wanted to see how God alone would bring it to pass without me adding my opinion or trying to "help" God perform His will. I wanted God to be able to trust me. For three years whenever I thought of the prophecy I also whispered a prayer like Mary, the precious mother of Jesus. "I am the handmaiden of the Lord! Let it be done to me according to Your Word. By faith I receive the grace to accomplish this." The Enemy can't read my mind so his spirits could only tell what God wanted after God continued to open doors and give me favor. He could see God's angels getting in position for my success before I could see anything happening.

Somewhere I read, "When the Lord knows that He can trust us with His secrets, He will reveal things to us that He cannot reveal to others." I want God to trust me with His strategies.

Luke 2:19 says of Mary: *But Mary kept all these things and pondered them in her heart.* She saw Jesus' calling develop as He grew up, but she didn't expose this to others before God's timing at the wedding in Cana of Galilee.

Now after three years God had our church prophetically demonstrate His plan to use me as a key person in this region. It was His plan to send the prayer troops to ambush the Enemy's strategy.

What God had done through us that night in 1992 angered the powers of darkness—a lot. A short time after I fell asleep, the Enemy sent some of his demons to frighten and intimidate me. Suddenly, my bed shook as the evil presences manifested themselves. They didn't say anything, but I smelled a peculiar stench like sour sulfur. I felt the presence of hatred, as though the room was filled with hatred because I was a woman who chose to obey God's call.

I reached for the lamp next to my bed and turned on the light. The room lit up, but I saw clouds of darkness. "I rebuke you, Devil! In the name and by the blood of Jesus! I grabbed my Bible from the nightstand and read aloud. I resist all the wiles of the Devil according to Ephesians 6:12-13: *For we do not wrestle against flesh and blood, but against principalities, against powers, against the rulers of the darkness of this age, against spiritual hosts of wickedness in the heavenly places. Therefore take up the whole armor of God, that you may be able to withstand in the evil day.* I substituted the word "I' for "we," making this passage my prayer.

Instead of leaving, they became angrier. They shook my bed more violently to the point that I was tossing around in the bed.

Ruth was awakened by the sound of my voice and told me later what happened. "Immediately, as I opened my eyes, I smelled a stench in the house and felt an evil presence. I heard you rebuke the Enemy.

So I threw back my covers, but before my feet could touch the floor, I heard the Lord speak to me. He said, *This is Diane's fight. You stay here and pray for her. She must win this battle on her own. You'll know when it's time to join her."*

Ruth prayed fervently for me and rebuked the Enemy aggressively from her bed.

I rolled out of bed onto the floor while I held tightly to my Bible. I could feel a heavy pressure on me that kept me pinned to the floor in a seated position. My bed was still shaking. This battle needed a more specific "sword of the Spirit." I needed the exact weapon that would truly become that sword to cut off the head of the serpent.

I asked the Lord, "I've had the Enemy try to intimidate me in many ways before, but this is the worst. Does the Enemy fight with this extreme warfare against *every* woman who accepts a greater call on her life—especially a call to become a senior pastor?"

Then I became as quiet as I could under the circumstances. My bed continued to shake and I was still pinned to the floor in an upright position.

No, the Adversary doesn't come with such force against every woman who accepts the call to be a senior pastor, but he does come. He is reacting this way because you have a global ministry.

These end times are a part of the fulfillment of Acts 2:17-18. I want to use my sons and daughters to their fullest extent. I want my sons and daughters in position to work together. I want my entire army mobile, all ages and both genders. I have anointed you with a specific message for women and a specific calling to the entire body of Christ for these last days. The Enemy is aware of this. You're a threat to his kingdom.

> *"And it shall come to pass in the last days, says God, That I will pour out of My Spirit upon all flesh; Your sons and your daughters shall prophesy, Your young men shall see visions, Your old men shall dream dreams. And on My menservants and on My maidservants I will pour out of My Spirit in those days; And they shall prophesy.* (Acts 2:17-18)

"Lord, I embrace the fullness of my calling!" I said. "What sword of the Spirit do I need to defeat *this* calculated assault against my calling?"

I was instructed to turn to Revelation Chapter 12 and read it aloud. *Chapter 12 is the chapter where for over six years, I have taught a message entitled, "Overcoming Satan's Assault on Women." In this message I expose the relentless assaults from the Enemy on women, which began when Eve agreed to bring forth the Messiah. She made a covenant on behalf of all women to bring forth a Seed that would crush the head of the Serpent.*

"Lord, You've done many miracles with this message. You have set women free from the affects of abuse, anger toward men, and unforgiveness. You've set women free from female trouble. Many became free from self-hatred. And all of these women realized Satan was their real enemy, not themselves or men.

"Is this a part of the warning You gave me in November? That's when You said in February I would see another level of Satan's assault on women. I feel I'm fighting for myself and other women also."

Yes, this assault is a part of what I revealed in November, but not the whole assault—there is more to come before this month is out.

My body was weak, but I felt fortified in my spirit by hearing Revelation 12 was my key weapon. I had what I needed, my specific sword, in hand. I read the entire chapter out loud—slowly, deliberately, and with boldness. Simultaneously, I imagined myself thrusting the Word of God as a spear into my enemies.

I saw myself as Jael when she nailed the tent stake into the head of Israel's sleeping enemy, Sisera, in Judges Chapter 4. She only had one chance to get it right or her enemy would have awakened and killed her. With precision and determination to move beyond her fear, with the tent peg in her hand and the mallet in the other she nailed Israel's enemy in the head.

As I spoke the last words of the last verse of Revelation 12, miraculously the assault stopped. All of it was gone. The darkness left, the bed stopped shaking, and I was able to stand up.

"Whoa! Thank You, Lord Jesus, for the release of power through Revelation 12. I praise You for the victory! There's more power in this chapter than I ever imagined!"

Then God changed the subject. *The power of My grace is here now for you to forgive Chuck. Unforgiveness will never be an issue if you accept this grace now. The Enemy will not be able to stop you because of unforgiveness. The same is true for you to forgive Lilly once and for all. If you'll do that now from the depths of your being, I will heal you and give you the grace. My grace will be sufficient for you to walk in liberty.*

I laid my Bible down and stretched my arms toward heaven. While tears streamed down my face, I cried out to the Lord. "I receive Your grace to forgive. I receive grace from the depths of my heart." Then I yelled because I felt like I had to push the words out of my mouth. "I *forgive* Chuck for choosing to be with another woman! I *forgive* Lilly for choosing to have a relationship with my husband, a married man and her pastor! I don't know if their choices will lead to Chuck getting a divorce, I hope not, but I forgive them no matter what happens.

"I forgive Chuck because he didn't turn to You when He started his midlife crisis a few years ago. I forgive him for teaching our sons to have pride instead of confident humility. I forgive him for showing them how to be disrespectful toward me and other women. I forgive Chuck for choosing to be self-centered and not care who he hurts. I forgive him for betraying the congregation.

"Lord, Your Word says in Colossians 3:19: *Husbands, love your wives and do not be bitter toward them.* I forgive him of accusing me for things that went wrong at home and at church. He allowed the Enemy, the Accuser, to accuse me without ever asking You what was the truth. Like Adam, he says the problem is the wife You gave him. I forgive him for not taking responsibility for his own actions. I forgive him for working to destroy my womanhood because he didn't understand the nature of a woman."

"I forgive now and forever! I choose not to allow unforgiveness to be a part of my future! Lord, destroy any way that the Enemy can use unforgiveness to destroy me. Thank You for doing for me what You alone can accomplish. Thank You for Your grace!"

I took several deep sighs and plopped down on the end of my bed. I struggled to mentally take in all that had happened in one night. I sat quietly with my eyes closed for what seemed like an hour, but was probably only twenty minutes.

I climbed back into bed and glanced at my clock which read 2:21 a.m. After I lay there a few minutes, I flipped over to my left side to get more comfortable. The moonlight shined on my mirrored closet door, and I saw a reflection of Chuck in the mirror. I rubbed my eyes and looked again. The reflection was still there. I sat up in bed, and I saw a vision of Chuck as he stood at his open closet. I knew he was actually out of town, so I rubbed my eyes, closed then opened them again.

This wasn't a dream, I was wide awake. This was an open-eyed vision. I saw him in slacks and a pastel long-sleeve dress shirt. He had a large box about waist high in front of him. Chuck is 6'4" tall, so waist high is a tall box. He methodically put all his shoes in the bottom of the box. Next his jackets, his sweaters, then his pants, and last his shirts and ties.

I didn't take my eyes off him as I slowly swung my legs around and put my feet on the floor. *What's going on?*

In the vision Chuck picked up the box, stared at me a moment, then walked slowly out our bedroom door and down the narrow hall. I jumped off the bed and chased after him, as I became hysterical.

"No! No! No! You don't have to do this. Chuck, God can heal your heart if you let Him." I pleaded and reasoned with the vision. "Why did you choose to go this path? You're going to hurt our kids and everyone else! I love you! I forgive you! You can forgive me! Don't leave! Don't do it, Chuck! Don't do it!"

He stopped for a moment at our front door and turned to face me. I stopped dead in my tracks. While clutching his box, he looked at me with such hatred it brought shivers up my spine. Without a word, he turned around and vanished through our closed front door.

"No, Chuck! No!"

Chapter 15

Moving Forward

For I know the thoughts that I think toward you, says the Lord, thoughts of peace and not of evil, to give you a future and a hope (Jeremiah 29:11).

R uth came running out of her bedroom in a panic. "Diane, what's happening? Why are you yelling I forgive you and screaming *no*, at Chuck? He's not here is he?"

She didn't know I was following an open vision.

"Are you OK?" she asked. "What's happening?"

I turned toward Ruth. "He's leaving! I had a vision of him leaving! He's really going to leave! He's not going to have a turnaround like we believed. I had a vision of him leaving and he looked at me with such hatred it was scary. Ruth, my heart feels like it's going to explode! I have to go pray, right now!"

I ran down the hall to my spare bedroom, where I fell on my face and sobbed uncontrollably in a way that felt like I would never stop. Ruth prayed for Chuck and me in her bedroom. As the uncontrollable grief subsided, I cried softly. The Comforter, which is the Holy Spirit, comforted me with the truth. He spoke a truth that broke my heart even further, but truth we don't want to hear may hurt more, but it also settles our hearts in a strange way because it's the answer.

I knew I needed to ask God some hard questions. I needed to gather the courage not to fear the answers, but accept whatever God said were the consequences of the vision. "Lord, I already feel this ripping away in my heart. What is this depth of loneliness hurting my heart? Has Chuck already turned his heart completely away from me?

"Lord, today You had Dr. Valerie speak on moving into the next dimension, no matter what it costs. While she was teaching, you deposited a new anointing in me. You are equipping me for my next position. I'm going to move forward, even though I am afraid."

I let out a big sigh. "God, I wanted Chuck to get back to the reverential fear of the Lord, and the passion and love he had for You and for me. I wanted Chuck to get healed. I had hoped he would stop criticizing me.

"Father, the vision of Chuck leaving is it permanent or temporary? Can I keep my marriage and fulfill your call and destiny for my life?"

The answer came back decisive and clear. *No, you cannot. So I am releasing you from the marriage because of Chuck's choices. His choices now are because of his choices over the years. Chuck has refused healing from the root of bitterness from the beginning of your relationship and bitterness from his relationship with his mother. His decisions over the years not to submit to Me and forgive, and his decision not to admit he had a problem has lead to his current decisions. He harbors deep pain and feelings of betrayal. I have unlocked the pain of betrayal many times and when I do he feels betrayed by everyone. He doesn't bring his pain to Me and allow Me to set him free. Instead, when he feels the pain of betrayal, he allows the Enemy to manipulate the pain so he will not trust anyone, which then causes him to isolate to protect himself from more pain. This is why his pain has gotten worse with age.*

The main reason Chuck is leaving is because you are no longer in unity of heart and purpose. You both know Chuck has allowed a dividing sword to be placed in the Enemy's hand, and he has not chosen to remove the source—a root of bitterness. He has been convinced by the Enemy that he can trust Lilly and not you.

One day, you will be thankful that he was seeing someone else before he left.

"I don't understand how I could be thankful about something that has caused me such pain, nevertheless, at Your Word, I choose to trust You, Lord."

Satan has full access to what is still hidden in the dark and not brought to My light. Chuck has refused to get free from the feeling of betrayal he has carried for twenty-four years concerning the question of whether Curtis is his natural child or not. So, when he leaves you, he will feel compelled to expose his pain so he can have his catharsis. People will call you to tell you what they've heard him say from the pulpit, be strong and courageous and don't defend yourself. Don't let the Enemy assault your heart with arrows of shame or pain.

Maintain your victory and talk openly when others mention this. You cannot rebuke this storm or cancel its effect. You must go through this.

"Yes, Lord, I hear and understand. I call on the Holy Spirit's help and Your grace to guide me." I dried my tears, got up from the floor, and slowly walked into Ruth's bedroom after two hours of prayer with the Lord.

"Ruth, I was yelling at Chuck because the vision was so real I could actually see him right in front of me. God just spoke to me and said he is going to justify his reason for leaving me by exposing something that we kept secret since before we married. Chuck will tell people he can't trust me and they can't either."

I told her about Curtis's conception—about how I regretted that I never took Curtis to counseling and he still doesn't know about this. How I obeyed Chuck's pride and my shame and overrode the promptings of my heart for us to expose this secret so God could have cleansed it years ago.

Ruth stared at me with wide-eyed amazement then said, "Please call Rev. Ev and tell her about your vision. Chuck was at her board meeting two weeks ago. Maybe he shared something with her. At any rate, you've got to talk to someone who can give you some wisdom. I don't know what to say."

I called Rev. Ev at 6:00 a.m., her usual prayer time. I asked her if Chuck had shared anything important with her about us when he was there for the board meeting.

"He said things are going well with your plans for the transition of you to become the senior pastor. I'm sad I won't make the installation service on May 3 he mentioned, I have a speaking engagement out of town."

I shared the vision with her.

"That's terrible! I hope that *doesn't* come to pass and it was a warning for prayer and not God showing what is about to happen! I can't wrap my mind around that. And you say he's seeing someone else? I can't believe my ears. Are you sure you're not overreacting to an unhealthy emotional attachment to a woman in the church? Sometimes men enjoy their ego being stroked by another female. Chuck's been a man of integrity, maybe God is warning us so we can pray and so He can intervene."

"No Ev," I said. "It has gone beyond an emotional attachment. I'm not saying they are sexually involved, but I am saying God let me know in no uncertain terms that he *will* leave. I don't know if it's sooner or later."

"I'm speech . . . less." She paused for a long time and then asked her husband to join us on the line. She briefly told him I had a vision of Chuck leaving me. He was stunned.

"Let's pray and ask God to expose the truth. We'll ask Him to cancel whatever can be cancelled and give grace and healing where you guys need healing."

We prayed. Ruth and I went to bed around 7:30 a.m. Monday morning. I took Dr. Valerie to lunch, but didn't say anything regarding the events of Sunday night because I didn't want to distract her from her ministry to the people at our prophetic school. Also I didn't know what God wanted me to say.

Our prophetic school included other ministers and many from other churches. Several said they learned a lot from Dr. Valerie that night. Chuck returned Tuesday morning. He and I visited with Dr. Valerie, and she shared about the powerful services we had while he was away. I didn't tell either of them about the visit from the demonic realm and the vision of Chuck from God on Sunday night. Chuck mentioned to her that the prophetic demonstration was concerning me becoming the senior pastor. She was shocked but at the same time congratulated me.

Then I understood why I needed to fast the whole month of February. I needed to concentrate to hear from God and obey Him. My focus would have been interrupted with me spending time overeating because of my anxiety.

The Holy Spirit made it clear that my Sunday night visit from the kingdom of darkness was the first phase of the February assault He had spoken about back in November. If there was more to come, I knew I needed to be spiritually and emotionally prepared for this next assault from the Enemy.

March, 1992

Before Chuck and I left for our scheduled counseling appointment that we decided on Valentines' Day to make with Dr. Dianne in Arizona, Chuck insisted we make an appointment with one of the most well respected women ministers in our nation, Dr. Iverna Tompkins.

Dr. Tompkins, a renowned leader to leaders and a dynamic Bible preacher and author, had spoken for us at one of our first pastor's luncheons in the early days of our ministry. We attended her Training Leaders for Christ (TLC) retreats in Arizona along with our friends Jill Austin and Revs John and Dana, in the late 80's.

We arrived at our Phoenix hotel the evening before our appointment. We had a pleasant dinner and a fun swim in the indoor pool. I momentarily forgot the reason we were there until later when I caught Chuck on the phone with his "lady friend," Lilly. At our appointment with Dr. Dianne, Chuck admitted he wanted to be with someone other than his wife.

Although I had forgiven him, I admitted to wanting to break his legs so he'd have to crawl out the front door when he left. I also admitted to wanting to kick Lilly out of the church even though I had forgiven her. I was not going to accuse her of anything, but I believed I had a Scriptural plan to take care of a problem in the church. Romans 16:17 says to *mark those* who cause discord and offences. I planned to have the ushers *mark her* one Sunday by escorting her out of the building and asking her never to return.

"Diane," Dr. Dianne said, "you're right about the passage in Romans 16:17: *Note* (mark) *those who cause divisions and offences, contrary to the doctrine which you learned, and avoid them.*

"But if you use this Scripture to have the ushers escort her out, no matter how wrong people may think she is, you'll become the bad guy, and it will backfire on you. People always sympathize with the perceived underdog. Pray about what God wants from you."

After counsel, I gave up on both of my ideas, concluding neither would have God's approval.

That afternoon, we left Dr. Dianne's office and drove to see Dr. Iverna. She stood up behind her desk to shake our hands. "Good afternoon, pastors, I was thrilled to see your names on my calendar for this week. Pastor Chuck, I haven't talked to you since you attended my retreat four years ago. Good to see you." She shook his hand, and then motioned toward a chair facing her desk.

"Pastor Diane, good to see you again. It's been a couple of years since my pastors' wives convention when I last saw you." We shook hands, and she motioned toward the other chair facing her desk.

She looked at Pastor Chuck. "How can I serve you fine pastors today?"

"Dr. Iverna, I have tremendous respect for you and your accomplishments," Chuck said. "God has spoken to Diane and me that she is to become the senior pastor, and I will be the overseer of the ministry. You have shared with those at your retreats that you took over a church when your brother Dr. Judson Cornwall stopped pastoring. God made it clear that you were to become the senior pastor. How many years were you the senior pastor?"

"I became the senior pastor and I served in that capacity for three years after serving as assistant pastor for a few years."

"Diane is going through the same transition, but from co-pastor to senior pastor. I thought it would be good for her to get some advice from a seasoned female senior pastor."

"Before I give Diane some insight, I'd like to ask you a question," Dr. Iverna said. "When God has truly spoken for a woman to head a ministry, I have *never* seen a single instance in which the Enemy did not come to divide the couple or bring accusations against her through the church members. He hates women, and even more, he hates women who are called to be in charge and make such a bold stand for God's grace in her life. I'm sure the Enemy has showed up in one way or another to tear at the foundation of your marriage and ministry. How are things going between you two?"

Chuck put on a big grin. "We are doing fine! The church is doing well, and Diane and I are fine. Thanks for asking. We just came from Dr. Dianne who gave us some wisdom and now we're here for Diane's senior pastor advice from you."

She stared at him for a moment, and then looked my way.

I stared straight ahead like a robot. *I want to submit to my husband and pastor, but I don't want to be like Sapphira in the Book of Acts who fell dead for lying to the Holy Spirit in agreement with her husband when he lied.*

> *But a man named Ananias—his wife, Sapphira, conniving in this with him—sold a piece of land, secretly kept part of the price for himself, and then brought the rest to the apostles and made an offering of it.*

> *Peter said, "Ananias, how did Satan get you to lie to the Holy Spirit and secretly keep back part of the price of the field? . . . the money was yours to do with as you wished . . . You didn't lie to men but to God.*

> *Ananias, when he heard these words, fell down dead . . .*

Not more than three hours later, his wife, not knowing of what had happened, came in. Peter said, "Tell me, were you given this price for your field?"

"Yes," she said, "that price."

Peter responded, "What's going on here that you connived to conspire against the Spirit of the Master?" . . . They carried her out and buried her beside her husband (Acts 5:1-10 MSG).

God was not expecting her to follow her husband into sin and death. That's not His nature. She was accountable on her own. If she wasn't she would have instantly fell dead when her husband died no matter where she was. Also Peter would not have asked her to answer from her own convictions. She could have said, "No, that's not the amount we sold the land for. This is the correct amount, but we only want to give this much." She would have been commended by Peter. Instead, she told the same lie to Peter and the Holy Spirit that her husband told. As a result she died too.

I won't disrespect Chuck, but I'm not going to lie to God's servant. I wonder if I should get up from my chair and stand against the wall in case Chuck falls over dead. I'm not going out that way! If Dr. Iverna asks me a direct question, I will answer truthfully.

I believe she could tell my dilemma, so she chose not to direct any specific questions to me. I reached for my notebook to show her I was ready to write her instructions. I took copious notes. Then, in her wise maturity, she asked as we were departing, "Pastor Chuck, I would like to continue to mentor Diane after today. You mentioned that you both saw Dr. Dianne before you came to my office. May I have your permission to ask Dr. Dianne anything that may help me understand you wife's transition in your specific ministry and personal concerns? If the answer is no, I completely understand. That is strictly client and counselor privileged information."

I'm sure he figured he would never see her again, and being the man of dignity he was, he didn't want to look like he had anything to hide. "By all means," he said. "We appreciate the help. I've laid a good foundation as the senior pastor for over nine years. Diane has a good example to follow, but I'm also glad you're here to help her be a success."

Sunday, May 3, 1992

We had the installation celebration on Sunday evening, May 3. Carlton was away at college, but Curtis joined us for the service. He laid hands on me also as the ministers prayed over me for my formal installation as senior pastor. Those who attended said it was a beautiful service. Several ministers were present. Rev. Joe Jordan waited to return to Oklahoma until after my service. It was a special blessing to have him and Barbara there because they have always encouraged me to become all God wants me to be.

Monday, May 4, 1992

Chuck called me while I was working in my office at church. "Diane, I received a call from Mother Dear that Aunt Joelle passed away this afternoon. Please teach the prophetic school tonight because I don't know how long I'll be with Mom."

"Please tell Mother Dear I'm sorry to hear about Aunt Joe, and I'll come see her tonight after class if you're still there, or I'll see her tomorrow. Tell her we'll pray tonight at class for her, and the rest of their family."

After class I received a message from Eric, one of our leaders, that Pastor Chuck had called the church office to say there was no need for me to go to his mom's house. He had already left and was heading for the gym, so he asked me not to wait up for him.

Chuck is a sentimental person and loves to reminisce about his close relationships. I knew he was not headed to the gym, but to be comforted and to reminisce with Lilly. Even though I knew we would be separated sometime in the near future, I couldn't stand the thought of him sharing his grief about losing the person who had also been my aunt for twenty-four years. I wanted to share my grief and laugh and cry about Aunt Joe with him. I felt betrayed, and infuriated. I didn't pray, and I didn't go home.

Instead, I drove through the gym parking lot to look for his car, but it wasn't there. I drove to Lilly's apartment building and waited for someone to open the pedestrian gate. I walked to her parking spot and saw his car in her guest stall. I sat on a bench next to her apartment for about thirty minutes. Then I realized I didn't need to talk to either one of them. That would accomplish nothing. He had made his choice. But in my flesh, I decided I couldn't come all that way without letting him know that I knew he had lied to me about the gym. I took my key to his car and moved his car outside the gate and parked it on the street. I felt numb as I drove home.

About an hour later Chuck called. "I need you to look into our insurance file and get the VIN number for my Camaro and my insurance policy number. Someone has stolen my car."

"Oh, where was it when it was stolen? Were you at the gym?"

"No, I went by the home of one of our members. That's where it was stolen."

"I know you're not at the gym. I knew where you were. I moved your car. It's outside the main entrance parked on the street to the left of the gate."

"You moved my car! You have betrayed me! You have embarrassed me in front of the police! What am I supposed to tell them after I reported it stolen?"

"Why not try the truth this time? Tell them your wife moved the car and you didn't know it. They'll totally understand."

Chuck came home at 1 a.m. and went directly to our garage. He came into our bedroom with a large box. "You have betrayed me for the last time! I'm moving out tonight and going to a motel. My job here is done. We installed you as pastor last night!"

He opened our mirrored closet door and methodically put his things in the box. First, his shoes and socks, then his jackets and sweaters, then his shirts and ties and set the big box aside. Then he got his toiletries from the bathroom and put them in a smaller box and stacked it on top of the larger box, all without a word.

"You don't have to leave like this!" I said. "I'm not pushing you out the door. Why are you acting this way? Why do you betray me, and then accuse me of betraying you?" I could feel the Holy Spirit bidding me to be quiet. When I got quiet, then I remembered the open-eyed vision I had back in February of Chuck leaving not with a suitcase but a large box.

Like the vision, I followed behind him to the front door. Clinging to his boxes, he turned to me with hatred in his eyes. "I'll get the rest of my stuff later. I'll still be working at church, so no one needs to know I've moved out. But I will never move back in."

We continued to work together at church. That was hard. Even Betty, our secretary, didn't know we were living apart. Chuck would arrive long before Betty and work until I arrived. He would come into my office and discuss whatever we needed to talk about then leave. Only Ruth and Curtis knew. Oh of course, Lilly knew too. Carlton was told when he came home on Memorial Day weekend, three weeks after his dad moved out. We didn't want it to affect his studies.

I received a membership resignation letter from Lilly the Thursday after Chuck moved out. It stated that Sunday, May 10th Mother's Day, would be her last day with us. She had been with us for six years. Traditionally when someone who served in any leadership capacity left our church, I always had my hospitality hostess purchase a gift for them on behalf of the congregation. This time was no different. It was hard to do, but a portion of Scripture kept rolling around in my heart. *But I say to you, love your enemies, bless those who curse you, do good to those who hate you, and pray for those who spitefully use you, that you may be sons of your Father in heaven* (Matthew 5:44-45a). My leaders and I prayed for God's direction for Lilly and the congregation hugged her and said goodbye.

My responsibility to the congregation was to model God's unconditional love. Pastor Chuck showed up at the service and stuck around until we finished praying for Lilly. I'm sure he wanted to make sure we treated her well. He said goodbye to the congregation after we prayed over Lilly and told them he needed to be with his mother after the loss of her sister.

I asked for God's grace to preach my Mother's Day sermon that day. The church family didn't know the significance of that day, but later, in July, when they knew Chuck left me on Monday and Lilly left the church that following Sunday—Mother's Day. And she received a parting gift. They marveled at the grace and love of God that filled the service. So God got the glory instead of the Enemy.

I continued my counseling until the end of July, but Chuck decided he was finished at the end of April. After we discussed with Dr. Dianne what we would do about a vacation cruise for May that the church had given us for our anniversary. We decided I would still take the vacation and take Ruth instead. At the conclusion of that discussion he decided he was done with counseling. Dr. Dianne helped us navigate through that difficult time. This was Chuck's plan all along and I was thankful for her.

Friday, June 5, 1992

My women's retreat in Lake Arrowhead, CA had barely gotten started when my speaker, Sister Frieda, asked the ladies from my church and their friends to surround me and pray for me. She felt God wanted to encourage me right that moment.

"The Lord says Diane that you have spoken many times to Him and asked, '*Lord, why does this have to be?*'

"God says to you, *My daughter, I have called you forward to do a work for Me. It is not an easy task that I have given unto thee. But, you shall be known throughout this land, as a woman who walks with Me hand in hand. The tongues of the unlearned I shall stop. Watch Me and see, for I am going to use you mightily.*"

She walked closer toward me. "God is showing me that there have been lies spoken against you. The lies were spoken by the ill-informed and the unlearned—by people who judged according to man. The Holy Spirit is showing me that He is undoing the Enemy's plan. Continue to strengthen people for Him, because He says He is going to turn the whole thing around.

"I also hear the words, 'Do *not* to be concerned about Chuck. You've got to let go of that concern.'"

Those words pierced my emotions like a knife. I was terrified about Chuck's relationship with Christ. I sobbed aloud as I exhaled all the pressure I held in from my conversation with Chuck that same morning just before I left for the retreat. No one knew he announced to me he was filing for divorce.

She instructed the women in the auditorium. "If you are someone who prays regularly for Diane, come now and surround her and pray softly over her." As I sobbed with my head in my hands she prayed. "Father, I thank You for strengthening her. I thank You for the virtue of the Almighty and the power that is found in Your hand. Father, Diane is Your handmaiden, so we surround her with our prayers, in the Name of Jesus.

We speak Your Word in Isaiah 54:17 which says: *No weapon formed against you shall prosper, And every tongue which rises against you in judgment You shall condemn. This is the heritage of the servants of the LORD, And their righteousness is of Me, says the LORD.*

"Father, You have said to us in Isaiah 49:25, *I will contend with him who contends with you, And I will save your children.*

"We hold onto the promises of God with Diane. I thank You Lord, that she will reverse the curse. You are gracious and kind. You will judge and do what is right, God.

"Pastor Diane, I see a dark cloud that has begun to swirl like a whirlwind. It is getting darker and bigger, but the Lord says He will see you through the storm, He'll see you through by His grace."

The pressure subsided. The ladies returned to their seats, and Sister Frieda taught her Bible message for the evening.

I hadn't planned to tell anyone—not even Sister Frieda of my concern about Chuck. I definitely was not going to say anything about our conversation that morning. But it became obvious to me that God didn't want me to carry the pressure and pain from our conversation alone. He loved me and wanted His grace to heal me right then instead of my plans to wait for a convenient time to call on Him to heal my heart after the retreat. I realized the Holy Spirit wanted me to share my plight with Sister Frieda.

She said, "Diane, I felt dread as I saw that dark whirlwind cloud that got bigger as it came toward you. I felt it was not going away soon. Do you have any idea what the cloud represents and why it's in your life?"

"Yeah, I do. This morning, before I left for the retreat, Chuck said he was going to file for divorce *today*."

"What? I can't believe it! I've known you guys for years, and he seemed to be in love with you. This is a shock! You two have served the Lord together for years. What happened?"

"The Lord revealed that Chuck had some serious betrayals he didn't allow Jesus to heal. His heart became hardened, and he lost some of the fear of the Lord. He became lukewarm in his walk with Christ. He's in his late forties, and I think also could be going through a midlife crisis."

"What has he been doing?"

"He has been cruel with his words to me over the last five years. He's said hateful things that he has not said since we've been saved. He has become more verbally abusive. He has never said a curse word, but spoken evil curses to intentionally hurt me. He moved out of the house in May."

"You're not going to tell me he's seeing someone else, are you?"

"Yes, for two years—a lady in our church named, Lilly."

Sister Frieda's mouth dropped open. We stared at each other as she struggled to embrace what she heard. Speechless she motioned with her hand for me to continue.

"I've counseled her over the years, and I don't think she can be faithful in a relationship. God has ministered to her through many speakers but she hasn't allowed Him to heal her completely. As a child, she was an incest victim for years who, as an, adult became a violator. She told us when she first came to the church six years ago that she had affairs with other pastors. I think for them to be together is a trap from the Enemy against Chuck's calling."

I got up from my chair and nervously paced the floor. "I'm worried Chuck will marry her and get betrayed by her unfaithful ways. He has accused me of being the kind of person she *actually is*. That scares me for him.

"I'm deeply concerned about his future with Christ. He has lost a lot of the fear of the Lord. He doesn't seem to have conviction for doing wrong. I'm not saying they are sexually involved. Chuck says they aren't, but he has been having an emotional affair. He came over this morning before I left for the retreat and said he is definitely filing for divorce today. I tried to give God those concerns as I drove to the retreat. Thanks for hearing from the Holy Spirit tonight, I feel much better after releasing my fears concerning Chuck."

Sister Frieda dropped her head into her hands. "Not Chuck!" She lifted her head to look up at me with a wrinkled forehead. "He has always seemed a man of integrity, and he always talked about integrity. It seemed important to him."

I stopped pacing and stood in front of her chair. "You're right. He actually prided himself on his walk of integrity. He was often critical of others who didn't walk in integrity. Lately, I've thought about the scripture passage that says: *Therefore let him who thinks he stands take heed lest he fall* (1 Corinthians 10:12)."

Again Frieda dropped her head down into her hands. "This breaks my heart. Of all my friends, I never would've thought this would happen to you guys."

"Me neither, I still love Chuck. I have to let God remove the love because if I try to do it I would harden my heart." I threw both hands in the air then plopped down onto the couch next to her chair. "God has used us to heal so many marriages. But . . . I guess it's all about a person's own will.

"This morning, Chuck told me, 'God has said that Moses gave a bill of divorcement because of the hardness of men's hearts.' My heart is hard toward you so I have Scriptural grounds for a divorce. I am not having an affair because I have not had sex with Lilly, so you cannot accuse me of that or say *you* have grounds for divorce."

"One of my nicknames for Chuck is Mr. Super Perfectionist, and because he's like that he gave me a list of things I should know because he's divorcing me." I recited how he read from his list.

"'First you need to change the locks on the door so I don't have a key to get in,' he told me. Can you believe that?

"'Second, Carlton is coming home for the summer so you can stay in the house for a while until we come to an agreement about when to sell it. Third, if you fall behind on any payment, then the house will become mine and you will move out. I'm putting that in the divorce papers. Fourth, I will only take my personal bills. The rest are yours. Fifth, since I have no job yet, there will be no spousal support for you. If you ever bring up spousal support then you will owe me a monthly payment.'

"I told him 'I don't care about spousal support. God has always taken care of me. Most of the time He used you and I was grateful.' But my trust is in the Lord, Frieda.

"I said, 'Chuck, I don't want a divorce. But I also don't want to live with you the way you are. The way things are now, no daughter of God deserves to be treated the way you've been treating me these last five years, and especially the last two years.'

"He said, 'Well, all that is over now. I have an appointment with a lawyer as soon as I leave the house this morning.' Then he was gone. And I left to drive up the mountain for this retreat."

Frieda and I both cried, prayed, and held onto each other. I told her I didn't think it was time to say anything to the women of my church yet. We prayed that the Lord would show me when to say something to our congregation. Chuck and I still worked together at church, but he was never there on Sundays.

July, 1992

Two people from two different states called the same morning before 9 a.m. and said virtually the same thing to me. "You have been praying about the time for an important decision you need to make. This Sunday is the time to do it." The messengers did not know what the message was about, but I did. This was God's confirmation to me that it was time to tell the congregation that their pastors were getting a divorce.

After the second call, I collapsed onto the foot of my bed. "Lord, I don't want to face the congregation with this news and see the grief on their faces. I don't know if I have the strength. Just rapture me out of here."

I felt all strength leave my body as I gave myself over to the care of what I faced. I felt as though I would faint. The more I thought about my circumstances, and how much I didn't want to move forward with this next step, the more lightheaded I became. As I fell forward because I had no strength left I felt a hard poke from an extremely large finger on my left shoulder.

"Ouch!"

Two more hard pokes pushed me over onto my right side on the bed. This was a big angel from the Lord. I'm sure he's the one that's probably been with me since birth and he's sent to keep me on track with my purpose. He probably gets paid overtime for working with me.

"What'd you want?" I asked as I recovered to an upright position.

I heard the angel speak audibly with a deep voice which sounded like a military officer. *Endure hardship as a good soldier of Jesus Christ!*

I recognized this as 2 Timothy 2:3: *You therefore must endure hardship as a good soldier of Jesus Christ.*

I jumped to a standing position. "Yes, sir! What do you want me to do?"

Your old assignment is over! Ask God for your next assignment! It's time to move forward!

Immediately my spirit, mind, and body were strengthened. I no longer felt as if I were going to faint. The Word of God through the angel gave me the grace and strength to walk through the closure to my former assignment as a wife and leading the ministry as a couple. I was strengthened with the fortitude to be a single woman head of a business—His church.

God gave me the grace the following Sunday to tell the church about my divorce. I felt no pain. "We'll endure this hardship as good soldiers of Jesus Christ. He will heal us and move us forward." This was my concluding remarks to the congregation.

End of July, 1992

I was served divorce papers in mid-June. In July we still worked together at church. We had switched salaries. He took the part-time salary. I received the senior pastor's salary.

In early July I flew to Arizona for my counseling appointment. Dr. Dianne asked, "When are you going to change hats?"

"What do you mean?"

"When are you going to stop thinking like a wife and fully put on the hat of a senior pastor? As a senior leader, you have a board member who has said to you and to his counselor that he has left his wife to start a life with someone else. What would you do with that board member if he were not your husband?"

"He would be brought before the board, asked for his keys, and be removed from the executive board immediately. As a board we have written him letters to come to a board meeting, but at the last minute he always says he had another commitment."

"Well, he keeps saying he's leaving the church soon, but he wants to keep receiving a salary until he has set himself up with some other income," Dr. Dianne said. "You need to change hats and stand in the position God has given you."

"I will!" I said emphatically. "I will send a letter this time which states it is mandatory for him to come to the next meeting for us to discuss his position at the church."

At the board meeting after my counseling I asked the board to draft a letter to ask Pastor Chuck to come to a mandatory board meeting to discuss his position at the church. Two weeks later we had that infamous board meeting at the home of one of the board members.

On my drive there, I had a conversation with God about having to take this specific next step. "Lord, every senior pastor who messed up either ran off with the church member and his wife or someone else became the senior pastor. Or he had a rendezvous out of town and didn't come back. I have seen where the pastor put his wife out of the church and took over the church with his mistress who soon became his new wife.

"But God, I have *never* heard of a wife becoming the senior pastor and having to *ask* her former pastor/husband to hand in his keys. I don't want to do this. I ask you for the grace to operate in the authority You've given me. I will wear the hat this position requires at this difficult time."

The board members and I arrived about half an hour before Chuck so we could pray. Chuck walked in and after the secretary made sure we had a quorum, I took charge. "Pastor Chuck, the purpose of this mandatory board meeting is to ask you to turn in your keys and ask for your written resignation from the board and from the church staff. Your decision to leave your wife and become involved with another woman has disqualified you for these two valuable positions. As you know according to our staff and board member qualifications you are now disqualified to serve."

He looked into the face of each board member.

I saw the pain in his eyes. I could hear the pain behind the hurtful words that came from his lips when I asked for the keys. It broke my heart. But the deception and pride in his mind were greater than his pain. There was no apology or repentance instead he blamed the board for his self-inflicted wounds. He used his displaced anger to project the majority of his false accusations toward me.

When Pastor Chuck finished accusing us of betraying him, without a word I put out my hand and he reluctantly handed me the church keys. Then he picked up the resignation form from the table. He said,

"I'll mail this form back to the church. I served faithfully for nine years as pastor to all of you and this is how you treat me. Goodbye."

At the next board meeting we received the signed resignation form, and a letter demanding severance and vacation pay. Myself and each board member received a separate letter from Pastor Chuck threatening a personal lawsuit. Some board members were frightened, and some were angry. I wanted to just tear the letters up and say, *leave us alone and just go your way. If you don't want us, then we don't want you.* But this would not be pleasing to God.

After each board member read their letter and I allowed them time to express their feelings. Then I asked them to go into the sanctuary to forgive him and pray. I asked us to pray audibly so we could agree with each other and so I could hear whether or not our hearts were clear. Some needed to forgive Pastor Chuck as well as Lilly, so we were there for a while—over three hours. "We'll stay on the altar until we have pure hearts and clean hands. I believe if our ways please the Lord we will not need to go to court." I said.

We prayed until all of us came up with close to the same amount of money to give Pastor Chuck as severance. It was well below what he had asked for, and we were taking bill money to do this, but we knew God would make it up to us. We drafted a letter for the secretary to type and left the church about 1 a.m.

Chuck sent us a letter of acceptance for the check we sent. He also expressed his disappointment that the amount was below what he expected. But God knew what he would accept.

Every Sunday evening we had regular repentance services with the whole congregation. We needed to move forward as a body to forgive him and forgive her. We also addressed any doors that had been opened to the Adversary through our former leader's disobedience, and through anything God wanted to remove from our hearts. We could not move forward without the favor of God.

Over a course of time I took three two-day trips to a secluded cabin in the mountains to pray through and release my grief. I was single-minded about getting free and I knew God would heal me if I was determined to be healed. I borrowed the money to pay for the cabin and did not wait on a "convenient" time. I wanted to show God how serious I was. I also needed to gain wisdom on how to move forward. The Lord was faithful. He spoke to me from Joshua 1:2: *Moses* [Chuck] *My servant is dead* [to this assignment]. *Now therefore, arise, go over this Jordan* [Inland Empire, Riverside, San Bernardino], *you and all this people, to the land which I am giving to them.*

The Holy Spirit spoke to me on my first trip. *You're their senior pastor, and they need to talk to their pastor about their feelings of betrayal from their former pastor. I'll so cover you that you will hear their words, and it will be like they are talking about someone else and not your husband. You will console and comfort them with My comfort.*

On my third trip, He spoke to me again. *You can quit looking for your grief now, because I have supernaturally removed it. Go back and tell the people that if they will choose to arise from their shame and grief, then I will supernaturally remove this from them as I did for you.*

That following Sunday we studied Isaiah 53:4a: *Surely he has borne our griefs and carried our sorrows.*

"God has supernaturally removed my grief and shame, and He will do the same for you today," I said. "Jesus carried our grief to the cross so we don't need to carry it. When Moses died, God gave them thirty days to grieve. Then He said, 'Pack up and move forward to the promised land.' God gave us time to grieve now our grieving season is over.

"In the name of Jesus, I break the back of grief and shame. I command you to leave this people!"

The power of God was awesome. Grief was broken off the church members. A visitor who was the mother of a congregant gave her testimony at the end of the service. "Pastor, my husband has been in a rest home for ten years. I see him every day, and every day I grieve over him. Grief has been with me constantly for the last ten years. I feel free today! All my grief is gone! I'll visit him today with a different attitude."

It took us a couple of years to fully resurrect our dry bones and become a mighty army again. The rumor around the city and in some other states was that we had folded as a church and I had left the ministry, but it was untrue. Instead, we moved forward, away from the shame, and we let go of the grief to become a healthy vibrant soul-winning, community-impacting, leadership-training church. We said to anyone who asked about us, "We're changing the world from here—changing lives in the Inland Empire and the world."

February – April, 1993

Calls flooded my home from famous ministry television personalities to former members of our church as people heard that Chuck and I were divorced. Most said, "I thought you would be the last couple to ever get a divorce. You seemed so much in love and worked so well together."

All but two of my speaking engagements were cancelled. A few friends called to genuinely find out if I had become a two-headed monster or not. But most called to accuse me because they believed I had put Pastor Chuck out of the church because I wanted to take over the ministry. Some pastors said I was a strong woman and I needed to be handled and he didn't know how to "handle" me, whatever that meant.

It was sad that only four or five persons asked me to tell them what happened. Instead, most accused me of jealousy, control, and turning the church into a ladies' meeting and kicking out the men. Not one came to visit to see the spiritual climate of the ministry. One pastor, his wife and two board members came to my office to talk to me face to face. They weren't sure if they should cancel me as the guest speaker for their ladies' retreat. They decided they would talk to me face to face before drawing any conclusion. Chuck had recently ministered at their church and he and his assistant accused me of "things" by innuendos.

I called them the tribunal. But they were sincere and open. Thank God they decided it was OK for me to speak to their ladies and we remain friends today.

Suddenly in early 1993 a few weeks after our divorce was final the calls took on a different tone. Several called to apologize to me because they had asked Chuck if another person was involved with him or with me as a part of our reason for the divorce. He was emphatic the answer was no. But now people had received a wedding invitation from Chuck.

With each call that was an apology I looked up toward heaven and said, "Lord, I'm grateful he was seeing someone before he left. You told me I would be grateful one day that he was seeing someone. I am thankful now. To some this is the only way I receive any compassion from them. Even though the real reason we are divorced is the condition of his heart toward me and You.The wedding invitation has saved me a lot of dialogue and restored many that had presumed I was a monster."

Others ways I moved forward:

We paid part of the $5,500 debt but had no more money. I prayed then asked the landlord of the industrial building to let us out of the lease with no penalty or forgive us of the $4000.32 debt. We were forgiven of the debt!

In April, 1996, our proposal for a larger building was chosen out of six other churches.

In 1989 and again in1992 God spoke to me about governmental favor and influence. Today I am the Chaplain for the base reuse commission of city and county officials, March Joint Powers Commission and staff (MJPC and MJPA)

I cannot use the name of Jesus so I close with, "In the name of Your Son." They have seen undeniable answers to my one-minute prayers.

I've held my Beautiful Women of God Seminars in other cities, states, and New Zealand.

In 2006 I finally received my Master of Theological Studies, and now I'm a Doctor of Ministry candidate with Vision International University.

God has anointed me to coach and train leaders whether in ministry or the marketplace on how to bring the kingdom of God and the person of the Holy Spirit into their sphere of influence.

Leader of a class for Faith Based Recidivism Ministry which helps men and women become grounded in Christ and not return to prison.

I'm on the Advisory Boards of Liberty Savard Ministries, Women United in Ministry (WUM), Christian Women in Media, (CWIMA), and Healing Advisory Board for March Life Care Development Campus.

I'm a published author, national and international speaker for men's and women's meetings, churches, spiritual life coach, and prison minister. Spiritual advisor to marketplace leaders and entrepreneurs.

My best days are still ahead.

I moved forward through God's grace and determination. I will count both failures and successes of the past as nothing to gain a fuller relationship with Christ. I will apprehend that for which Christ apprehended me and saved my life that I may serve Him as an overcomer.

Not that I have already attained, or am already perfected; but I press on, that I may lay hold of that for which Christ Jesus has also laid hold of me. Brethren, I do not count myself to have apprehended; but one thing I do, forgetting those things which are behind and reaching forward to those things which are ahead, I press toward the goal for the prize of the upward call of God in Christ Jesus (Philippians 3:12-14).

PART V

Grace

Chapter 16

Sufficient Grace

*And God is able to make all grace abound toward you, that
you, always having all sufficiency in all things, may have
an abundance for every good work* (2 Corinthians 9:8).

can't imagine living without calling on the grace of God. Early
on I was given four powerful visions that changed my entire view
of grace. I know for a fact that the storms of adversity would
have pulled me under if I didn't know how to access the power of His
grace. Every storm the Enemy sent my way took grace to walk through
and grace to overcome.

To overcome means to struggle successfully against a difficulty; to
defeat somebody in a conflict in spite of obstacles.

Revelation 3:21 says: *To him who overcomes I will grant to sit with
Me on My throne, as I also overcame and sat down with My Father on
His throne.*

Many other rewards are promised to us if we choose to be an
overcomer. Christ says to the overcomer, "Well done good and faithful
servant." I determined to be faithful to His Word and do whatever it
took to learn how to obey it. No matter how many times I failed, I got
up and tried again. I also knew I could not succeed without God's grace.

Grace is a tangible force in the unseen spirit realm. There's *power* in
the grace of God. There's enough power to accomplish what we need
and enough power to accomplish what God desires. When our storms

and trials last for years and there isn't an end in sight, grace is our sustaining force—our answer. When we are petitioning God for closure and there is none, He says to us what He said to the Apostle Paul: *"My grace is sufficient for you, for My strength is made perfect* [complete] *in weakness."*

Paul's response was awesome: *Therefore most gladly I will rather boast in my infirmities* [weaknesses], *that the power of Christ may rest upon me.*

Here are the four illuminating visions about His grace:

First Vision

I saw the entire earth as a big globe and from heaven came what looked like pulsating radio waves. These waves showered down upon the earth with great force. They were intense when they left heaven and intense when they entered earth's atmosphere. These pulsating waves went into every home, church, synagogue, and mosque, every school, as well as every bar, night club, crack house, prison, even cult, and occult gatherings. It surrounded those who lived on the street. They permeated virtually everywhere there was life.

These waves encircled each person as if to search for a place to enter their lives. Although the waves surrounded them constantly, they never entered a person's life uninvited.

Whether the need was small or great, the only way the waves could enter someone's life was if they turned their will toward God in faith. The *faith* that caused the waves to increase and enter someone's life came from the person in need, or someone who prayed for them. Unfortunately, most people were oblivious to the pulsating waves around them. Others felt something prick their conscience—like inward pressure from God—but they rejected it.

In a flash, the vision was over.

"Lord, what were those waves from heaven that pulsated with such force and went everywhere?"

His answer: *My grace.*

Then a Scripture came to me: *Let us therefore come boldly to the throne of grace, that we may obtain mercy and find grace to help in time of need* (Hebrews 4:16).

God sits on a throne named grace and dispenses mercy and grace to help us whenever we need it, but we must do our part first. We need to approach His throne via humble prayer and ask for help. Our pride or our rebellion will keep us from seeking God. We need to ask, listen, and obey.

The words "grace to help" stood out to me.

Then a revelation came: No matter what the need, we can find grace to help. No matter how frequently we call on God for His grace, it's there for us every time. It already surrounds us.

Another Scripture opened my thinking: *But by the grace of God I am what I am, and His grace toward me was not in vain; but I labored more abundantly than they all, yet not I, but the grace of God which was with me* (1 Corinthians 15:10).

The Apostle Paul told us he did not take for granted or ignore the grace that came *toward* him and was *with* him. So the presence of those waves of grace was not in vain or unused. Paul was a powerful leader and the writer of two-thirds of the New Testament. He attributed who he was and what he accomplished to the grace of God—the divine assistance that was *with* him. He knew that to access the grace he had to simply talk to God in humble trust, admit he needed His help, and obey the Bible, then do the instructions he sensed God wanted.

In this vision the waves of grace infused into people the moment they turned their hearts in faith toward God. Most people I saw in the vision rejected the grace. They did this by saying to themselves one of the following:

- "God doesn't want to hear from me because I only talk to Him when I'm in trouble."
- "God is in control of everything, so why should I talk to Him when He's the one who caused the problem?"
- "I got myself into this, so I need to get myself out."

- "I don't need God to help me if I can help myself. He gave me common sense and a logical mind."
- "I don't believe there is a God, and if there is, then He doesn't care or He would do something about all the evil in the world."
- "I prayed and nothing happened, so God didn't answer my prayer."
- "I can pray for others, but I have a hard time believing for myself."

Then we blame God because He didn't rescue us from our problem in *our* way and in *our* timing. But God was waiting for us to use the faith He provided us according to Romans 12:3: *Through the grace given to me, to everyone who is among you . . . God has dealt to each one a measure of faith.*

Our faith is a gift, and the grace our faith activates is a gift, too! I basically understood grace to be God's undeserved favor. The Holy Spirit brought this to mind: *For by grace you have been saved through faith, and that not of yourselves; it is the gift of God* (Ephesians 2:8).

I knew I was saved by grace through faith, but obviously this vision showed me that the force behind grace is more powerful than I imagined. I looked grace up in my dictionary. The definition read: Grace is unmerited divine assistance given humans by God; a virtue that comes from God.

I meditated on what I had seen about the pulsating grace. I wrote the vision down in my prayer journal notebook along with the definition and some thoughts. I sat quietly in my chair to allow the Holy Spirit to expand on this. "Lord, how do I cooperate with You to activate that pulsating grace? What do you want me to do?"

The Holy Spirit impressed me with this thought. *Grace is all around everyone. When Christ's blood was shed, it released grace for all. Each one must choose grace. Pray for others to receive the grace that already surrounds them. The Enemy blinds their eyes to simple words of faith that will access My grace. Pray for their hearts to turn toward Me no matter where they are or what they've done. That's the quality of grace—it's undeserved, unmerited, unearned. It is a gift, so you can't work for it—only receive it. If anyone turns in the slightest way in their hearts toward Me, I will send laborers to touch their lives. Pray for the laborers to listen and obey the voice of My grace to minister to those who want help.*

Second Vision

A lady was crouched in the corner of a living room in a crack house. She was strung-out, frail, and looked as though she could die at any time. The pulsating grace filled the house in every room where people were present, and it was all around her also. In her weakened state, she looked around the room in disgust at everyone in the crack house. Then she looked up. "Lord Jesus, I'm sorry. Help me. I don't want to die like this. If you will take me, I give You what's left of me."

She felt nothing outwardly, but I saw some of those waves of grace intensify and enter her body the moment she turned her faith toward the Lord. Then she found the strength to slide up the wall, open the door, and leave that house. She headed toward a rehab center only three blocks away. Then the second vision ended.

The grace of God was there, but it could only be activated by her faith. Although she felt nothing, her smallest cry for help allowed the grace of God to infuse her life immediately. We should never judge His grace by our outward feelings. It must be accepted as a fact of faith.

Third Vision

I saw a man in an expensive business suit sitting on a stool at an upscale exclusive bar—extremely drunk. He was waiting for closing time to leave. He put his head down on his right arm that rested on the bar counter.

Without speaking a word, he said in his heart, "God, if You're real, I know You don't want me to live like this. I've lost my family because of my pride and my drinking. With the increase of money, success, and public recognition, my drinking got worse instead of better. I have everything I ever wanted: I own my own airplane. I own vacation homes and residences where I work around the world; I have companies on different continents. I have the respect of heads of nations and heads of industries. Women are chasing after me. I have everything—except peace and genuine love.

"I finally understand I can't change on my own. Please help me change. Please, I'm willing to give up my pride and get help. So if you can hear me please do something."

The pulsating grace had already filled the bar and was available to the dozen or so people who sat there. But this man was the only one who received the waves of grace. The moment he finished his words, his cold heart melted, and he wept. "God, I know You're real because I haven't cried since I was a teenager. Somehow you touched me." And he wept some more.

The bartender became concerned. He served this guy for years and never saw him act like he wasn't in total control, "Hey, man, you OK?"

The businessman looked up. "No, I'm not OK, but I believe I will be." He put his head down and continued to weep. He finally spoke, "Oh God, I'm so sorry."

The grace of God brought hope to him, something he hadn't felt in years.

God's nature was revealed to me when He said: *I've encountered the ones in your visions through My grace. That grace comes from My goodness and will extend to them to carry them through their current trials, but they still must take the next step. Now that they have received My grace by faith, I will reveal to them their need for a Savior. Then, they'll decide if they are going to become born-again and make their personal commitment to My Son. They will choose whether they want Me to only fix their current problem or change their lives forever. They must choose to humble themselves to My Word and My will.*

The vision ended.

I picked up my Bible and turned to a familiar scripture in Romans 2:4: *Or do you despise the riches of His goodness, forbearance, and longsuffering, not knowing that the goodness of God leads you to repentance?*

Seeing these visions filled my heart with hope for my family and others who seemed so far from God. Now I knew for sure that no one was beyond the reach of grace. I understood that I didn't have to pray grace down from heaven to reach someone. Grace was with them, always surrounding them. When they rejected God, and rejected those whom He sent to tell them about Him, they rejected the grace to help. But, in a split second, they could have a change of heart and by faith access the grace to enter their lives and change them—just like 1 John 5:14-15 says: *Now this is the confidence that we have in Him, that if we ask according to His will, He hears us. And if we know that He hears us, whatever we ask, we know that we have the petitions that we have asked of Him.*

Sometime after the visions, I was praying at home. "Lord, you have grace for every personal problem and every sin. You need partners on the earth to pray for that grace to be activated in people's lives and to pray for laborers to tell others about Your grace. I will become more of a laborer. I can be more effective if I choose two areas to help You instead of trying to scatter shoot and hope I hit something. You can count on me to be Your consistent partner." I thought for a few moments.

"Jesus, I will focus the release of grace into the lives of those who are feeling hopeless—especially those Satan is tormenting with thoughts of suicide. I'll also pray specifically for those who have lost hope because of domestic violence. I'll pray for the victim and the violator. Lord, You don't need to ask me to pray. I will pray each time I think about hopeless people. I'll pray for grace to bring hope because without hope, they can't have faith in You. I'll pray for their hearts to open to receive the grace and pray for Satan to no longer blind their eyes to the grace You have for them."

Now faith is the substance of things hoped for, the evidence of things not seen (Hebrews 11:1).

One day as I prayed for someone who felt hopeless, I had my fourth vision.

Fourth Vision

A lady clutched a bottle of prescription pills. She told God she didn't want to live any longer with the pain in her body and in her heart. She opened the bottle of pills, and then closed it. Finally, she returned the bottle to the cabinet. "Lord, I'm going to try one more time to find some kind of hope. If I don't feel any different, then I'll take this whole bottle of pills."

This vision upset me and I prayed aggressively against the Enemy's assault on her mind. I called upon God's grace to minister hope. I declared that she would live and not die and that she would one day declare the works of the Lord. I cancelled the assignment of death against her and demanded the spirit of death to leave her. Then I prayed for her heart to receive the grace that surrounded her and not reject it. I surrendered her life to Jesus. I prayed until the Holy Spirit ministered to my heart that I could quit. I had to win this battle for her. I felt we had won the victory over her life. The agitation left my spirit and I had peace.

Months later, I spoke at a Woman's Aglow meeting in a nearby city. The meeting was nice, but uneventful. Almost a year later, I spoke at another Aglow meeting in another city. When the meeting was over two ladies approached me and one said she had a question.

"Rev. Diane, did you speak at an Aglow meeting in Hemet a few months ago and you taught on the person of the Holy Spirit?"

"Yes, I most certainly did. Were you there?"

"Yes, I was, but I had no memory of what the speaker looked like. But I remembered your voice. I heard every word that night. I was so drunk I could hardly hold my head up. I laid my head down on the table in the back of the room so no one could see that my eyes were red from drinking and from crying. I purposely drank a lot of alcohol and took a bottle of pills from my cabinet and placed it on my table to take them when I returned home. You're not to mix them with alcohol.

"I had no hope and wanted to commit suicide. When I took the pills in my hand I yelled at God and cried about my circumstances. I lost my good paying job because of sever back problems and they are not sure surgery will help. My dad was dying and I had to take care of him and he's verbally abusive. And I was behind in all my bills. I told the Lord I was tired of the pain in my body and the pain in my heart.

"Somehow I found the strength to put the pills back in the cabinet and then I said, 'Lord, I'm going to try one more time to find some kind of hope. Shirley, my friend," she pointed to the lady standing behind her, "invited me to that Aglow meeting. So I said to God, 'If I don't feel any different when I get home, then I'm taking the whole bottle of pills.'

"I went to the meeting and sat alone at the back table. I didn't want you to see me. I didn't want to talk to anyone either. I left when you started praying for people because I didn't want you to pray for me. When I got home I went straight to bed. In the morning all my problems were the same, but I had hope. Sometime during the meeting, the pressure I felt from the Enemy to commit suicide left and I began to sober up some. I left there a different person.

"Shirley brought me here today because she said she thought you were the one from that meeting in Hemet."

I was speechless as she thanked me over and over again. We exchanged phone numbers.

On the drive home, my mind went over the scenario. *I knew that vision was from God. I knew He ministered to whomever He had me pray for. But never in a million years did I think I would ever meet the person from the vision. That is truly the gift of grace. His grace was sufficient to rescue her with no one touching her or praying with her. Grace was poured in her because she chose faith. No matter how feeble her faith was she acted on it and that accessed the grace she needed to help her come to the meeting and receive hope.*

Although she lived an hour away, she became a member of my church. She also joined the staff of my Beautiful Women of God

Seminars and traveled with us to various cities throughout the state where we held seminars. When the Holy Spirit directed me, I had her share her testimony. We asked for those who felt hopeless to come forward for prayer. God's grace entered their lives and drove out the fear and hopelessness. We saw many miracles.

We stood by her when she had back surgery and it went well. We prayed for her dad and he began to treat her a little better, but mainly she was healed emotionally and his words didn't hurt her like before. Her financial situation improved and she received money when her dad passed.

Today, I am determined with the Holy Spirit's help not to allow grace to surround me in vain. I want to access grace, accept grace by faith, and use grace by acting on it. Here's the key: access grace, accept grace, and act upon that grace.

My passion is to glorify God in the way I navigate through the storms of life. I look to the Word of God and ask the Holy Spirit for the Scriptures He wants me to embrace. I refuse to allow my emotions, Satan, or circumstances to define my existence. I desire to have a testimony that Jesus can use to help others see the power of His grace.

I found that I cannot hold onto self-pity, sympathy, or my self-serving ways and still glorify God. I've learned to cancel my doubt, depression, discouragement, shame, and fear with my own words. What turns things around for me is when I am alert and perceive them as they creep into my life. And then I must choose to fight these enemies of my faith. In those moment by moment choices I fight to be an overcomer. So let's choose life, healing, and His overcoming grace!

There are times my heart is overwhelmed with the cares of this life. Singing to God is a good way for me to release my faith and access His grace. When I'm in a hard place a song may come to mind as I awaken or at some time during the day. If I sing it out loud to the Lord, I can sense faith arises and grace fills my mind.

The Bible admonishes us to sing to the Lord a new song. That's a song we make up. We know every song was a "new" song the first time it was sung. I'm not a singer but God loves my joyful noise and the devil gets nervous when I sing. My new song is a song from my heart with my own words of victory. The Psalms are my pattern, I declare my enemy's defeat, and proclaim my trust in God. Often I sing a Psalm that fits my heart's cry.

I use part of a Psalm as my springboard by making up my own tune to the words. I look for the part that announces my Enemy's defeat. I look for the words which help me repent and words which help me surrender my cares to the Lord. I pick a verse or two and use them as my chorus. When I do this I encourage myself and change the atmosphere around me.

I'm continually inspired by these words from John Newton's popular hymn *Amazing Grace*.

> *T'was Grace that taught*
> *my heart to* [have reverential] *fear* [of the Lord].
> *And Grace, my* [unhealthy anxious] *fears relieved.*
> *How precious did that Grace appear*
> *The hour I first* [humbled my will in faith and] *believed.*
> *Through many dangers, toils and snares*
> *we have already come.*
> *T'was Grace that brought me safe thus far*
> *and Grace will lead me home.*

God's grace is sufficient in the face of the Enemy's storms. Access, accept, and act upon His grace—it already surrounds you like a pulsating force. Don't let any storm ever stop you! Your will is the deciding factor not the devil and not your circumstances. Be determined and write down your victory testimony!

The next generation needs to hear and read your testimony. They will be encouraged in their fight of faith. They will learn how to overcome the Enemy.

But the people who know their God shall be strong, and carry out great exploits (Daniel 11:32b).

The Lord of Hosts (God of the Armies of angels) is fighting on your behalf. If God be for you who can be against you? Think of new ways to praise Him for His greatness, His grace, and His goodness.

You've finished this book so I know you are full of faith! You have the faith to walk on the water with Jesus. You have the ammunition you need to defeat the storms and live the life of an overcomer. Every victory whether small or great is a victory testimony of His grace!

Other Work by **Diane Gardner**

Contributing Author

Extraordinary Answers to Prayer Series:
The Healing Touch

By

Guideposts
Stories Edited by James Stuart Bell

Contributing Author

Breaking Invisible Chains
The Way to Freedom from Domestic Abuse

By

Susan Titus Osborn

CPSIA information can be obtained
at www.ICGtesting.com
Printed in the USA
FSOW02n1613290415
6804FS

9 781490 815015